ECHOES of TRAUMA

A masterful writer and clinician, Charles has penned a volume that illuminates principles integral to psychoanalysis and depth psychology. With rich case histories that offer expert attention to eating disorders, narcissism, and psychosis, Charles stays close to her subject in a manner that demonstrates a style of gentle in vivo development in response to early traumas. While simultaneously providing ample footing for graduate students and analytic candidates seeking integration of theory and practice, this is a book that seasoned clinicians will also find illuminating. I highly recommend it and hope that it will become a sought-after cornerstone in supervisory seminars.

—**Louis Rothschild, PhD,** independent practice, Northern Baltimore County, MD; author of *Rapprochement Between Fathers and Sons: Breakdowns, Reunions, Potentialities*

In this work, Dr. Charles leads us on a guided tour through what psychoanalysis has to offer patients in the wake of early relational trauma. With clinical wisdom and sophistication, she weaves together theory and clinical examples in ways that are at once sweeping and simple. Dr. Charles's expertise and synthesis of the literature will fill gaps in the knowledge of experienced clinicians while also inspiring students to think about the nature of engagement. As in her other works, here Dr. Charles demonstrates her steadfast commitment to carrying the best of psychoanalysis forward in her own voice.

—**Christina Biedermann, PsyD, ABAP,** Associate Professor, Illinois School of Professional Psychology at National Louis University, Chicago, IL

Echoes of Trauma is equally evocative and accessible, bringing to life the legacy of trauma in the consulting room. It promises to inspire clinicians of all levels of experience to immerse themselves more authentically in the art of this work. An essential reading for anyone who works with traumatized individuals.

—**Stephanie Kors, PhD,** Assistant Professor, Loyola University Maryland, Baltimore

Reading this book is like listening while a fine musician explores the possibilities of an instrument. The melodies that Marilyn Charles plays are familiar, but the ways she engages with them are creative and moving. Anyone interested in applied psychoanalytic theory and practice will find *Echoes of Trauma* both clinically useful and personally enlightening.

—**Nancy McWilliams, PhD, ABPP,** Visiting Professor Emerita, Rutgers Graduate School of Applied & Professional Psychology, New Brunswick, NJ

With "trauma" literature proliferating over the last few decades, the subject can get rather tired and one dimensional. In *Echoes of Trauma*, however, Charles returns our formulations about trauma to a more sophisticated, developmental, embodied, and generously conceptualized form. Charles's text is a treasure of theoretical depth with tremendous clinical application. This is the very best of contemporary psychoanalysis.

—**David M. Goodman, PhD,** Dean, Woods College of Advancing Studies at Boston College, Chestnut Hill, MA

Echoes of Trauma is a scholarly work by a master clinician that will be studied for years to come. The author's integrative approach may well represent the future of psychoanalysis.

—**Deborah Anna Luepnitz, PhD,** Institute for Relational Psychoanalysis of Philadelphia, Philadelphia, PA

Marilyn Charles weaves her wealth of clinical experience working with the most complex patients, her sophisticated knowledge of psychoanalysis, and elements of her own life story into a narrative that illustrates how therapists can accompany their patients on a journey into meaning. She demonstrates how trust, respect, attunement to mourning, and deep humility can create a space that invites even the most vulnerable patients into a journey toward healing and toward drawing wisdom from their own lived experience.

—**Michael O'Loughlin, PhD,** Professor, Derner School of Psychology, Adelphi University, Garden City, NY; coeditor of the journal *Psychoanalysis, Culture & Society*

ECHOES of TRAUMA

Meaning and Identity in Psychoanalysis

MARILYN CHARLES

AMERICAN PSYCHOLOGICAL ASSOCIATION

Published by
American Psychological Association
750 First Street, NE
Washington, DC 20002
https://www.apa.org

Order Department
https://www.apa.org/pubs/books
order@apa.org

Typeset in Charter and Interstate by Circle Graphics, Inc., Reisterstown, MD

Printer: Sheridan Books, Chelsea, MI
Cover Designer: Gwen J. Grafft, Minneapolis, MN
Cover collage by Marilyn Charles. Photograph by Doug Bush.

Library of Congress Cataloging-in-Publication Data

Names: Charles, Marilyn, author.
Title: Echoes of trauma : meaning and identity in psychoanalysis / by Marilyn Charles.
Description: Washington, DC : American Psychological Association, [2025] | Includes bibliographical references and index.
Identifiers: LCCN 2024045831 (print) | LCCN 2024045832 (ebook) | ISBN 9781433841996 (paperback) | ISBN 9781433842009 (ebook)
Subjects: LCSH: Identity (Psychology) | Psychic trauma. | Psychoanalysis. | Developmental psychology.
Classification: LCC BF697 .C484 2025 (print) | LCC BF697 (ebook) | DDC 616.85/21--dc23/eng/20250215
LC record available at https://lccn.loc.gov/2024045831
LC ebook record available at https://lccn.loc.gov/2024045832

https://doi.org/10.1037/0000455-000

Printed in the United States of America

10 9 8 7 6 5 4 3 2 1

To Laura,
Whose vision breathed life beyond her limits

Contents

Acknowledgments

I am grateful to all of those with whom I have learned so much over the years, in whatever roles we have played with one another. This is highly personal work, requiring intense intimacy and authenticity to break through the layers of debris that accumulate over time, obscuring what is most precious and unique in each of us. In finding ourselves, we can find one another.

I would like to express particular gratitude to those at APA Books who have shepherded this process, first Susan Reynolds, who has always believed in my voice and vision, and Beth Hatch and Laurel Vincenty for their help refining the manuscript into its current form. Their patience and feedback have been invaluable.

I would also like to thank those who read and commented on portions of the manuscript-in-progress for their insights: Zane Dodd, David Neal, Vivian Chan, and Sharin Kazimov. Appreciation is also due to colleagues who have helped me think through thorny issues over time, Angela Allen-Peck, Carrie Atikune, Jeremy Bloomfield, Ellen Chazdon, Noemi Ford, Danielle Frank, Lynn Higgins, Caryn Schorr, Sandra Ullman, and Sarah Winchester, to name a few; and members of my Eating Disorders Study Group, Rubén Benavides, Carolina De Los Santos, Sandra Delgado, Andrea Madero, María Mirón, Lina Ponder, and Claudia Quintero, for all we have learned together in our research.

Finally, I thank my family: my sisters, Karen and Ellie, with whom I have survived childhood and learned to thrive; my children, Devon, Justin, and Jonathan, who have taught me so many lessons; and my grandchildren,

Grant and Carson, with whom I continue to learn what it means to become oneself in this challenging world; and their dad, Bryan, who helps me see things from another side. And always, my rock and soulmate, Bruce, who has made possible life as it has become.

Those I work with now benefit from those who joined me before in this strange and wondrous journey.

ECHOES of TRAUMA

INTRODUCTION

Companions on a Journey

It is of the essence of our impossible profession that in a very singular way we do not know what we are doing. [At] the heart of our work . . . is a mystery.

—Coltart (1992, p. 2) in *Slouching Towards Bethlehem*

Not only can man's being not be understood without madness, it would not be man's being if it did not bear madness within itself as the limit of his freedom.

—Lacan (1955–1956/1977d, p. 179), in "On a Question Preliminary to Any Possible Treatment of Psychosis"

Psychoanalysis affords a unique lens through which to recognize the complexities of personal, familial, and sociocultural layerings and to investigate ways in which these levels of experience intertwine. Psychoanalysis also offers a method that can help us work our way through our traumatic antecedents, both personal and cultural. Recognizing the story that courses through us provides a ground on which to build a more solid and resilient identity. Crucial

https://doi.org/10.1037/0000455-001
Echoes of Trauma: Meaning and Identity in Psychoanalysis, by M. Charles

to these efforts is a recognition of the impact of trauma on the development of affect regulation, metacognitive capacities and reflective function, and identity itself.

Although Freud (1923/1961) grounded psychoanalytic theory in his recognition of the body at the core of all human meaning, there has been a tendency to lose touch with these moorings in our theorizing. Current trends toward the cognitive threaten to leave behind the nonverbal systems through which essential meanings are registered and, in this way, to also leave behind the signs we are offered to help a person put together the keys to their life story, keys that have eluded them. And yet, as Iain McGilchrist (2009) has reminded us, to be fully human, we need to be able to use both sides of our brain. As the move toward the rigidly rational increasingly overtakes psychology, our solutions to problems become increasingly disembodied and mechanistic. This alienation from self and other is itself insidiously traumatic.

Psychoanalysis is a personal journey made possible by a structure that supports the individual's capacities to learn and to grow. The psychoanalytic canon has been burdened by an overreliance on the male voices that, together, create an authority that threatens to obscure and obstruct the development of an internal authority guided by conscience. We seem to be in an adolescent passage in which Freud's authority is being stamped out by the voices of those who feel marginalized by it. In this volume, I hope instead to invite you to consider how, in light of your own experience, you might make use of the ideas and methods you find within psychoanalytic texts to immerse yourself in your own meaning-making and find your own way. That, to my mind, is the true path of psychoanalysis: an immersion into an embodied psychic reality with sufficient companionship to be able to map out the terrain and make meaning from the experiences.

With these ideas in mind, I offer you this volume with the hope of inviting you into an investigation of these issues. To that end, I look at the impact of trauma across the lifespan and at its intricacies and manifestations. I hope to contextualize the language of psychopathology within the more pressing issues regarding how adaptations to distress can lead development astray. I argue for an embodied view of human development, highlighting ways in which unmourned and unexplored trauma repeats itself across the generations. As the source moves further into the remote past, the "problem," rather than being visible and potentially resolvable, becomes instead the family *até*—the unexpiated misfortune passed along the generations—experienced as a curse that formulates the phantoms haunting at our heels in the form of unresolved trauma masquerading as destiny.

FINDING OURSELVES IN OTHERS' DILEMMAS

There are many books about trauma. This volume is intended for clinicians who engage deeply and personally in the work and who recognize the importance of being able to find ourselves sufficiently in the dilemmas of those who seek our assistance in order to be authentic in our engagements—not imposing our own ideas or sensibilities, but rather inviting people to engage more deeply with their own. Although it will likely be helpful to have a grounding in psychoanalytic theory, I hope that you will persist despite unfamiliar jargon and discover the basic principles of human meaning and becoming that it marks.

This struggle with the unfamiliar and the unknown is precisely the work of psychoanalysis. As Bion (1977) noted, we are always at the crossroads between growth and evasion, fending off what can seem like catastrophic change in relation to challenges not yet faced. The arena of *catastrophic change* marks the spaces we have not yet successfully mastered in our developmental efforts thus far and, therefore, it is precisely the arena into which psychoanalytic and other insight-oriented therapies invite us. For those with histories of the type of *small-t trauma* (the type of serial onslaught of unresolved distressing events often thought of as complex trauma) that results from dysfunctional parenting, developmental challenges can feel like demands for catastrophic change.

We consider ways in which trauma is an inevitable part of life, marking and shaping the human experience. From that perspective, we can perhaps meet those who seek our assistance respectfully and empathically in even the most terrible and terrifying places they find themselves. I believe that good clinical practice is based on experience—tempered, moderated, and augmented by what we learn from others but always grounded in our own histories of what it means to be a human being in the world.

From that vantage point, we can integrate new ideas and perspectives into a framework with a humanistic integrity at the core that is grounded in the truth of personal experience. If we look at the major psychoanalytic theorists, what is salient is the recognition of the importance of individual truth, from Winnicott's (1971) view of the play space through which growth might emerge, to Bion's (1990) view of internal truth as the star we steer by—something we can only perhaps glimpse in the present moment—to Lacan's (1975–1976/2016) later writings about the *sinthome*, the unique construction of self built from one's experiences as a person. The sinthome marks our trail as surely as our fingerprints identify us. From that perspective, our job as a clinician is to be a companion on a journey guided by the other person's internal compass in relation to the truths of their own experience. We might add signposts and anchors along the way but always in relation to the map they are building that shows their unique construction of a universe that is also populated by other points of view and frames of reference.

For Bion and Lacan, perhaps the greatest hazard is that we will put more faith in theory than in whatever is happening in the moment: "The *practice* of psychoanalysis is the only place where it is possible to read people, not books" (Bion, 1990, pp. 63–64). This statement suggests that our practice must be guided by the exigencies of the present moment—as best we can locate ourselves and the other person within them given that the essential problem is not their relationship to us, but rather their relationship to themselves, "which may be so bad that he cannot even make use of what he already knows" (Bion, 1990, p. 50).

BLENDING DEVELOPMENTAL AND PSYCHOANALYTICAL THEORY

My model is a developmental one based on the idea that the meaning of any event is predicated on the history of experiences for that individual, only some of which are accessible to conscious reflection. Development is never final but can become waylaid. To understand any person's problem at a particular moment in time, we need to learn something about the history that has given rise to it, some of which they may be able to tell us directly, but some we may have to intuit from signs and symptoms. As Tronick (2022) suggested, dysfunction emerges not from singular events, but rather from experiences that are chronic and repeated, shaped by both "external interpersonal relational experiences and internal somatic and brain—neurosomatic—processes" (p. 661).

Following Freud, psychoanalysis has skewed toward the rational despite the recognition that what is often most crucial to our learning comes from the unconscious registers. The model offered here is based in a commitment to a maternal pedagogy that recognizes the essential value of lived experience in meaning-making (see Crociani-Windland & Charles, 2022a). Meanings are moored in the body:

> To solve the problem of what it means to be a human subject, a self-reflective self, we should not consider the brain in isolation, but focus on its tight interrelated connections with the body. We should also abandon the solipsistic stance and address the issue from a social point of view. (Gallese, 2014, p. 2)

The patriarchal turn in Western culture has led to a valorizing of the male voice despite repeated calls to attend more carefully to "women's ways of knowing." Freud recognized early on that his views were informed and limited by his person, but it has taken many decades to begin to take his question "What does a woman want?" seriously and to refine our ideas regarding the impact of culture on lived meanings. Notable women did speak back. To name just a few, Shoshana Felman (1993) addressed Freud's question directly, insisting that only a woman could answer it as subject rather than object. Joan Riviere (2019) theorized about women as persons in their own right, and her translations of Freud carry the poetry of his words. Karen Horney (1950, 1967) considered the impact of culture on meaning and being, and Marian Milner (1969, 1987) followed Freud's model, learning through her own experience how to foster development in those who came to her seeking assistance. Nina Coltart (1992) affirmed the essential mystery at the heart of this work that requires us to tolerate the paradox of intuition and not knowing. Julia Kristeva (1986) traveled alongside Lacan, highlighting the feminine and maternal aspects of development and meaning. Although Melanie Klein (1930/1981a, 1940/1981b, 1957/1975) has persisted in the psychoanalytic canon, intrepid freethinkers, such as Milner and even Kristeva, tend to be glossed over as we turn to the authority of their male counterparts. In that turn, we have unbalanced ourselves, and I hope to soften that imbalance by including some of those missing voices—or at least to sound their echoes in my own work. I do carry them with me.

To illuminate this complex territory, I trace some of the threads from psychoanalysis and developmental theories that help make sense of how we become who we are and how we might grow beyond the places we get stuck. Psychology and psychoanalysis are each grounded in developmental views that oppose any mechanistic stance regarding disease models of human suffering. Insight-oriented approaches rest on the notion that building reflective capacity is the key toward greater well-being. For me, the strength of these theories, as opposed to medicalized formulations, is precisely that they *are* developmental, inviting us to consider how we might mobilize our capacities for growth and change in the service of building more viable and satisfying lives. We do not get to choose the challenges that confront us, but psychoanalytic work helps afford us choices in meeting those challenges. Growth requires facing the sticking points rather than merely trying to manage or override them.

Medical formulations have invited us to focus on diagnostic categories that tend to obscure the developmental aspects of the person's dilemmas. In my work at the Austen Riggs Center, a small hospital where psychoanalytic treatment is offered within the holding environment of a therapeutic community, I have the opportunity to work intensively and extensively with individuals for whom psychiatric offerings have not resolved their problems. Rather, there is often a confluence of difficulties that were not attenuated sufficiently by parental offerings to have provided the type of mastery experiences so crucial for tenacity under pressure. The recognition that reflective functions can develop during insight-oriented psychotherapy has led to a body of research using Lysaker et al.'s (2005) Metacognition Assessment Scale–Abbreviated that tracks particular aspects of reflective capacities as they develop. This development parallels Bion's (1977/1989, "The Grid") Grid progression from *notation* toward more active thinking and integration of meanings, affirming that, despite very different language structures, efforts to provide people opportunities to grow beyond where they have become caught have meaningful commonalities at the core.

My research into metacognitive changes over time in individuals who have engaged in psychoanalytic psychotherapy has shown interesting patterns that have implications for technique and for expectations we might have for those whose symptoms fall within various diagnostic categories (Neal et al., 2023). Recognizing a person's particular strengths and vulnerabilities is crucial to being able to meet them where they are, something that both the attachment and psychoanalytic literatures mark as essential to building a viable relationship. That point of meeting is a human juncture of great intimacy, one that requires clinicians to be sufficiently familiar with their own internal workings to make use of their own thoughts and feelings in adaptive ways and to recognize the other person's vantage point sufficiently to sustain and enhance engagement, thereby modeling their own reflective functions.

Freud offered us a method of recognizing parallels between ourselves and others. Over time, locating Freud in his own context has helped us deepen our appreciation for the impact of contextual factors on individual development and on theory so that we can find our own way in this complex and evolving terrain. As clinicians, being able to find ourselves sufficiently in the individual and collective dilemmas described by those seeking our assistance helps afford us the wherewithal to stand beside them in their journeys without imagining that our job is to "solve the problem." We cannot know another's truths in the same way they can know them for themselves, and we cannot impose our understanding on another without undermining their autonomy and development. That recognition helps us have faith that they can encounter the information they need to the extent that we can leave room for it. We also need to be able to locate ourselves in time so that we can apply Freud's method to current data and disentangle ourselves from some of the more limiting presumptions embedded in his theories and be able to recognize that "truth" continues to evolve in relation to changing times. We need to be able to encounter theory with interest without imposing injunctions, in order to move out into the unknown with both faith and humility. In these efforts, a developmental, contextual view of the troubles that ail us is crucial in our work with those we encounter in our consulting rooms today.

THE OVERARCHING MAP OF THE JOURNEY

In this volume, we look at the intra- and interpersonal contexts in which identity develops. We consider how development is shaped, including relational and meaning-making aspects. Research into parent–child relationships has taught us a great deal about the interpersonal processes that underlie meaning-making from the very basic rhythms of experience that form the relational matrix of parent and child (Sander, 1977). These rhythms are put into play before birth, the patterned elements of early life forming the interpersonal context that undergirds the beginnings of language. Familial and cultural legacies infuse the language as it is communicated, shaping the meanings of life stories as they evolve interactively between parent and child.

Psychoanalysis has taught us a great deal about the process of meaning-making itself from what Bion (1977) termed *beta elements*, aspects of experience that are present but have not yet been thought about and reflectively integrated into our conceptions of self and world; or what Aulagnier (2001) termed *pictograms*, referring to our earliest experiences of self in relation to other that are suffused with affect and that underlie personal and interpersonal meanings. We use Bion's (1977/1989, "The Grid") *Grid* as a matrix through which to consider these two interrelated matrixes of meaning-making. Across the horizontal axis, Bion has outlined the affective-relational trajectory that tracks the increasingly complex functions to which thinking addresses itself from *attention* to *action*, as noted in Freud's (1911/1958b) "Formulations on the Two Principles of Mental Functioning." Down the vertical axis, Bion has tracked the evolution of the complexity of thought from proto-symbols, through images and myth, to algebraic patterns of meaning. I hope that using the frame of the grid helps you track the two vertices of development I then illustrate for you: the relational and the cognitive. Each, importantly, is linked to the earliest rhythms of experience that underlie the patterned, affectively driven meanings through which we come to know self and world.

Earliest experiences of self-with-other optimally provide the type of containment necessary for building the basic affective self-regulation on which cognitive development depends. We see how disruptions in early life impact development, leading to various types of symptom pictures, many of which may be more usefully conceptualized through the lens of the complex trauma that results from repeated disruptions (Van Nieuwenhove & Meganck, 2019). These disruptions also have profound implications for identity, which is formed within the context of interpersonal relationships. We learn who we are from how we are treated. Over time, given sufficient attention to our own developing capacities, we begin to recognize that others have their own characters and perspectives that shape their perceptions of us. We learn that small-t truth is personal and that we need to be able to stand for our own—that our stand is stronger to the extent that we can consider alternate ideas and integrate them. People often think of trauma in terms of major life events, but those major life events may be difficult ordeals without necessarily derailing us. Crucial to resilience are the relational underpinnings that help us to self-regulate under pressure and to believe in our own capacities to endure and to thrive, turning challenges into opportunities for mastery.

To investigate the impact of complex trauma requires an exploration into the development of self that underlies all issues of identity. As Stern (1985) and many others have shown, the self is developed in relationship to others at the levels of both physiology and meaning-making. Physiologically, the infant depends on caregivers to attend to and attenuate distress, in this way developing communication channels and the capacity for affective self-regulation. Even before the caesura of birth, however, the developing fetus begins to regulate in relation to the rhythms of the mother. In the last trimester, an enhanced interconnected rhythmicity develops that becomes the precursor for the establishment of a safe containing space through which rhythms of meaning can evolve between parent and child (R. Feldman, 2006).

These rhythms may be seen as the presymbolic structures that undergird the possibility of communication between human beings. Rhythmic coordination between parent and child is not only crucial for relational development but also forms the timing patterns that become the type of procedural knowledge that underlies many human activities (Jaffe et al., 2001). The discovery of mirror neurons (Gallese, 2009) affirms the importance of what is learned through being-with others, highlighting that much of what we learn is taken in directly and absorbed without conscious awareness. That lack of conscious awareness eases the integration but can be confusing when known "truths" are challenged by alternative data. Those moments of challenge become opportunities for growth to the extent that space can be held for learning. For the young child, that space requires an attentive other who can recognize the dilemma and hold hope for its resolution, a relational pattern we also find in psychotherapy in which our job is often to hold hope for the possibility of growth beyond the place where the person finds themselves caught. This growth is catalyzed by the learning that occurs between persons as they engage meaningfully and respectfully with one another.

Freud (1900/1953b) has helped us organize our understanding of the underbelly of experienced meanings through his term *primary process*, referring to the amassed data that we store without necessarily knowing what is there but draw on in making meaning from our daily lives. This is the realm of Laplanche's (1997) *enigmatic messages* transmitted from adult to child, meanings that have an impact but cannot be parsed from the perspective of a child's mind or experience. Aulagnier (2001) has dipped even further to detail a layer she termed *primal experience*, suggesting that the foundations of experienced meanings are laid in the earliest moments of food- and warmth-seeking in the meeting of the infant's body with that of the caregiver, taking in not only the physical encounter but also the affective infusions attendant to that encounter. That affect, suggested Aulagnier, becomes a template on which all later renderings of self are built. The unconscious becomes the repository of rich confluences of meaning, parsed and unparsed, that forms the background from which each person's vantage point or, in Lacan's (1964/1977e) terms, the *Imaginary*, is constructed.

THE PATH FORWARD

To elucidate this territory, we begin in Part I with an exploration of the intra- and interpersonal contexts in which identity develops. Using Bion's (1977/1989, "The Grid") Grid, I offer a way of thinking about the clinical work as an enterprise in which we might stand alongside the person as a way of better understanding the predicaments that have brought them into treatment (Chapter 1). After offering a view of emotional development grounded in research on attachment theory and early child development (Chapter 2), I discuss the development of the complexity of thought, from proto-symbols, through symbol formation, to more complex verbal language structures (Chapter 3). We then broaden the field to discuss ways in which culture impacts identity development (Chapter 4). In these efforts, I weave together the personal, theoretical, and clinical, drawing on previous writing I have done on memory and identity, emotional development, and the impact of individual and collective trauma on identity development.

In Part II, we look at transference and countertransference as essential lenses through which to make sense of the interpersonal aspects of psychoanalysis. Transference helps us recognize ways in which repetition is also a communication that helps us make sense of the other person's interpersonal world-as-lived. From that perspective, the transference/countertransference matrix can be seen as a useful tool for better understanding a particular individual and locating them in their own unique social and emotional environment (Chapter 5). We then consider interpretation as a means for offering back to the person another perspective that might break into fixed ideas about the trouble and invite greater reflectivity rather than imposing meanings in ways that further obstruct learning and growth (Chapter 6). Our developmental model recognizes that our shared formulations, offered with curiosity and interest, invite those we work with to reflect along with us, adding data from their own feelings and sensibilities in ways that help illuminate the terrain and enhance their reflective capacities while also enriching and refining the formulations.

As we proceed, I highlight theoretical conceptualizations I have found particularly useful, drawing on threads from various psychoanalytic thinkers and schools and using brief clinical vignettes to illustrate how we might use our theories to facilitate the development of those we work with.[1] Part of what I am promoting is a feminine, maternal model of psychotherapy that foregrounds the containing environment as crucial to engendering creative participation (e.g., Baraitser, 2023; Crociani-Windland & Charles, 2022b). This model emphasizes making use of one's own experience to better understand others, promoting development through a process of modeling as we make use of our own reflective capacities. Essential in this regard is our attention to maintaining a reflective stance but also recognizing the communicative value of "noise" in the system—being open to odd thoughts and feelings that can give us data beyond the words being spoken. This stance also includes being open to the metaphors that evolve in the work as it transpires between the participants, most particularly the symbols that arise through dreams and reverie—always most attentive to those coming from the other person—remembering that they are in a privileged position in relation to their own internal truths. In this way, we can support a truly developmental model rather than one that moves toward normalcy at the expense of creativity (McDougall, 1978).

In Part III, we look at the relevance of a developmental view for understanding ways in which symptoms appear, turning our lens toward salient problems emerging in the clinical encounter today. Being able to mark symptoms as failed communicative efforts can usefully inform our work with

[1] All names and persons in case illustrations have been fictionalized to protect confidentiality.

troubles that might best be read in terms of developmental difficulties in affective and identity development rather than through a disease model. We consider ways in which trauma may be represented, focusing on symptoms and defenses, beginning with the somatic complaints that mark difficulties that accrue over time, registering in the body because they cannot be symbolized (Chapter 7). Eating disorders are explored as a particular way of managing distress that becomes addictive because it eases the distress temporarily without resolving the underlying issues (Chapter 8).

We then turn to the crucial juncture between feeling and thinking that Freud (1895/1955d, 1905/1953a, 1909/1955a, 1909/1955c) originally took up in his cases on hysteria and obsessions (Chapter 9). From that vantage point, we look at distinctions between the borderline and the narcissistic positions, elaborating on the obsessive defenses that leave people unknown to themselves. That exploration will lead to a more extensive consideration of issues we encounter with individuals caught in the narcissistic position (Chapter 10). We end this part with a consideration of the complex social and developmental challenges of those who find themselves in the psychotic position (Chapter 11).

In Part IV, we consider applications of our model. We begin with an example of how theory might enlarge and enhance our reflective and creative capacities rather than close them down, looking at the intersections between personal experience and evolving metaphors as they play out in the consulting room (Chapter 12). We then explore ways in which ideas about dreams and the psychoanalytic field can enlarge our creative capacities within the session (Chapter 13). We then consider how ideas of time can enhance the work (Chapter 14). In exploring intersections between meaning and being, I hope to bring you full circle in a process that invites you to reflect more deeply on your own relationships to small-t trauma in your own life. I hope this process will invite you to recognize ways in which the interplay of embodied experience, interpersonal engagement, and transference/countertransference, as well as reflection, dream work and narrative, and primary and secondary process, work together to provide the wherewithal for a more creative engagement in the challenges that living brings, including those we encounter in our consulting rooms.

PART I THE INTRA- AND INTERPERSONAL CONTEXTS IN WHICH IDENTITY DEVELOPS

1 BION'S GRID

Tracking Relational Versus Cognitive Development

In trying to think through the threads important in understanding the impact of complex, small-t trauma on human development, I realize that this problem is precisely what Bion (1963, 1965, 1977/1989) was pointing to in his formidable grid (see Figure 1.1). From Bion's perspective, we learn ambivalently, always fending off the trauma of contending with ideas that might lead to catastrophic change. We see this hesitation in the face of major change in Gesell's (1933) graph of child development, in which major changes are preceded by a breakdown in what had been a steady state of functioning. Optimally, early parent–child relationships provide a container that makes room for the frustration that accompanies growth while fending off the overstimulation that shuts down cognitive processes and can even be experienced as traumatic. That external containment helps the child develop the internal capacities for affective self-regulation that undergird cognitive development and make possible experiences of mastery that encourage curiosity and further learning.

In this chapter, I explain how Bion's Grid can serve as a tool for transformation. His Grid shows how a person's statements reflect both conscious

---

This chapter is adapted from "Bion's Grid: A Tool for Transformation," by M. Charles, 2002a, *Journal of the American Academy of Psychoanalysis, 30*(3), pp. 429–445 (https://doi.org/10.1521/jaap.30.3.429.21971). Copyright 2002 by the Guilford Press. Adapted with permission.

https://doi.org/10.1037/0000455-002
Echoes of Trauma: Meaning and Identity in Psychoanalysis, by M. Charles

FIGURE 1.1. Bion's Grid

	Definitory Hypotheses 1	ψ 2	Notation 3	Attention 4	Inquiry 5	Action 6	. . . n.
A β-elements	A1	A2				A6	
B α-elements	B1	B2	B3	B4	B5	B6	. . . Bn
C Dream Thoughts Dreams, Myths	C1	C2	C3	C4	C5	C6	. . . Cn
D Pre-conception	D1	D2	D3	D4	D5	D6	. . . Dn
E Conception	E1	E2	E3	E4	E5	E6	. . . En
F Concept	F1	F2	F3	F4	F5	F6	. . . Fn
G Scientific Deductive System		G2					
H Algebraic Calculus							

Note. From *Elements of Psychoanalysis* (p. 434), by W. R. Bion, 1963, William Heinemann Medical Books Ltd.

and unconscious experience. It also helps us to organize the two threads we will be following, explored more fully in Chapters 2 and 3. By applying our understanding of this Grid to those seeking our assistance, we gain greater insight and can process new meanings as they emerge.

DISTINGUISHING THE COMPLEXITY OF A THOUGHT FROM ITS USES

Much like Lacan's view of the *Real* (whatever exists beyond the limits of what is symbolized or symbolizable), Bion (1962) viewed thoughts as existing prior to thinking. In this way, he anticipated the territory we explore in Chapter 3 regarding the development of symbolic thought. Crucial to Bion's perspective is consideration of how the thinking is being used to deal with the *problem* of thoughts that may "be evaded or modified or used as part of an attempt to evade or modify something else" (Bion, 1962, p. 83). We have all had the experience of noticing unwanted thoughts lurking at the periphery of our mind and wanting to just wave them away. Recognizing this ambivalence in ourselves better positions us to consider how the other person's speech—or silence—may represent an attempt to communicate or, alternatively, to get rid of unwelcome thoughts or feelings.

The Grid (see Figure 1.1) shows Bion's attempt to move away from the content of the psychoanalytic material and focus instead on distinctions between the complexity of a thought and the uses to which it is being put. The horizontal axis represents the developmental progression of thinking, the uses or "functions that a statement is being made to perform" (Bion, 1963, p. 71). These functions are patterned after Freud's (1911/1958b) descriptions of attending to—versus turning away from—stimuli encountered in the external world, his recognition that the unconscious contains perceptions that have not been afforded sufficient attention to be able to call them to mind. Here, we find the stuff that dreams are made of, both the detritus of daily life and the important elements that call to us from the unconscious, speaking through symptoms or haunting us in our dreams.

In tracking these progressions of the development and complexity of thinking, the Grid helps us recognize that statements that are the same in form may serve quite different purposes. They become more active and directed as we move across the horizontal axis, beginning with simple definitory statements, then moving to falsehoods that serve a defensive function. Column 3, *Notation*, marks the beginning of a realization of meaning that gives rise to more directed *Attention* in Column 4, affording illumination and expansion of the material already gathered and leading to *Inquiry* in

Column 5, statements that actively probe for more material. In Column 6, *Action*, we find statements that aim toward effecting solutions to problems in development. I invite you to use the horizontal axis of the Grid as a rough frame through which to consider the territory covered in Chapter 4: the development of self, mind, and interpersonal meanings within a relational context.

In juxtaposition to the tracking of the quality of the thought on the horizontal axis of the Grid, the vertical axis tracks the evolution of the complexity of the thought. On this axis, the uses to which statements are being put remain constant, whereas the terms themselves vary, becoming increasingly more complex and abstract. In Row A, we find what Bion has termed *Beta-elements*, basic sense impressions that have the quality of concrete objects not yet actively thought about. In Row B, we find *Alpha-elements*, the most basic products of thinking, elements to which we have turned our attention. These basic units become *proto-symbols*, elements that can be used in the formation of dreams and waking thoughts. In Row C, we find those dream thoughts in the form of images that have become more fully elaborated. These are the symbols encountered in the manifest content of dreams and also in myths. The narrative form of dreams, stories, and myths provides a structure that helps us locate elements in relation to one another so we might go back and forth between the part and the whole, in this way also noting the patterns that emerge through these relationships. In Row D, we find what Bion called the *Pre-conception*, a state of expectation in which the mind is adapted toward receiving a restricted range of phenomena. When a preconception is joined with a realization, suggested Bion, this results in the *Conception*, found in Row E, which can also become a preconception for the realization of further conceptions. In Row F, we find *Concept*, which is a further refined and validated conception. It is at this level that Bion places psychoanalytic theories along with other logical or scientific formulations that provide a statement regarding the meaning of the patterns.

You can see how the vertical axis tracks the further elaboration of ideas from their basic constituents into increasingly complex and nuanced forms that can be reshaped and reconfigured as new ideas are encountered and assimilated. Rows D, E, and F represent essential aspects of the analytic process in which an observation (the "realization") becomes integrated with previous awareness (preconception or conception) in such a way that the previous knowledge does not preclude new awareness, but rather facilitates it. Keep in mind Bion's (1967a) admonition to avoid memory or desire, to avoid saturating the space with ideas we already have so we can be open to the new idea that might emerge if we have sufficient openness to *realize* (as an active verb) something new. In Row G, we find the *Scientific Deductive System*, a combination of concepts or systems of hypotheses that are logically related to each other. At this level, the logical relation of one concept with another and of one hypothesis with another enhances the meaning of each idea thus linked and expresses a meaning that the concepts, hypotheses, and links do not individually possess (Bion, 1963).

In Row H, we find scientific deductive systems that Bion thought could be represented by an *Algebraic Calculus*, according to formal rules. Here, we see his basic presumption of a formal, patterned structure of relationships between elements underlying human experience. Bion (1962) had hoped to encourage discussions regarding form and function by illuminating rules governing the psychoanalytic process that often get lost behind our fascination with aspects of content. He was well aware that our theories easily become preconceptions that impede our ability to learn from experience. Bion (1980) was also aware of the tendency to defer to authority rather than learn to think for ourselves, a hazard that also preoccupied Lacan (1964/1977e)—a reminder of the importance of thinking for ourselves even in the face of uncertainty.

As Bion (1977/1989) put it, "As I became more able to silence my prejudices, I also became able to be aware of the evidence that was there rather than to regret the evidence that was not" (p. 22). Although a personal analysis can help shed light on our preconceptions, these may be replaced by conceptions we learn through our training. He described the dilemma:

> The effect of my own analysis was that it diminished the obstructive force of unconscious memories and though I acquired new ones, usually believed to be the theories of my analyst, the effects of such recently acquired memories were of a different kind than those usually characterized as inhibitions; these last could be more fruitfully, though more vaguely, described as column 2 categories—that is to say, psycho-analytical objects feared as liable to trigger off developments of a catastrophic nature, to initiate "catastrophic change." (Bion, 1977/1989, pp. 16–17)

MAKING USE OF THE GRID

Although our theories help us better understand intra- and interpersonal dilemmas, they also can inhibit us from seeing other "truths" that might emerge if we could be open to them. Bion's Grid reminds us in simple and pragmatic terms that, regardless of its elegance or complexity, any theory can be used for either evasive or constructive ends. Just as it is important to be able to consider the value of a given statement in terms of its complexity (vertical axis), it is also important to consider it in terms of the purpose for which it is being used (horizontal axis). Is it an attempt at definition, a negation of meaning, a notation of meaning, or an active attempt to discern meaning?

Take as an example the statement "I don't know." In any particular moment, I don't know what this person means by this statement because it has meant various things in the past, including: "I do not want to know and am actively erasing the meaning from my mind" or "I know that there is some meaning here, but it is slipping away even as I try to find it," or "I am unable to tell you that right now," or "I do not want to tell you that right now." Each of these statements has a particular flavor that indicates the stance the person is taking toward knowing whatever is eluding them and us in the moment. This is the arena of Winnicott's (1971) false self and of Lacan's (1964/1977e) recognition that we come to treatment largely seeking misrecognition rather than whatever truths might lead to catastrophic change. This is also the terrain of Lacan's *oblique angle* in which we try to look from the side to see how the person is aiming their statement rather than merely being caught by the force of it (see Chapter 12 for further exploration of this concept). Thinking of the Grid categories reminds us that there are possibilities of meaning to be explored together and helps afford sufficient containment to invite greater inquiry and self-knowledge rather than close both down.

Notable for our purposes here, moving too close to the traumatic without sufficient scaffolding can feel traumatic. It is crucial to recognize that profound impending change can invoke a sense of dread in relation to what feels like catastrophic change or imminent annihilation. Although profound transformation accompanies growth, it also subverts the prevailing order. We need to recognize the deep ambivalence we all hold as we move toward attaining greater insight in precisely those areas we have avoided because they are also the places of fear or shame. Recognizing that seeing ourselves more clearly can feel shameful, particularly in an interpersonal context in which we have already been seen, is crucial in trying to provide a space in which inconvenient truths might be encountered (Charles, 2012).

Recognizing this challenge, Winnicott (1971) marked the importance of providing a play space, in which what Milner (1987) described in terms of the uniqueness of the individual and their creative capacities might be discovered. Lacan (1975–1976/2016) seemed to arrive at a similar place in his depiction of the *sinthome*, the unique ways in which the Real, the Imaginary, and the *Symbolic* (governed by the social rules linked together by language) come together for a particular individual. Rather than seeing symptoms as pointing to problems to be resolved, they become ways of orienting toward a deeper understanding of the individual who suffers, recognizing that suffering is a fundamental aspect of human experience.

For Bion (1962), meanings are inevitably personal, learned from experience. The discovery of an orienting principle—or, as he termed it, a *selected fact*—is always idiosyncratic and affectively driven, pointing toward greater coherence and clarity of meaning. Meaning is not only dependent on perspective but is also a function of linking, whether of object to object, idea to idea, or self to other (Bion, 1962, 1963). For Bion, *unlinking* is a defense that moves against coherence when knowing would be too scary. From that place, the symptom, rather than providing an orienting point, becomes alienating. For both Lacan and Bion, the process of naming is itself important. Lacan viewed naming as a core element of identity and defense in relation to the sociocultural groups to which we belong (Verhaeghe, 1999), whereas Bion viewed naming as a more general process through which similar phenomena are linked together. Names become selected facts that foreground particular aspects of reality, dictating how links are to be patterned, organized, and understood. We encounter this idea again in Chapter 3 as we consider the development of symbolic thought and language as well as ways in which trauma impedes this process.

For those arrested in the process of becoming autonomous, individual beings, there are always, in the history, conditions that inhibit or actively prohibit the development of one's own narrative (Davoine & Gaudillière, 2004). Knowing one's story requires anchors in space and time. Just as a name can indicate the categories in which something belongs, stories identify relationships among elements of experience. Because of this function, myth serves a privileged function in Bion's schema, providing a shorthand form of a more complex configuration of meanings. Whereas Freud used myths in very particular ways, Bion looked at the larger pattern of human experience revealed by the myth. In his hands, for example, the oedipal myth became a heuristic marker for the larger issue of ways in which we move toward a willful blindness—toward unlinking—to not know whatever might be too painful to face. He located the oedipal dilemma in relation to the symbol of the sphinx, an enigmatic figure "from whom disaster emanates" (Bion, 1961, p. 162). Learning to face our humanness, our suffering, and our limits becomes an essential part of the psychoanalytic journey.

THE POWER OF METAPHOR AND MYTH

Psychoanalysis is particularly suited to this type of self-exploration because of the respectful recognition of the unconscious, where, as Bion (1992) noted, our most important processing takes place. This deeper level of processing enables us to take in and metabolize the "facts" of our experience rather than merely "think about" them through the relatively less efficient rational mode (Charles, 2002b). Recognizing the dual tracks through which meanings are made, Bion highlighted ways in which the nonverbal and verbal, primary and secondary process work together to make rational sense of experienced reality. He posited learning as a function of transformations of experience through which meaning is deduced via the interplay of intuition and reason (Bion, 1965), noting that it is largely in the realm of metaphor (which Bion referred to primarily as "myth" or "visual models"; see also Bion, 1963, p. 63) that these complex meanings are most productively passed along and digested. Whether these are personal myths (e.g., dreams) or more publicly shared myths, they provide a condensed statement of complex phenomena in ways that facilitate both understanding and communication. From this perspective, the Tower of Babel story is one exemplar of a wider range of myths, including the story of Oedipus, that warn against the pursuit of knowledge. These myths "provide a succinct statement of psycho-analytic theories which are relevant in aiding the analyst both to perceive growth and to achieve interpretations that illuminate aspects of the patient's problems that belong to growth" (Bion, 1963, p. 63).

Bion's metaphors are quite striking, revealing his views of the processes by which growth in understanding occurs. For him, process is much more important than content, and the relationship between elements is crucial for any real understanding of the parts. For Bion (1970), the concrete gives foundational meaning, whereas the abstract provides rules for using that knowledge, so that, in Grid terms, *intuition* is the vehicle whereby the analyst *realizes* the products of nonsensuous experience. In this way, metaphor serves the somewhat paradoxical function of containing our more intangible experiences. The move toward verbalizing these experiences further contains them in a medium through which they can be more explicitly communicated: via the word. As we abstract the essential meanings from the experience, we devise categories by which to order and organize them. In this way, the intangible intuition is translated into a concrete abstraction: the word.

Through this interplay between intuition (based on the "facts" of our experience) and abstraction (providing a means for organizing these facts), we derive greater perspective from which we might move beyond what is currently *known* in a derivative sense to what might *become* known in the sense of *understanding* (Bion hated that word [Grotstein, 2009], but I do not know of a better one in this context; I think he wanted to emphasize that learning is an active experience, not an attainment). Bion's Grid represents one attempt to provide tools in the form of abstract rules and principles, whereby the concrete facts of experience might be usefully transformed. Symbolically, it represents how we process insights: "how we *unconsciously* process new ideas, correlate them with already established ones, and confront the 'catastrophic change' that emerges on the frontier between the new and the old" (Grotstein, 2000, p. 300).

From this framework, myth enables us to communicate with one another about essential truths in a form that allows us to keep the various aspects in mind. Unpacking the myth helps us appreciate the ramifications of the various elements. Because these elements are also found in the personal myths that make up the content of the psychoanalytic session, myth provides the most constructive mode of representing these personal and universal truths. That idea forms the core of the Bionian field theory discussed in Chapter 13. In some ways, Bion's thoughts on myth parallel Milner's (1987) recognition of the unique patternings of meaning for each individual, which is also the point Lacan (1975–1976/2016) came to in his exegesis of the sinthome. Psychoanalysis is uniquely suited to highlight the particularities of meaning that both hide and reveal the individual's suffering. Coming to respect our uniqueness in relation to the particularities of our histories is key to living well.

RELATING ELEMENTS OF MEANING

Bion's views are profoundly relational, positing a dynamic relationship between elements of meaning. Through this lens, we can see that transference is not just about relationships between persons but, more profoundly, about relationships between aspects of experience that come to have meaning. Although meaning is built between persons in relational space (the focus of Chapter 2), over time, these meanings generalize, forming symbols that move beyond the concrete representation to refer to objects and elements of experience not physically present (the focus of Chapter 3; see also Beebe et al., 1997).

For Bion (1963), learning occurs through the dynamic relationship between container and contained, neither of which can be understood without reference to both aspects. Notably, whatever is contained from one perspective will also be seen to be contained from another. This concept is essential for understanding how meanings develop and evolve. The second crucial element pointed to by Bion is the relationship between processes of fragmentation and integration. These processes, too, can reverse perspective, each impacting the other depending on the context—what Bion (1962) termed the *selected fact* that organizes the elements, introducing order into chaos. Notable for our purposes here is that moving too close to the traumatic without sufficient scaffolding can feel dangerous, invoking a sense of dread as we move toward subverting the prevailing order to effect the profound transformation that accompanies growth (Bion, 1965).

For Bion (1977), myth brings to our attention aspects of experience that tend to co-occur while also marking their relational contexts. If we do not saturate the elements by taking them literally and constricting their meaning, the elements offer themselves up for our consideration and encourage constructive thinking. For example, think of the Oedipus complex and how it has become particularized to refer to parent–child entanglements. Bion (1977), however, pulled back to recognize the larger configuration of not-knowing, or of turning a blind eye, as Steiner (1985) referred to it. Keeping in mind the larger pattern of the story helps us bring the details into focus without losing sight of the frame in which the elements occur. Equating myth with model (Grid Category C) and contrasting these with more sophisticated theoretical formulations (Grid Category F), Bion suggested that the more myths we have at our disposal, the easier it becomes to illustrate and bring to our awareness essential aspects of human dilemmas that can be both elusive and essential to think about. As we progress along our journey, we will see that metaphors also serve this function (Charles, 2001). The metaphors, myths, and dream images shared and inhabited in our interactions in the consulting room become important reference points that ground us in our work together as the person builds more complex, nuanced stories that mark their own development (Fivush et al., 2011).

MAKING SENSE OF FALSE STATEMENTS

In working with trauma, Bion's (1962) distinction between evasion and modification when confronted with pain is a crucial one. *Evasion* precludes growth; it "is intended not to affirm but to deny reality, not to represent an emotional experience but to misrepresent it to make it appear to be a fulfillment rather than a striving for fulfillment" (Bion, 1962, p. 49). In the Grid, the categories are based on the individual's experience of the act in question. Thus, our judgments "must hinge on whether the solutions attempted are growth-producing or the reverse" (Bion, 1965, p. 66). A statement may be made not to mislead but to fill the function of evocation. Thus, a lying report may be evocative or provocative, accusatory or defensive, to name only a few of the more obvious uses. If the aim of psychoanalysis is seen as truth, the lying person may be seen as a problem. However, the lie may also be a way of bringing important defenses to our attention. In this sense, the lie becomes a potentially useful enactment: a definitory statement of sorts, pointing to the nature of the problem.

This is where our own experience of being human is essential to any understanding of others. Our ability to engage deeply and empathically affords us the sensory data we need to follow the story being told at the nonverbal, along with the verbal, level. In being willing to take note of data as they come to our attention and to check in with the other person regarding the meaning of whatever we are noticing, we hope to build a space in which greater engagement (in the sense of the horizontal axis) and meaning-making (in the sense of the vertical axis) can occur. From this framework, what we call "countertransference" is the instrument through which the nonverbal meanings can register, and our job is to attempt to think about what our common senses are telling us, always checking in for validation or modification. In this process, we are hoping to build a containing relationship that might attenuate the fear and shame that can obstruct the curiosity needed to most adaptively learn from our experience. With that learning comes the sense of pride and mastery that encourages curiosity and further learning.

CONCLUSION

Bion's Grid helps us transform the concrete "facts" of others' statements into greater insights and meanings. By considering both the complexity of a statement and the ways in which that statement is used, we can relate different elements of meaning together. Metaphors and myths are particularly powerful reflections of unconscious thoughts. By processing the meanings of metaphors and myths, we move toward verbalizing our more intangible experiences of those seeking our assistance, thereby facilitating growth and understanding. In the following chapter, I look at the affective underpinnings that form the core of both cognitive and relational development.

2 AFFECTIVE DEVELOPMENT

In this chapter, I look at the impact of the early relational environment, focusing particularly on the affective underpinnings that undergird cognitive, relational, and identity development. Human beings come into the world incompletely formed and utterly dependent on caregivers for survival. Birth itself changes everything, making the early moments of life integral to building the type of solid foundation on which later resilience will rest. Although we do not have explicit memories of these moments, they form the background melodies on which meanings are built. For Aulagnier (2001), these earliest moments of life are critical to all later being and meaning as the infant seeks comfort in the containment of the parental embrace, reeling from the onslaught of sensations that accompany the birth process. Those first moments of seeking warmth and nourishment, she contended, are imprinted with the affective charge that infuses the experience, conveying an enduring message as to whether one is desired as an anticipated source of pleasure and interest or is unwelcome and unacceptable.

Although these early experiences cannot be consciously remembered, they become a template on which all later experience is written. In this way, parental ambivalence can become the trauma that disrupts development

https://doi.org/10.1037/0000455-003
Echoes of Trauma: Meaning and Identity in Psychoanalysis, by M. Charles

without being recognizable, aside from the ways these early messages communicate themselves through the bodily memories, symptoms, and recollected, affectively charged moments that link with and structure lived experience. For the clinician, recognizing and taking seriously this information as it manifests in real time in the consulting room can be crucial in helping a person make sense of their relationship to self, even the type of self-loathing that may be an empathic tie to a disturbed parent. That type of unreliable parenting tends to accompany parental deficits in mentalization that interfere with the development of the embodied knowing and epistemic trust so crucial to meaning-making (Fonagy & Allison, 2023; Gallese, 2009), making relationship building an essential first step in any therapeutic process.

THE RELATIONAL CONTEXT

The early relational matrix is the context in which identity is built through the evolving narratives between parent and child in relation to the history as it happens. Because there is always more perceptual data than we can possibly take in or make sense of, learning depends on our ability to selectively attend to and manage the too-much of daily existence. The attuned parent is attentive to the child's experience in relation to their own, trying to read the child's nonverbal communications in attempts to accommodate to their needs and feelings. The inevitable gaps afford frustration, which helps build the child's affect tolerance and sustains the caregiver's interest in this new person who may be like them but is also different in important ways. Profound parental deficits, however, can lead to the difficulties in self- and identity development associated with character disorders and psychopathology more generally (Luyten et al., 2020). In this chapter, I focus on this early relational context in which communication between persons becomes possible; I reserve for later chapters the symbol formation and identity development that is also taking place during these crucial early years.

As parent and child come to know one another, familiarity builds a sense of comfort and trust. Over time, what once might have startled the infant is either not noticed or else is noticed with whatever pleasure or discomfort has been linked with the event. These repeated moments of pleasure and displeasure, novelty and familiarity, become the rhythms of experience that begin to organize meanings in the world (Beebe et al., 2003). The anticipation of startle ending with a positive resolution helps the child to meet novelty receptively rather than fearfully, knowing that there is someone to turn to if need be. Here, we find the patterns of rupture and repair that lead to games like peekaboo and hide-and-seek: The excitement at a mystery that can be resolved encourages the curiosity needed for engaged learning.

In this type of back-and-forth prosody, we see how resilience is built in the intersections between protection from distress and the soothing that attenuates it as the child builds their capacity for frustration tolerance and affect regulation and also actively attempts to obtain what they need from caregivers (Tronick, 2007). The caregiver's *empathic attunement* (Stern, 1985) tells the child that their efforts have value and that their distress is recognized, cared about, and endurable. That early relational containment helps build the trust necessary for moving out into the world with interest rather than fear.

AFFECT REGULATION AND INTRAMODAL PROCESSING

Affect plays a crucial role in structuring nonverbal meanings. Affect registers and is recognized directly and consistently across modalities, "the supra-modal currency into which stimulation in any modality can be translated" (Stern, 1985, p. 53). Tomkins (1982) offered a way of making sense of these implicit meanings, suggesting that each affect has its own clearly discernable melody that evokes the feeling it marks, undergirding the procedural memory that guides behavior (Tronick, 2007). Beyond our capacity to decode them verbally, affective meanings become reference points, melodies we recognize implicitly in changes in tone, touch, or gesture (Charles, 2002b). These affective prosodies are highly patterned and evocative, intuited directly through "the dimensions of experience such as shape, texture, and location in space [that] all come to carry meanings beyond any specific representation. We learn to 'read' nuances of line in works of art as in faces" (Charles, 2002b, p. 111). The slope, turn, sweep, and rhythm, therefore, all become important reference points (Charles, 2002b).

From our earliest beginnings, we need assistance in orienting toward signals versus noise as we learn to make meaning from the plethora of perceptions impinging on us. Beginning life as sensory, meaning-making beings, we initially take in the world primarily through taste, touch, sound, and smell. These early experiences form a template against which all later experience is tested and understood, infused by the affective undertones and overtones we take in directly without initially being able to make sense of them. Over time, words are attached to those experiences and become a means for indexing and talking with others about them, shaping both language and experience.

Early moments of resonance with a responsive other underlie the amodal experiences through which information from one sensory modality is translated into another while preserving the essence of the communication (Stern, 1985). Our innate capacities for *embodied simulation* (our innate ability to know through doing) afford the capacity to generalize, across modalities, visual or other sensory data into visceral and motoric sensations and sequences (Gallese et al., 2007). The interpenetration of meanings found in this nonverbal intramodal processing underlies Freud's (1900/1953b) conception of *primary process* in which apparent distinctions blur, leaving other aspects of conceptual linkages more apparent. Meanings are condensed, or, as Matte-Blanco (1975) termed it, *symmetrized*, in ways that can highlight important conceptual threads. Psychoanalytic theory has rested on the idea that the linking of meanings in the unconscious is highly personalized, a presumption that is borne out by empirical data that show a processing preference for self-representational stimuli without fidelity to details (Constable et al., 2019).

We see this symmetrization of meanings perhaps most clearly in dreams in which something can stand for something else while clearly not being that thing (e.g., "It was your office but did not look like your office"). An important thread in this process is affect, which functions at a presymbolic level and is linked across different domains of sensory experience (Bucci, 1997, 2001). Affect is prior to and to some extent separate from cognitive memory. Affect influences our thinking even when the affect is not conscious (Krystal, 1988); it is recognized intuitively through its patterns in terms of both our internal experience and our ability to perceive its traces on faces or in body position or gesture (Ekman, 1982).

Affect can be recognized across cultures by reference to its prosody and intensity (Tomkins, 1982). Optimally, we learn to read affect like a signal and to notice those signals at relatively low levels so that we can respond accordingly and keep our affect within tolerable limits. From this state of relative equilibrium, spikes of affect are useful signals that tell us that something is wrong and needs our attention. This signaling system helps us mark pleasurable and unpleasurable experiences and organize our ideas about how to encourage or avoid them. In the consulting room, it is crucial to notice when a person cannot downshift in moments of dysregulation so that we can at least mark the distress rather than inundate the person with words that they may be unable to parse in that moment.

Experiences stored within the body provide a complex coding system. We respond affectively to meanings we may not consciously recognize, and our capacity for affective resonance helps us communicate without conscious awareness or verbal language. The deficits associated with complex trauma leave the person at the mercy of signals that cannot be parsed, interfering with the affective resonance that includes all aspects of experience associated with those states. That resonance may best be conceptualized in terms of *contours* of feeling in which the form and pattern come to have both evocative and symbolic functions (Stern, 1985). Notably, those contours are also infused by the messages received from those around us regarding our place in the social world—the extent to which we are desired or valued (Aulagnier, 2001). We can watch the transfer of these contours in the interactions between parent and child and also in our own interactions, in the impact we have on one another. For example, we can notice how the mother's regulatory function is internalized as when the child comforts themselves through a doll, using the mother's soothing tone to say, "It's all right. Mama will be right back." In this vignette, we see not only the contour of the soothing but also the underlying message that the child's distress is worth soothing, that the child and their well-being matter.

Our early sensory experiences become integrated as models that guide and constrain all later understandings. Our innate facility for *intramodal processing* enables implicit communications to be transmitted in ways that, over time, themselves evoke responsiveness and also provide criteria regarding what is to be perceived as useful information and what is to be warded off as "noise" or "threat" (Beebe & Lachmann, 1988, 1994, 1998; Stern, 1985). These messages may be skewed away from useful reality testing by parental or cultural aversions or injunctions, making it difficult for the child to obtain data veridical to the situation being encountered. Fear and shame are particularly virulent emotions because they invite us to avoid precisely the data we might need to reduce the emotional intensity.

As we grow older, our appreciation for the nonverbal elements of meaning tends to diminish, and yet the meanings persist. Tone, for example, comes to carry meaning beyond—and often in disjunction to—the words expressed. Often, our words are eclipsed by the tone, which conveys important elements of meaning, like the child who complains about being "yelled at" in relation to not an increase in volume, but rather a note of disapproval in the tone. With children, nonverbal meanings tend to carry more weight than the words themselves. Denial of these nonverbal elements of meanings can be literally crazy-making, whereas acknowledgment can provide opportunities for the child to recognize the validity and potential value of their perceptions and make sense of contradictions when they occur (Bowen, 1978). When the early relational environment has been depriving, affective signals easily become noise to be managed or erased rather than adaptively attended to.

Part of what psychoanalytic therapy offers to those who have not been afforded sufficient opportunities to learn this coding system is the opportunity to slow things down and begin to make sense of the sequences of experiences through which meanings are marked. From that position, they might be able to register an impending difficulty earlier on in the sequence before they are so saturated by affect that they cannot think. Insight-oriented therapies provide these types of marked meanings, helping to build a scaffolding on which reflective capacities can be built. Even an ostensibly simple intervention, such as "You seem to have had a feeling just then?" can invite the person to more actively register a feeling that was too paired with danger to even notice.

LEARNING FROM EXPERIENCE

For the child who grows up in a family in which there are strong inhibitions or prohibitions against knowing, learning is impeded. Lack of acknowledgment is profoundly destabilizing. Studies show that discrepant data can result in confusion regarding even the contours and limits of our own bodies (Petkova & Ehrsson, 2008). Such difficulties impede the fundamental discriminations between self and other that are a precondition for self-knowledge and undermine the embodied simulation through which emotional experience (and its avoidance or inhibition) is communicated directly from parent to child (Gallese, 2009).

Language helps us sort our experiences into categories, organizing the complexities of daily life but also infusing those experiences with the values taken in from family and culture, much of which remains unconscious (Fonagy & Allison, 2023). Many of our activities are driven by the implicit, procedural knowledge that guides routinized activities, such as riding a bicycle or driving a car. The implicit memory system depends on our ability to recognize patterns that provide cues to help us navigate the complexity of signals coming our way. These patterns become nonverbal units of meaning that are read intuitively without necessarily invoking conscious attention (Charles, 2002b), patterned experiences that become attached to learned values (Tomkins, 1978). Without sufficient reflective capacity, these values can become rigid obstructions to learning rather than evolving markers of ethical principles.

Bucci (2018) suggested that the implicit meanings undergirding the nonverbal realm that we term *primary process* are best understood in terms of affect activation that occurs at both symbolic and subsymbolic levels.

In the *subsymbolic* system, learning occurs in relation to not discrete symbolic elements but rather variations along continuous dimensions (Bucci, 2002). This processing "occurs in motoric, visceral, and sensory forms, as sounds, smells, feelings of many different sorts, rather than as symbols or words . . . communicable directly within the sensory modality itself, and indirectly through analogic representations in other modalities" (Bucci, 2002, p. 769). The term *emotion schemas* describes "clusters of representations of events incorporating similar bodily, sensory and motoric processes, symbolic images and words" (Bucci et al., 2016, p. 359). These clusters become prototypes of meaning structures, such as those we find in Bion's Grid Category C (see Figure 1.1 in Chapter 1), the dream elements and other condensed symbols that are recognized intuitively. Driven by their affective charge, they coalesce into scripts that control how lived meanings are parsed and structured (Tomkins, 1978)—Lacan's (1964/1977e) Imaginary realm of personalized human experience.

This type of direct recognition occurs at the subsymbolic level and is processed through the nonverbal, implicit memory system that functions most efficiently in moments of relative inattention. At times of disequilibrium or startle, when our expectancies do not match our experience, we are drawn to more focused attention, which can be useful in a crisis but constrains our ability to attend to other data. Being able to make sense of our experience is inherently soothing, whereas unpredictable environments leave us in states of distress and "dis-ease." Excessive instability becomes a precursor for the complex trauma linked to disorders of self (Luyten et al., 2020). At the extreme, other people become markers of threat rather than sustenance, resulting in a hypervigilant focus on others' affect that makes it even more difficult to make use of internal sensory data.

Increasingly, neuroscience has affirmed many of the suppositions underlying psychoanalytic treatment, illustrating ways that early experiences shape the organization of our brains, particularly those functions that affect nonverbal learning (A. N. Schore, 2003). Research into mirror neurons has provided useful insights into some of the dilemmas encountered by the child who does not receive sufficient, adaptive attention (Gallese, 2009), the type of marked mirroring that psychoanalysts describe in relation to the crucial experience of being able to find oneself in the eyes, and therefore, the mind, of another person (Gergely & Watson, 1996; Winnicott, 1971). We experience this type of recognition when our feelings are acknowledged, that moment of meeting so crucial to the subsequent moving on (Stern, Bruschweiler-Stern, et al., 1998). Although the capacity for recognition of and responsiveness to the human face seems to be hardwired, trust in these capacities is built in real time. For example, one can watch a child playing with their tongue in response to the "La, la, la" being crooned by the parent. We can observe an infant begin to initiate smiling in the presence of other people and see the delight that occurs when the smile is returned, but we can also see the disorganization that sets in when the infant cannot engender smiling in the other.

These identification processes are strong and far-reaching. A functional magnetic resonance imaging study assessing responses to one's own and others' facial affect, for example, suggests that mirror neurons aid in empathic engagement at the level of the brain through mimicry of the emotion on the face of the other (Schulte-Rüther et al., 2007). This translation process occurs across modalities through our innate capacity for embodied simulation (Gallese et al., 2007). One can watch a young child watching their parent and see the sequence of behavioral moments play out embryonically in the child's body. In later years, one can then see ways in which the child's behavior imitates in form the behavior of the parent in gesture, tone, and the rhythms of speech and movement. We are indeed our parents' children.

When all goes well, the mirror neuron system helps us to make sense of self in world and, vicariously, to imagine how others might be both like and different from us. On the one hand, the body "constitutes the basic sense of self. On the other, it shapes our perceptions and pre-reflective conceptions of others" in line with our own experiences (Gallese, 2014, p. 2). This system depends on our ability to adequately take in data that is sufficiently consistent with previous experience to make sense of. Given the confusion that can arise when we are offered discrepant data, even about our own bodies, the relational context can be even more perplexing.

We can conjecture that when failures to mourn leave some data unintegrated, the affective messages in a given moment may be highly discrepant to what can be overtly recognized or discussed. The parent who has worked through past difficulties can mark a moment of distressed distraction in ways that assist the child in transitioning from distress back to equilibrium, but the mixed messages that are prevalent in families with unintegrated trauma make it difficult for the child to make sense of their experience and therefore also to generalize intention in accordance with categories of experience (Knox, 2009). These failures become a vehicle through which intergenerational trauma interferes with the development of the capacities for abstraction and generalization that facilitate learning. Complicating the picture are what Laplanche (1997) called the *enigmatic messages* that parents offer to children through the affective loadings that speak from the parent's unconscious to that of the child. These messages not only speak from unintegrated trauma but also from the cultural injunctions and fear- or shame-bound aversions that have shaped the parent's mind and being (Apprey, 2024).

AFFECT REGULATION AND TRAUMA

Factors that inhibit active engagement with self or other, such as stress and trauma, constrain our attention and disrupt the fluid interplay of explicit and implicit understandings, interfering with our ability to make sense of self and world and also undermining our faith in our ability to do so. This uncertainty creates "noise" in the machine, distancing us from making use of capacities that are more effective when largely unconscious. At the extreme, the novelty that should invite curiosity, exploration, and new learning instead may invite fear, vigilance, and uncertainty. Because it disrupts our ability to be present in the moment, trauma interferes with the integration and consolidation of memories and the development of a coherent worldview.

Although we often think of trauma in relation to major events that might shake the person's world, more critical are the small-t traumas that insidiously interfere with the individual's capacity to cope with life events as they occur (Main & Hesse, 1990) and cumulatively contribute to the symptom picture known as *complex trauma* (Stubley & Young, 2021). Parental failures to integrate their own experiences result in disruptions in the child's experience as the parent turns inward to cope with their own distress and becomes unavailable to the child in ways that are inscrutable and therefore seem random (Dozio et al., 2020). The young child depends on being able to find the parent's receptive face in moments of uncertainty. We all know this moment of pause as a young child waits to see the parent's reaction to a surprising event, such as an unexpected fall, to ascertain whether this is a moment for tears, laughter, or just moving on.

The developmental literature marks the importance of these early relational experiences in building resilience and facilitating the implicit relational knowing and epistemic trust so crucial to normal development (Fonagy & Allison, 2023; Stern, Sander, et al., 1998). In tandem, psychoanalytic theory, built on experiences with those whose development has been disrupted, shows the importance of early relationships in symptom formation and of the therapeutic relationship in making meaning from those symptoms.

We learn through our experience, and experience itself is complicated, particularly when trauma and shame preclude learning. Deficits in the capacity for affect regulation put us at risk. Survival depends on our ability to respond quickly and efficiently to the signal qualities of affect, which are integrated far more rapidly than conscious, verbal awareness. In the moment, the prosody of affective patterns provides important cues as to one's relative safety and the likely trajectory of a given interaction. Overstimulation disrupts this feedback system, encouraging a shutting down when dysregulation occurs rather than the fine-tuning of emotion that might take place with sufficient resilience.

Experiences of overwhelming affect, unmoderated, are themselves traumatic, interfering with our ability make sense of and organize our experience (Krystal, 1988; LeDoux, 1999; A. N. Schore, 1994), thus disrupting the signal functions of affect by blurring the features by which the signal might be recognized. As the child shuts down in the face of overstimulation, they are cut off not only from what is happening in the moment but also from building the self-regulatory capacities that might help them cope in future. These moments of shutting down can be seen as precursors for the capacity for dissociation. Distancing ourselves from self and experience can help us survive a difficult moment, but when there is no integration and repair, doing so obstructs the experiences of mastery that build resilience and self-esteem.

These failures also invite shame, undermining the sense of potency that undergirds the optimism and interest so crucial for new learning. Shame not only inhibits the relational engagement that is crucial to healthy development but also can impede adaptive efforts in ways that make attempts at repair traumatic. Repetitive traumatic experiences become anticipated insidiously in a process of "self-generated reoccurrence, self-generation of triggers" that are part of the "continuous never-ending meaning making processes, processes that feed upon themselves" (Tronick, 2022, p. 666).

In the extreme case, affect can become a signal for avoidance, further impeding our ability to encounter and use affective signals and becoming a generalized anxiety that cannot be parsed, thus inviting defensive maneuvers aimed at numbing rather than resolving. This dilemma is amplified in fear reactions, which tend to be entrenched and are particularly difficult to overcome because of their inherent survival functions (LeDoux, 2002). Shame is also highly resistant to change because of its virulence and avoidant properties.

Much as Bion (1977) highlighted the crucial choice between seeking knowledge or avoiding it, Tomkins (1978) described shame as a function of a sudden interpersonal break that inhibits curiosity and engagement. Shame not only casts down our eyes but also amplifies emotion, leading to the magnification of particular scripts that carry meanings forward in ways that can preclude reflection or integration. In Bion's terms, meanings become saturated as though all is known and there is no point in inquiring further. In the transference (discussed further in Chapter 5), we encounter these scripts as they play out in real time in the relationship.

Such presumptions inhibit reflective function, making it difficult to sustain curiosity and take the risks required for new learning and the experiences of mastery that build positive self-regard and metacognitive capacities (Fonagy et al., 2002; Lysaker, Erickson, et al., 2010, 2011). Shame inhibits the ability to look outward, closing down the perspective necessary to make sense of self in relation to others. Recurrent experiences of shame can result in internalized scripts in which expectations of humiliation, defeat, and victimization are self-validating and resist moderation or repair (Tomkins, 1978). These expectations become self-validating because they inhibit reengagement with others in ways that might ease the distress or alter the expectation, so that even our efforts to make meaning from them can be self-perpetuating (Tronick, 2022).

TRAUMA AND THE RELATIONAL MATRIX

Adverse early life circumstances have a physiological impact. These effects can be moderated by the parent–infant attachment bond and also by empathic containment in psychotherapy (A. N. Schore, 1994, 2003) in part by building the epistemic trust so crucial to the development of reflective capacities (Fonagy & Allison, 2014). Secure attachment is linked not only with higher levels of affect regulation and self-reliance but also with greater social competence and resilience (Sroufe, 2005), whereas low maternal sensitivity and high intrusiveness are linked to decrements in both cognitive and social development (R. Feldman, 2010). Difficulties with affect regulation impede recovery from stressful events across the lifespan (Burke et al., 2005).

These data show the crucial importance of the quality of parental care for the development and well-being of the child. Infants are active learners. Not merely responsive to and imitative of the gestures of others, they also come to anticipate and invite a continued exchange from those around them. In anticipation of the expected response, newborns spontaneously produce gestures they have previously imitated (Nagy & Molnár, 2004). Such observations show the importance of the ability to elicit responses from the parent in ongoing exchanges of meaning-making. Trauma impedes the parent's ability to respond empathically and effectively to inevitable moments of misattunement that optimally afford the moments of rupture and repair that are crucial to the development of resilience. When the parent is too preoccupied with their own distress to effectively turn their attention to the needs and feelings of the child (Beebe & Lachmann, 1994; Dozio et al., 2020), this repair process is hindered.

Trauma disrupts the intersubjective rhythmicity that structures the intermodal processing through which meanings are exchanged with the preverbal child (Trevarthen, 2005). In this way, it also disrupts the parent–child synchrony that underlies the intersubjectivity at the heart of human relationships (R. Feldman, 2007). "Viewed as a formative experience for the maturation of the social brain, synchrony impacts the development of self-regulation, symbol use, and empathy across childhood and adolescence" (p. 329). This synchrony is integral to the nonverbal underpinnings of meaning that include the temporal aspects of interpersonal reciprocity,

> the rhythmic repetitions, the ongoing match of affective states, the sequential mirroring of the infant's communicative signals, and the parent's transformation of the infant's social bids into a variety of sensory modalities that preserve the intensity, shape, and rhythms of the original message. (R. Feldman, 2007, pp. 329–330)

Child and infant optimally form a unit in which each person's actions are continually modified through interaction with the other in the system Fogel (1992) termed *coregulation*. Maternal depression and anxiety interfere with the development of synchrony through overintrusive, controlling behaviors and a lack of responsivity (R. Feldman, 2007; Field, 1992; Lima et al., 2014).

Unresolved trauma or loss can make the parent unavailable in moments of distress (Field, 1992), disrupting both narrative coherence and self-development (van Ijzendoorn et al., 1999). Because of the importance of imitation and interaction in the early months and years, the child's failure to engage the parent has significant consequences for their social and emotional development (Tronick & Reck, 2009). The child who cannot elicit responsiveness from the parent can become disorganized and lose their self-regulatory capacities under strain (Main & Hesse, 1990); the child may become preoccupied with the environment at the expense of self-knowledge and with self-soothing at the expense of interpersonal engagement and the development of self-knowledge (Tronick, 1989; Winnicott, 1971). At the extreme, hypervigilance for danger disrupts intramodal processing and impedes learning to make the fundamental discriminations between self and other that are a precondition for self-knowledge and for building our metacognitive capacities.

In families characterized by pushing past mourning rather than facing it, a toll is taken that haunts successive generations. The parent who cannot face their own traumatic past turns that blind eye to the difficulties faced by the child. In turn, the child registers the difficulty, but, without the words to speak about it, the unrecognized knowledge often lodges in the body itself through physical symptoms, disorganization, or heightened distress (Liotti, 2004; McDougall, 1985), a topic explored further in later chapters. Communal trauma takes an even larger toll because the extended family and community have fewer resources to help attenuate difficulties encountered with parents. The impact of communal trauma is exacerbated by the shame and negative self-identity associated with marginalization that can be passed along the generations somewhat invisibly. In Abraham's (Abraham & Torok, 1975/1994) formulation, it is "the dead who were shamed during their lifetime or who took unspeakable secrets to the grave" (p. 171) who are most likely to haunt us. Failure to face these phantoms can take a terrible toll on identity development, as discussed in Chapter 4.

IMPLICATIONS FOR TREATMENT

The early child literature highlights the debilitating, insidious effects of trauma, disruption, and neglect on the developing child in terms of the affective development so crucial to identity, interpersonal relatedness, and a sense of embeddedness within the social world (Fonagy & Allison, 2023; J. R. Schore & Schore, 2008). Too much stress interferes with the child's affective and cognitive development and is exacerbated by parental failures (Fonagy et al., 2002). These developmental failures inhibit learning and decrease resilience, thereby increasing the negative impact of later traumatic or disruptive events. Development is further impeded when children are exposed to the frightening or overwhelming experiences with caregivers that are linked to a disorganized attachment style, characterized by dissociative behavior and a tendency to freeze and be unable to manage challenges as they arise (Lyons-Ruth, 2003; Main & Hesse, 1990).

One consequence of such disruption is difficulty in recognizing or making adaptive use of the internal signals and external cues that otherwise might guide behavior rather than merely inhibit or provoke. Interventions that invite us to encounter and reflect on these internal and external cues help develop resilience by building the metacognitive capacities that provide a stronger foundation from which to encounter the world. Psychoanalytically informed therapies have as a major goal the development of insight: the ability to take oneself and one's feelings, thoughts, and desires seriously. This intention takes a stand against hierarchical models in which one might come to an authority to obtain received knowledge. Rather, this is a model that contends that we can learn to be more resilient and make more adaptive choices to the extent that we are aware of our feelings, desires, and motivations. For those who have been severely traumatized, coming to the point of thinking of oneself as the primary frame of reference can demand a fundamental shift from avoiding the aggressor (or searching for a savior) to respecting one's vulnerability as well as one's strengths. This shift can only occur within the context of a relationship that is safe enough to risk allowing oneself and one's struggles to be known. Clinically, these data invite us to focus most directly on building a containing relationship in which capacities for affect regulation can develop. These capacities become the ground on which metacognition and a more cogent and adaptive identity can be built.

CONCLUSION

In this chapter, I highlighted how available and empathic caregiving helps to moderate stress, whereas children whose parents are either unavailable or not empathically responsive to the child's needs and feelings show elevated levels of stress (Gunnar & Fisher, 2006). Deficits in caregiving have an impact on the child's ability to organize and effectively manage their activities and behavior, the *executive functions* (Curtis & Cicchetti, 2003), or metacognitive capacities, that are crucial in making one's way in the world. The ability to reflect on one's own thoughts and feelings in relation to the thoughts and feelings of others is integral to both self-esteem and healthy relationships.

The tendency to freeze and dissociate that is linked to severe abuse and neglect interferes with the ability to be aware of one's own perceptions, feelings, and thoughts, as we will see in the chapters that follow. Interventions that recognize the primary importance of affect and the relative inaccessibility of trauma to verbal language are much more likely to be successful in facilitating self-development than those that focus on cognition or behavior alone. Recognizing the fundamental links between affective self-regulation and cognitive capacities reminds us to pay close attention to levels of affective activation in the consulting room so that we can invite greater respect for the person's own feelings in ways that enhance their reflective capacities. Guiding our efforts is recognition of the importance of building the type of trusting and trustworthy relationship that can support the person as they build the capacities for self-reflection and awareness of others so crucial to well-being. We turn now to symbolization, the development of the consensual language essential for making sense of experience and finding one's way in the world.

3 SYMBOLIZATION

In this chapter, I expand on the foundation created in Chapter 2, recognizing how the early embodied experiences that build interpersonal safety and relatedness also make possible the transformation of these experiences into the symbols that form the bedrock of consensual verbal language. I then explore how recognition of these processes might inform our clinical work with those whose development has been waylaid such that important meanings may be expressed in symptoms rather than in words.

MAKING SENSE OF EMBODIED EXPERIENCE

Parallel to the development of nonverbal interpersonal communication occurring in the early days and months of life is the development of verbal language. This process evolves through engagement with other speaking beings, transforming primary experience into the symbols that underlie the

---

Portions of this chapter have been adapted from "Somatization and Symbolization," by M. Charles, 2024, *American Journal of Psychoanalysis*, *84*, pp. 57–78 (https://doi.org/10.1057/s11231-024-09441-1). Copyright 2024 by Springer Nature. Adapted with permission.

https://doi.org/10.1037/0000455-004
Echoes of Trauma: Meaning and Identity in Psychoanalysis, by M. Charles

construction of verbal language. Establishing our identity as a separate and unique person in relation to other persons requires real engagements through which interpersonal meanings can be established—Lacan's realm of the Symbolic. Otherwise, we are left accommodating to others' constructions or inhabiting an overly personalized, imaginary universe that excludes others. For Lacan (1975–1976/2016), meaning resides precisely in the intersections between the Imaginary and the Symbolic, the places where experience meets language, where minds might link.

Symbols not only transmit information but also, as Bion (1977/1989) demonstrated in his Grid (see Figure 1.1, Chapter 1), become vehicles for thinking, enabling the transformation and elaboration of meanings necessary for adaptive living (Cassirer, 1957). Psychoanalysis has positioned the body at the core of meaning, stressing that "mind and mental functions emerge from sensory and emotional data rather than the other way around" (Carignani, 2012, p. 311). Taking this seriously, we see how the relationships with others so crucial to human development provide a containing function that supports but is subsidiary to this primary relationship with one's own body (Ferrari, 2004). From this perspective, verbal language develops in the interplay between beings in relation to the embodied experience that grounds it through the patterned rhythms that form the core of all human meaning-making.

Despite Freud's (1923/1961) emphasis on the ego as forged in and through the body, in his hands, psychoanalysis became an exploration that valorized the word over nonverbal experience. Various thinkers have theorized toward this gap between body and mind. Klein (1940/1981b, 1946), for example, examined the terrain in which early drives and conflicts determine actions, and Bion (1967b) extended that work to consider how thinking, as an active process, develops from the primary bits of data that assail us. Lacan (1964/1977e), in his focus on the *gap* as a locus of lost meanings, went back to Freud in positioning the unconscious as the driving force recognizable indirectly through omissions, slips, and symptoms. Freud's (1900/1953b) *kernel*—the unassimilable nugget at the core of human meaning—became Lacan's *hole* into which we can fall in our impossible quest for a Truth not conditioned by our human be-ing.

The field of psychosomatics arose precisely in relation to symptoms lodged in and expressed through the body that could not be thought about, symptoms that mark a hole in meaning. These explorations of the nonverbal domain have relevance for clinicians who are trying to understand experiences that are not fully symbolized. In this chapter, I focus on ideas regarding the symbolization process itself, beginning from the most concrete elements to increasingly refined mental products that can be communicated and engaged with between persons. The flow of this enterprise is toward Bion's

(1977) goal in psychoanalysis of developing greater capacity to make use of one's experience to further the capacities to think and to *dream* in the sense that Winnicott (1971) used the term. At the extreme, fantasies can be ruminative and obsessive, destroying possibilities rather than allowing us to play with them. Winnicott (1971) described this hazard in terms of a type of empty, repetitive fantasying that may be self-soothing but goes nowhere versus a dream that can be used in creative ways because it is layered with meanings that relate "to past, present, and future, and to inner and outer"; self and other (p. 35). Keeping in mind Bion's Grid, we recognize that the person's intent is pivotal: Are they moving toward growth or evasion?

Bionian field theorists, such as Civitarese and Ferro (2013), have made use of this idea of developing the capacity to dream in their practice, actively engaging in creative "dreaming" during the sessions as an invitation to the analysand to engage in their own dreaming. The realm of dreams is the realm of images, which may be seen as proto-meanings that can develop over time into rich and more fully elaborated symbols and stories within the context of reliable relationships. Without such a foundation, images become signs that may not be useful beyond the confines of one's own dream or fantasy, and the most crucial data may be held so privately that no one else has access. Truths thus guarded come to seem like lies because they cannot be shared without putting at risk what feels like a deep and fragile anchor. Under such conditions, the clinician's respect for signs of danger or openness to preliminary attempts at making meaning can help to mark the interpersonal moment in ways that facilitate the symbolization process.

Truths held at that primary level likely relate back to meanings that have not been fully metabolized and may not be consciously known. This would seem to be the realm of Kristeva's (1986) *chora*, the primary rhythms that structure all meanings. Aulagnier (2001) suggested that, underneath conscious memory, early infantile experiences of flesh upon flesh, infused by the caretaker's pleasure or displeasure, form a template, a *pictogram*, on which all meanings become patterned. The pictogram, for Aulagnier, is the representational system of what she termed the *primal* process, the underbelly of all sensory experience and human meaning. Her view argued for the particularity of human meaning and experience, demanding a person-centered approach to treatment. As we will see when we consider transference and countertransference in Chapter 5, such embodied meanings are often *felt* rather than consciously *known*. The receptive clinician can help contain anxiety by thinking about feelings experienced during sessions without trying to manage them or shut them down. Gallese's (2009) work on mirror neurons helped sustain the clinician's efforts at self-soothing during difficult moments by validating the impact of our own reflectivity on those around us.

Being respectful of the embodied, underlying layers of meaning infusing experienced reality is essential in work with those whose own embodied experience has become inscrutable. When affect has lost its signal functions, becoming something to avoid, manage, or control, people may present with symptoms of panic, somatization, or posttraumatic stress disorder. These presentations have in common the type of primary, developmentally driven deficits that Freud subsumed under the rubric of the *actual neuroses* (Verhaeghe & Vanheule, 2005; Verhaeghe et al., 2007).

With people who are limited in their reflective capacities, I often find myself imagining and describing to them my fantasy of what might have led to symptoms that seem unfathomable. This stance affirms my belief that there is significance to their symptoms, meanings to which they uniquely hold the key. Difficulties in early development leave people unknown to themselves, unable to read their own communicative efforts, much less contextualize their experience into a life story that makes sufficient sense to afford hope or possibility.

THE RELATIONAL CONTEXT

When children are offered a good-enough early environment, there is a normal progression from primary sensation to verbal language. As we have seen, the attentive, attuned parent learns the child's language, differentiating among cries that signal pain, hunger, or the desire for social engagement. The parent who meets and mirrors the child's feelings helps the child organize an understanding of self and other that is based on the primary sensory and emotional experiences we all share and can recognize in one another. This fundamental self-knowledge is the bedrock of the development of reflective function, a relationship with embodied experience that allows us to symbolize an increasingly nuanced understanding of self and other in the service of managing daily life and enjoying social interactions (Fonagy et al., 2002).

The attuned parent who meets the child's distress with attention and then soothing helps the child learn to soothe themselves; the basic functions of care and attention are internalized and can be linked to primary sensory and emotional experience. As basic trust in the availability of assistance is built, the development of verbal language enables the child to turn more actively to others and ask directly for what is desired or needed. Words become an important medium of exchange through which increasingly complex needs can be recognized and filled. Essential to this process is the development of a separate self, the culmination of the type of engagement Winnicott (1971) described in his ideas about the use of an object. From his perspective, we must be able to get rid of the other's mind sufficiently to find our own.

Separateness is essential to agency. Once autonomy is established, experiences can be shared, helping us organize our understandings in ways that promote reality testing, enrich our reflective capacities and our ability to master challenges, and build empathically attuned and sustaining relationships. When parents are not attuned to the child, language becomes a means of attenuating a gap that may be so profound that the person is unable to make sense of or adaptively make use of their feelings as signals mindfully guiding behavior. The clinical work, then, begins with an attempt to orient to something that, for all intents and purposes, is not there: the person's mindful, respectful interest in their own internal experience. At the extreme, needs and feelings may be experienced as dangerous to acknowledge, much less show to others.

With those who have not developed a language for speaking about internal experience, behavior tends to be driven rather than reflected on. Even speech that seems consensual and agreed on may have profoundly different referents when inquired into. For example, take Olivia, a woman in her early twenties who entered treatment because she had been told her ideas were delusional. Olivia is uncertain how to make sense of her experience and what and whom she might trust if she cannot trust her own mind. A part of her wants to believe she is delusional because then she might be "fixed," and the people she relies on for comfort might be less angry. She is irritated when I inquire into her experience of the events in question because this clearly shows that I do not understand the problem. She does not know anything, she insists—that is why she is here. Despite her reluctance, I continue to inquire into her experience while also tracking it, noting affect as it plays across her face and being interested in what it might mean. In a given moment, she might freeze at being recognized but then shift into a beaming smile when the recognition is not accompanied by reproof or rejection. My smile seems to invite her into being. Her hunger for it becomes its own hazard as she looks to me to fill the void.

Opportunities occur for Olivia's questions to be answered in real time, but she is so afraid of being seen that she runs away from engagement. She would like to present another self instead of the empty, devouring need she finds inside. Who is she? She doesn't know. "Find out," I tell her. "Try to be present in the moment; notice your reactions; see what you think, even if you can't say it. And try to speak and see what happens."

Olivia listens. In a group, someone seems angry, and Olivia says so. The person wants to know why she said that. Olivia shuts down, frightened, sure that the person's question is an aggressive attack rather than an attempt at engagement. "How *did* you know?" I ask. "Her face, her tone," says Olivia. "Oh," I say, "You know a great deal about that," thinking of her parents' faces in a family meeting. Her face lights up at having her internal knowing recognized by another as valuable. She finds my hope for her utterly enigmatic but also compelling, helping her move from the places she gets caught. When she can be more present, she is able to collect data about herself in relation to others. Through these efforts, she is learning to symbolize her experience and speak from it, but meanings can still disappear when the threat feels too dire.

Having the family context in mind helps the clinician better understand some of the impediments to meaning-making we encounter. Olivia's story is one of well-intentioned parents who were preoccupied with their own troubles during her early life. Although they loved her and delighted in her precocious brilliance, they were not sufficiently attentive to her struggles to help her effectively work through them. She learned to rely on appearances rather than to become more actively engaged in the making of meaning. She reminds me of another young woman with whom I worked, Lina, who kept searching for the "right clothes" that would present her in the way she desired (see the explication of this case in Chapter 5). How would you know what to wear, I would ask her, if you do not know who you are, what you like? It took her many months of struggle to be able to settle into the legitimacy of this question. At that point, the real work began.

MOVING TOWARD SYMBOLIZATION

In working with people so caught by early failures, it is useful to have in mind Aulagnier's (2001) primal level of experience that includes both the sense of body on body and the affective infusions attendant to those early experiences. Her depiction of representations occurring at this level as *pictograms*, however, may be misleading. Perhaps more experience-near would be Tustin's (1984) term *auto-sensuous shapes*, which refers to the type of *unmentalized experience* (Mitrani, 1995), often libidinally charged, that is used toward self-soothing. These bits of experience that are not yet mentalized would seem to be the territory that Bion (1977) referred to in terms of *beta-elements* (defined in the introduction to this volume).

Early memories that are not easily accessible to conscious awareness remain, forming a *language of the body* (Charles, 2002b) whose meanings are linked by affect. Affective memory exists prior to, and to some extent separate from, cognitive memory, exerting an influence on secondary processes whether or not the affect becomes conscious (Bower, 1981; Krystal, 1988). Bodily memories may be expressed in numerous ways, including as unexplained pain or repetitive, patterned movements. Although these types of *primitive communications* (McDougall, 1974) may be difficult to understand, they may also help us recognize nonverbal memories and unconscious fantasies as they emerge in the moment so that we might begin to symbolize what has remained unformulated.

Symbol formation and communication depend on the ability to transform these sensory and affective experiences first into the condensed, affectively driven elements of primary process and then into the more distinctive elaborations of secondary process. As elements of primary experience become further elaborated, they not only help us communicate to others but also provide conceptual anchors that help us learn from our experience. For those whose early experience did not afford sufficient grounding, the clinician's interest in the variousness of signals of affective memory can facilitate greater conscious awareness, respectful attention, and integration of disparate and disowned experiences, helping to build a conceptual map through which to make sense of self and world (Charles, 2010). Often, this requires slowing down the process when we see the person jumping past an elusive or uncomfortable thought or sensation. "Whoa," I might say. "Something just happened there. What was going on?" Our active interest is a designation of value that can help the person to persist as they encounter perplexing or dangerous territory.

In normal development, confluences of sensation become related to the structures of actual objects in the world and form the basis for object relations. Secure relational containment allows separation, and with it the rudiments of meaning-making, to occur. Failures in containment, however, invite *false-self constructions* (Bick, 1968) in which rigid defenses allow for a sense of coherency but at the price of self-knowledge and integration. What remain, then, are unmentalized experiences that provide the rudiments of meaning if we can orient toward them and unpack them.

Affirming psychoanalytic observations regarding the essential nature of the unconscious events or fantasies that underlie all mental processes (Freud, 1900/1953b; Isaacs, 1948), the developmental literature describes generalized episodes that are abstracted from specific occurrences and become prototypical expectations against which all later events are gauged (Stern, 1985). The generalized pattern becomes a meaningful structure, which can be modified, further elaborated, or encapsulated—depending on the individual's later experiences and how and whether they can be integrated. When isolated from the original experiences, these patterns may be highly idiosyncratic, resulting in symbols best interpreted by the individual themselves until we become familiar enough with them that our interpretations are more likely to be meaningful, as happens over time in insight-oriented therapies. The ability to form and modify generalized conceptions in an ongoing fashion helps build the sense of a core or cohesive self in relation to a coherent other that is an essential underpinning of identity development (Stern, 1985).

These patterned meanings are not only shaped by interpersonal engagements within families but are also infused by cultural presumptions that circumscribe the parameters of what might be known. Psychoanalysis had its origins at a time when sexuality was problematic, particularly for women, whose psychological struggles were manifesting through their bodies while they remained unconscious of the sources of their distress. These early beginnings have led to ongoing investigations regarding the splits that occur between body and mind, which I explore more directly in Chapter 7.

A DUAL LANGUAGE STRUCTURE

As a clinical enterprise, psychoanalysis works toward resolving this type of split by recognizing the existence of a dual language structure that includes both body and mind as constituents of the fabric of embodied meanings. From that perspective, the body may be seen as the locus of the aesthetic underpinnings of meanings, reminding us of the roots of knowledge that mark essential truths. These truths are grounded in patterns through which more fully elaborated meanings are constituted (Charles, 2002b), the prosodies of affective, personalized constructions marked in the stochastic structure of the unconscious, each with their own unique rhythms (Kristeva, 1986; Lacan, 1964/1977e; Matte-Blanco, 1975).

Patterns are recognized at very basic levels, increasingly organizing our perceptions as we make sense of the world. Affect is known through its rhythms, each having its own particular prosody. Infant and caregiver speak to one another through these primary rhythm structures, receiving and anticipating meanings in cross-modal communications that evolve over time (Stern, 1985). Even before verbal language, meanings are being structured in the ongoing call and response between parent and child (Wermke & Mende, 2009), the melody of language speaking truer than words in our early lives (Fernald, 1993; Papoušek et al., 1990).

Bucci (2018) moved beyond the dual structure of primary and secondary process to propose a *multiple code theory* that can be useful in helping us track and make sense of the multiple ways in which meanings are represented. At the core of her theory are the *emotion schemas* that "constitute the desires, expectations, and beliefs one has about other people, which develop through interactions with others from the beginning of life" (Bucci, 1997, pp. 156–157). Bucci suggested that meanings are made through a referential process that includes *affective arousal,* which occurs in subsymbolic form; *symbolizing,* which occurs both nonverbally in the form of imagery and verbally in the form of narrative; and *reflection/organization,* which occurs through the active process of attempting to make meaning from the experience. In this progression, we find referents in Bion's Grid (see Chapter 1), reminding us that theory points toward realities of human be-ing, so that we might integrate the pieces that are most useful to us without necessarily looking for the most "correct" theory.

Bucci's theory implied that, for those dissociated from their experience, the therapeutic process entails linking sensory experience to memories and fantasies such that they can be reflected on and meaning made between individuals within the psychoanalytic field (Civitarese & Ferro, 2013). In this context, bodily symptoms provide opportunities to imagine and recognize emotions that have been dissociated or unrecognized as connections are built "within the nonverbal system between subsymbolic somatic activation and images of objects" so that "meaningful verbal communication can occur" (Bucci, 1997, p. 165). These connections could not be built without reference to some other person who can link sensation with words and thereby bring previously unformulated experience into the realm of the conscious, reflective mind—someone who can notice both similarity and disjunction.

Bucci's formulations are in line with research and clinical evidence that has shown how integrally the evolution of our cognitive capacities is linked to our ability to make meaning from somatic experience (e.g., Lysaker et al., 2020). Reflective capacity depends on one's ability to be grounded in and make sense of primary sensory and affective experience, a lack we find in the subjects of Freud's early studies of hysteria (Breuer & Freud, 1895/1955). Through that lens, hysterical displays were seen in relation to bodily sensations that could not find direct expression, but rather spoke through the language of the symptom.

Psychoanalysis helps us make sense of this type of unformulated communication, suggesting that psychosomatic illness marks communicative efforts that come from unmetabolized experience, "an archaic form of mental functioning that does not use language" (McDougall, 1989, p. 10). These primal language registers take the form of Aulagnier's (2001) embodied, affect-laden pictograms that mark the most basic underlying relation between self and other, the basic link or lack thereof. Leikert (2021) termed this region one of *encapsulated body engrams,* unsymbolized substructures within the unconscious that govern meanings even more powerfully because of their inaccessibility to conscious thought. This is also the terrain explored by Aulagnier in which the embodied experience is the fundamental starting point, but the receptivity of another person is required for nascent meanings to evolve into knowledge that can be held in mind and communicated in verbal language.

Saturated by meanings that cannot yet be parsed, Aulagnier's (2001) pictograms may form the underlying essence of Laplanche's (1997) *enigmatic signifiers* in which traces of the caregiver's messages "remain, acting as precursors of the secondary, obscure 'witnesses' to the existence of alterity, otherness" (P. Miller, 2015, p. 1364). For Aulagnier (2015), at the core of psychosomatic and psychotic disturbance we find an object relation that was not sufficiently flexible to enable the infant to encounter self in relation to other, therefore also obstructing the crucial transition to being able to use others in the service of meaning-making, in Winnicott's (1971) sense.

Without sufficient subject status, the infant is at the mercy of the desire of the caregiver, who must be sufficiently empathically available that the suffering of the child invites attention to the particularity of that other being. The caregiver's interest enables a transition from a primary relation with the body to an embodied relation with others (P. Miller, 2015). Without that scaffolding, "symptoms are seen as signs, not symbols, and follow somatic rather than psychic laws" (McDougall, 1974, p. 441). In such cases, the therapist's focus on bodily experience, perception, sensation, and affect invites the person to notice and recognize embodied, patterned meanings and "to find a language, or indeed to notice the language(s) which they are already using" (Carvalho, 2012, p. 422). At the core of this work is the recognition of the body as "*still a concrete object, the reintegration of which into the analytic process enables the patient to open up to experience, change and life, even before opening up to thought*" (Lombardi, 2008, p. 106).

SYMBOLIZATION

The transition from sign to symbol is a complex one. In the consulting room, it is important to be able to recognize what Lacan (1964/1977e) termed *empty speech* that marks missing data. In this regard, da Rocha Barros (2000) suggested that three interconnected levels of meaning may be operating simultaneously: hidden, absent, and potential meanings. "'Hidden' meaning [results] from dynamic forms of repression, absent meaning from a pregnant pressure exerted on psychic life by unconscious internal objects whenever any new emotional situation confronts the ego" (da Rocha Barros, 2000, p. 1087). Whereas hidden meaning is posited as resulting from depression and as accessible to conscious thought, absent meaning requires interpretation to come to consciousness. Another mind is required to realize the potential.

da Rocha Barros lodged this fundamental human dilemma of representing internal experience to another person in precisely the arena we have been discussing: the communication system that seems to be present even before birth in the early interchanges of sensation that pass between mother and child. The presence of a receptive other invites further activity without the excess of tension that arises when the need for response is frustrated. How the communication is read matters, as in the mother who accuses her child of being impossible when the child's frustration reaches its upper limits. We see this type of double message in Olivia's interactions with her mother, where the verbal message is "I love you" while the face expresses hateful aggression. At the point at which the system fails, the communications can become noisy indeed.

Freezing makes sense when there is insufficient trust to work through a troubling or confusing encounter. When direct communication seems dangerous, working in the displacement can provide a transitional space to reflect on difficult material. Dreams are particularly useful in providing imagery to communicate primary experience. Because they are the dreamer's own product, the metaphors derived from them are experience-near. Access to embodied meanings in this way can be crucial for individuals such as Olivia, who has trouble even knowing what is real given the disjunction between her own experience and what she is being told by those she depends on. For da Rocha Barros (2000), this type of tension marks an absent meaning needing to be discovered. In daily life, we try to reduce the tension, which is all well and good, but, in psychoanalysis, we also need to explore those points of tension as important kernels of meaning awaiting investigation. Recognizing the sources of tension provides opportunities to work through problems rather than merely try to avoid them.

da Rocha Barros's formulation invites us to move beyond the archaeological metaphors of the hidden meanings once thought to be the prize of psychoanalytic exploration to recognize the absent meanings carried in the unconscious as potential meanings awaiting construction (rather than *re*construction). Recognizing these incipient *meanings in search of characterization*, as Ferro (2009) put it, helps us symbolize the affective underpinnings in ways that are generative rather than reductive. This type of process respects how profoundly early experience structures meaning for each individual, resulting in the unique creative potential marked by Milner (1987) and explored further by Lacan (1975–1976/2016) in his depiction of the sinthome. Recognizing the roots structuring these personalized meanings helps us track the patterns respectfully, in close relation to the person's history, rather than overriding incipient meanings through our own formulations.

da Rocha Barros (2000) used the term *affective pictogram* to refer to representations of early experience laden with emotional meanings that are present in image form but not yet expressed in thought. From this perspective, dream images are condensations and constellations of meaning structures held in mind and awaiting mentalization. In a primary stage, a dream maps out undigested feelings revolving around the more basic structures of the ego that constitute the kernels of meaning of emotional experience. Apprehending these kernels of meaning in the form of pictographic images is a first step in the process of articulation of affects in the mind (da Rocha Barros, 2000). This transformation process moves from primary affect, to image, toward greater abstraction and elaboration in the presence of a receptive other (Meltzer, 1984). For those for whom meanings have been denied, however, the internalized opposition can result in destructive impulses that obstruct symbol construction (da Rocha Barros & da Rocha Barros, 2011).

Matte-Blanco (1975) refined our ideas of primary and secondary process by pointing out that each realm has its own logic. *Primary process,* he suggested, is governed by *symmetry*, focusing on links between seemingly unlike things, whereas *secondary process* builds categories by focusing on the *asymmetry*, the differences between groups. Mancia (2008) picked up on Matte-Blanco's ideas regarding symmetrical relationships, suggesting that the early unrepressed unconscious is the site of implicit memories, a storehouse of our "conscious and unconscious history . . . where our affects, emotions, thoughts, and even our dreams are stored" (Mancia, 2008, pp. 201–202).

This storehouse includes sensory experiences from the womb, particularly the tone and cadence of the mother's voice (R. Feldman, 2006). In the early months of life, "the mother's vocality and rhythms of language build up an area of affective and emotional interaction, where introjections and projections between the mother and child converge" (Mancia, 2008, p. 202). Much like Aulagnier's (2001) formulations, for Mancia, the prosody of the mother's language is linked to her feelings in ways that influence the child's internalization of meanings. This view is also in line with Winnicott's (1971) recognition of how the child mirrors not only the facial expressions of the mother but also tone and gesture, each of which carries emotional meanings based on the experiences held between the two. At times, the clinician can catch glimpses of this mirrored image, which helps us to recognize the face of the internalized mother in the person before us. I learned this lesson quite dramatically when I recognized the look of repulsion I was seeing mirrored from one woman's previous encounters with her own mother (see Chapter 6 in Charles, 2004, for an explication of this case).

Mancia (2008) suggested that early traumas, especially if repeated, result in defenses that are stored in implicit memory in ways that may impede the development of symbolic process and reflective functions. As he put it,

> Continuous or repeated frustrations and disappointments can also contribute to organizing a young child's fantasies and defenses, which will be deposited in the preverbal and presymbolic implicit memory, where they will mold the structure of an *unrepressed unconscious nucleus of self*. (Mancia, 2008, p. 203)

The internalizations from these early, preverbal years come to structure memory, meaning, and the self. The clinician's sensitivity to the musicality of the other person's speech allows contact even with "deep-down unconscious elements that cannot be recalled, connected to the early and most significant relational experiences dominated by the mother's voice, and stored in implicit memory as structural components of the unrepressed unconscious" (Mancia, 2008, p. 204).

In the consulting room, we try to formulate in verbal terms what we can only have access to in the nonverbal domain of elements of experience, to translate beta-elements into mentalized alpha-elements (Bion, 1977). These nonverbal elements cannot properly be remembered but perhaps can be recognized, that is, "emotionally re-lived in the intersubjective relationship that enables the patient to identify himself, in the transference, with early infantile parts of his self that revive preverbal emotions he cannot recall" (Mancia, 2008, p. 205). In this way of working, attention to countertransference experiences and to the recounting of dreams helps provide a play space through which to recognize and reconstruct meanings held in implicit memory, as discussed in later chapters.

Freud (1910/1957a) focused a great deal on repression, which presumed a logic that underlies the capacity to reject information. Following Matte-Blanco's (1975) ideas regarding the symmetrization that occurs when emotion prevails over reason in organizing experience, Mancia (2008) suggested that the early memories Aulagnier (2001) referred to as primal cannot be recalled because there are no figurative representations, only embodied memories that implicitly affect how the person derives meanings in their current life. Ideas regarding the primal layer of experience and the unrepressed unconscious point to the underpinnings of experience that have been lived but not metabolized. Winnicott (1974) suggested that this process also occurs with traumatic events that were not lived through and therefore cannot be remembered. In psychoanalysis, part of what we are searching for is the story underneath the story that makes sense of the person's troubles as they have emerged. As we begin to formulate the story and speak to it, we provide a conceptual scaffolding that can be modified and moderated by the person themselves as they develop their own internal sense of truth in relation to the authenticity of lived experience.

CONSTRUCTION OF MEANINGS

Having in mind how formative these early experiences are despite not being directly accessible through conscious reflection helps us pay attention to the data we do have access to through feelings and dreams, noticing what seems to *touch* the person in real time and being open to inquiring into those moments as they occur. The living-through and subsequent working-through is facilitated in psychoanalysis by having another person present to mark meanings and also gaps. For Olivia, my recognition of forces that obstruct conversation in her family helps her recognize the impasses as relational rather than personal. We can encounter the story-as-it-has-been-told and question it in light of real-world data. Much as her mother gives mixed messages, Olivia's father imposes messages in a repetitive fashion that leaves no room for any engagement at all. Having a witness to the impossibility of conversation in her family—without denigration—helps Olivia recognize that her inability to connect with others can be traced to functions she never learned rather than to some essential internal deficiency.

Even when we do not have direct information from the family available, we can still conjecture about developmental failures from the data at hand, as when I sensed that the look of repulsion I was seeing on the woman's face was a reflection of what she had seen in her mother's face (see Chapter 6 in Charles, 2004). The important thing is to be able to mark the moment and invite the person to consider the particularities of their development in ways that invite reflection and growth, a reconstruction that moves not toward placing blame, but rather toward discerning the threads of meanings configuring current experience.

When data are missing, we can make use of dream imagery, which can mark elements of mental life that have not been made conscious and yet may organize our understanding of reality in relation to our earliest experience (Mancia, 1989). Bion (1962) suggested that transformations toward greater symbolization occur during the dream work as elements of experience are processed and metabolized. That formulation shifts the focus of the dream-work from censorship and repression to a process that affords greater access to unconscious contents through an easing of the stimulus barrier. In Chapter 13, I look more closely at dreams and at the Bionian field theory that makes rich use of the dream as a primary access point to the unconscious.

To facilitate this type of transformative process in the consulting room, our offerings need to be sufficiently experience-near to be parsable (da Rocha Barros & da Rocha Barros, 2011), in Bucci's (2018) terms, to allow "the arousal to be sufficiently powerful but not overwhelming" so that thinking and feeling can be adequately integrated to allow symbolization. To be transformative, the interactive process needs to move from the primary affect, to image, toward greater abstraction and elaboration (Meltzer, 1984).

This focus on the development of symbolization is in line with current recognition of the interactive development of metacognitive capacities in psychoanalytic psychotherapy (e.g., Charles, 2021b; Neal et al., 2023). In keeping with this developmental view of psychoanalytic process, Ferrari (2004) suggested a focus on *analytical propositions* rather than interpretations. Whereas the notion of interpretation presumes a privileged knowledge position, the idea of propositions privileges the individual's own internal knowing. This focus integrates a Kleinian recognition of the value of countertransference as a knowledge function—a language register (Ferrari, 2004)—and a Lacanian insistence on the primacy of the subject as privileged knower (Lacan, 1964/1977e). Such a stance presumes that

> the analyst is putting forward his own (sensational and affective) experience of the process in the consulting room so as to facilitate the person's own experience of it of the vertical axis, rather than obtrude an interpretation as a "truth" which might obstruct his access to it. (Carvalho, 2012, p. 422)

This orientation also aligns with Winnicott's (1971) admonition not to steal the person's learning by imposing our own ideas.

This type of stance entails a profound being-with that meets the call of the analysand's body with the receptivity of the analyst's own, in this way allowing communications that could not be parsed previously to be received and responded to. If not, we run the risk that archaic, destructive modes of relating that have not been metabolized will merely repeat themselves given that—much as Winnicott (1974) described regarding trauma—in the words of Aulagnier (2015), "*in the constructions of the primal, the effects of the encounter take the place of the encounter*" (p. 1384). At the extreme, both pleasure and suffering become self-generated and resist any attempt at interpretation. The pictogram, in effect, "has metabolized a somatic state into the presentation of a psychical affect, *experienced and depicted at one and the same time as self-engendered*" (Aulagnier, 2015, p. 1385). At this level, somatic meanings have primacy; they are experienced as truths that are not open to consideration.

With those who have deficits in their capacities for symbolization, we must be able to recognize the disturbed and undeveloped relationship with the body at the core (see Chapter 7). Otherwise, deficits in symbolization interfere with making meaning from sensory experience so that whatever has not been developed into more fully articulated emotion or thought—"*something concrete* that awaits the means for symbolic unfolding"—is expressed by the body (Lombardi, 2009, p. 128). When sensory experience and symbolic elaboration are not well integrated, we must be able to find "*theoretical and operational tools with which to help them feel and discriminate within their own sensations*, as an indispensable precondition to personal growth and to the capacity to form relationships" (Lombardi, 2009, p. 125).

The analyst's willingness to enter deeply into the transference enables them to register sensations that the other person may not even consciously recognize and to formulate thoughts in relation to those sensations. We find ourselves in the position of the early parental figure whose empathic, attuned reactivity was required but not sufficiently encountered. Our concentrated reflective activity enables us to offer "a clearer *distinction between*, on the one hand, *a sensation that was a concrete bodily fact* . . . and, on the other hand, *[their] bodily emotional participation, which was of a symbolic nature*" (Lombardi, 2009, p. 135).

This type of distinction is crucial for those whose experience is so unformulated that the somatic complaint can form a needed bulwark against psychotic disorganization (Aulagnier, 2001). In noting certain similarities between psychosis and psychosomatic illness, McDougall (1989) suggested that "both states serve an underlying reparative aim in the face of an overwhelming, though often unrecognized, sense of danger" (p. 29). Psychosomatic symptoms can be a last bulwark of self-preservation, an attempt to survive by speaking "'in the mind's place' . . . obeying messages that, while they did not pass through the language structures of the mind, were a stimulus to a somatic response, as in infancy" (McDougall, 1989, p. 30). In this way, we find McDougall theorizing closely alongside those who have suggested that the impetus in psychosomatic disorders may be difficult to parse because it addresses the impassive, unresponsive other of infancy who should have been available to contain, metabolize, and make meaning from the infant's experience. For the clinician, recognizing—in words—the legitimate need that was not met at the proper time can help the person to respect the archaic need that can never be met. That recognition helps to free the adult self to learn to meet current needs and thereby attenuate their own suffering.

THE RELATIONAL CONTEXT

In the consulting room, we are charged with making meaning from these types of addresses. Useful in this regard are Fischbein's (2011) distinctions between *types* of somatic complaints, which have important ramifications for technique. Similar to Winnicott's (1974) position that we must be able to provide the conceptual framework that enables the person not only to formulate unthinkable thoughts but also to recognize that the feared event has already occurred, Fischbein suggested that the analyst must work toward describing the stressful situation that could not previously be registered sufficiently for meaning to be made. Crucial to our efforts is an appreciation of the need to build sufficient epistemic trust within the dyad to afford some ground on which the person might build (Fonagy & Allison, 2014).

Notably, and paradoxically, it is the person themselves who potentially knows most about what is happening inside their body, and yet, as we have been learning, there are those who are functionally incapable of making meaning from somatic experience. For those who have not developed sufficient capacity to be curious about their sensory experience or to learn something about what the body might be telling them, another person is required to provide the needed ballast and the directional flow to mark that meanings might be made. The analyst's interest in the bodily experience, and their willingness to imagine it as they hear about it, provides a containing space within which the two might consider how that bodily experience might be relevant to the life story as it has and has not evolved, in this way allowing possible meanings to unfold. Taking Aulagnier's (2001) warnings seriously, however, we must also be open to the possibility that our receptivity alone may not be sufficient for meaning to be made or suffering to be attenuated. This has certainly been the case in my work with Emily, a woman now in her early thirties, described shortly.

With people who are limited in their reflective capacities, I often find myself imagining and describing to them my fantasy of what might have led to symptoms that seem unfathomable. For example, Emily spent her first 8 weeks of life in a pediatric intensive care unit with intense abdominal pain that required surgery. The early deprivation of human contact, along with recurrent pain throughout her childhood that was treated by "knocking her out" with medication until the pain subsided, resulted in her moving toward shutting herself down and knocking herself out when faced with psychic pain. Inviting her to imagine her early experience and to recognize that her life story has implications for her somatic and psychic experience has been a long and arduous task, though it is something that she is finally becoming interested in more actively exploring. Her concrete denial of meaning is giving way to curiosity.

As I investigate further into this territory of psychosomatic illness, I have been able to appreciate some of the impasses in which I find myself in my work with Emily. Increasingly, I have had to pull back from the idea that knowing the story would be the key to relief from suffering. Rather, I use my own understanding of the story to invite her to find her way into the consulting room and to tolerate her very primal need to be in the presence of another. She finds these basic and desperate needs so abhorrent and incomprehensible that it is often all I can do to induce her to just try as best she can to inhabit the space. Following Aulagnier, I have tried to reconstruct, in my own mind, the conditions under which Emily's body can find the proof it needs of the possibility of being loved and protected despite her ongoing suffering. In this sense, an important part of my work is to suffer alongside, to remain empathic, and try to tolerate my inability to save her from her suffering.

A breakthrough occurred when I read R. Feldman's (2006) work on premature infants who miss the last trimester, during which interactive rhythms of experience develop between mother and fetus. Suddenly, I had a frame of reference through which to make meaning of the intransigence of Emily's symptoms. We had retold the story of her birth but had never made sense of the primary context in which that birth had occurred that left her feeling unsoothed and unsoothable. Her desire to curl up in my office and find something she had been seeking began to make greater sense.

I told Emily that I thought that, underneath the story as we had known it thus far, there seemed to be another story: one of an infant who, deprived of the final months of interactive rhythmic communications with her mother, was left instead with the rhythms of the machines that were keeping her alive. Adjusting to the world as it had been presented left an empty space that she had never, and could never, have known how to fill. Unfortunately, neither parent had been sufficiently attuned to her rhythms to have moderated the damage.

This interpretation seemed to hit at a level that sufficiently met Emily's experience to provide some relief. We are left with less frustration, guilt, and discomfort in the moments during which she seeks soothing rather than speech in my office. Making sense is itself inherently soothing, Sirois's (2012) interpretations that *touch*. The fact of this type of relief reminds the clinician to take our countertransference experiences even more seriously with those who do not seem to have the words to speak to their troubles so that we can catch the communications, as best we might, at the level at which they touch us.

LANGUAGE DEVELOPMENT

To better understand the development of language, we can look at salient concepts from the literature. Bion (1977) described *beta-elements*, the bits of experience that are always present, awaiting recognition and representation by an attentive other who can mentalize them. In building a relationship with another person, we need to be attentive to how they do and do not register these bits and also how they communicate their experience so that we might provide sufficient containment for the bits to be mentalized and integrated. The development of the capacity to use the symbols derived from these interchanges was described by Klein (1930/1981a) and Segal (1957) in terms of a transition from the *symbolic equation* in which the thing is felt to be a concrete object, in and of itself, to the symbol proper, a representation of an idea that can be worked with and played with. We see this process developmentally, from the child whose attachment to the mother's presence is direct and dire when threatened, to the recognition of a mother who can be represented in mind and called for when needed, to the internalization of a soothing presence that can be called on when the mother is unavailable.

In investigations at the Austen Riggs Center by my research group into the development of reflective function, we have found that it is important to recognize which aspects of reflective capacity are stunted (Neal et al., 2023). For example, those we would term *borderline* often have ideas about their own and others' internal experience, but they are not sufficiently grounded to be reliable. In contrast, people who are narcissistically organized have great difficulty gaining insight into their minds and feelings. And yet, even with those whose development has been severely stunted, the provisions of psychoanalytically oriented psychotherapy—in the context of an attuned and attentive relational space that includes intense interest in the person's relationship with their own embodied sensory and affective experience—can afford significant gains in reflective capacity.

As experience becomes able to be symbolized and meanings parsed between two separate persons, people can begin to develop a narrative of their lives in which they are the central subject. As Aulagnier (2001) said,

> If I can perceive the intelligibility of the image of a dream, a fantasy, a daydream, even if it is to criticize it for being senseless, it is because I may discover in it the work of a reason that, while not its own, nevertheless obeys a certain logic. (p. 62)

That logic is cast in relation to Milner's (1987) unique psychophysical, patterned rhythms of the individual. In the consulting room, the analyst becomes the voice of the other that insists that meaning can be made from what seems, at first glance, senseless. That insistence helps the person to capture the enigmatic messages held in the unconscious and marked in their dreams. This is the realm of myth, the enigmatic meanings we recognize but cannot parse.

For Aulagnier, primal, libidinal meanings always maintain priority over linguistic meanings. "Whatever the voice is saying, it will always be perceived as a desire for pleasure or as a persecuting intention" (Aulagnier, 2001, p. 65). In that way, she marked the importance of recognizing ways in which our relation to ourselves is colored by the messages received from those charged with caring for us. This perspective is similar to Klein's (1930/1981a) depictions of early object relations in which the maternal desire looms large and conditions all possibilities for the developing child.

CONCLUSION

In the consulting room, we hope to enhance the symbolization process through our interest in the meanings awaiting recognition so that they can begin to take shape and emerge as thoughts that can be considered, brought into words, and built on. The spoken word is powerful, embedded in agreements of meaning that mark us as part of the social world. For those who find themselves on the margins of the social world, making meaning from experience together can provide an invitation into a world from which they have felt excluded, aiding in the process of a self-discovery that can include, perhaps most importantly, healing their relationship with themselves. In the next chapter, the focus is on the development of identity with a particular eye toward considering how to apply what we have learned thus far to our clinical work with those who have not been afforded sufficient grounding to build a solid, adaptive identity.

4 IDENTITY DEVELOPMENT

Identity begins to develop very early on with children able to differentiate between self and other during the second year of life. As young as age 3, a shift occurs in which memories begin to be organized around a relatively stable psychological sense of self (Welch-Ross, 1995). As described in previous chapters, children learn best when caregivers are attuned to and appropriately responsive to the child's needs and feelings. Such relational engagement helps the child meet challenges, including the development of an identity that can grow and transform in relation to ongoing life experience. In this chapter, I outline the normative processes underlying adaptive identity development and then consider how we might best work with those for whom this process has been foreclosed by trauma or neglect. I also look at the impact of the intergenerational transmission of trauma and ways in which explicit and implicit messages affect how particular aspects of cultural identifications are internalized. The clinician's sensitivity to cultural injunctions and disjunctions can be particularly critical for those caught between two cultures or even between different generational values (see Strenger, 2005).

https://doi.org/10.1037/0000455-005
Echoes of Trauma: Meaning and Identity in Psychoanalysis, by M. Charles

THE RELATIONAL CONTEXT

Children whose parents are not emotionally and empathically available tend to have higher stress levels, which interferes with the child's capacity to freely explore the environment and learn from those explorations (Gunnar & Fisher, 2006). As we have seen, unresolved familial grief is a key factor that impedes development. Even otherwise attuned and responsive parents whose own dilemmas are unresolved are less accessible as resources to their children and may even impede growth through disorganized or dysregulated behaviors that are frightening and confusing to the child (Main & Hesse, 1990). At the extreme, the child learns to attune to others' needs rather than their own, accommodating to messages inhibiting or even actively prohibiting recognition of particular communications or other aspects of their environment.

Intergenerational transmission of trauma interferes with identity development across the generations in part because of the tendency for parents to dissociate or become preoccupied in moments of high affective arousal, leaving them unavailable to the child as resources or adaptive models (Main & Hesse, 1990). The dissociative response to trauma is particularly toxic in the parent–child relationship. Whereas the preoccupied parent shifts the focus away from the child's needs and experiences toward that of the parent, the dissociated parent presents the child with a terrible absence that cannot be penetrated and is difficult to endure. "If the mother's face is unresponsive, then a mirror is a thing to be looked at but not to be looked into," said Winnicott (1971, p. 113). Survival, then, depends not on turning to the parent to develop and sustain consistent and organized strategies for affective self-regulation, but rather on learning to empty out, like the parent, when overloaded with emotion. In the absence of more adaptive strategies, bumps in the road can become calamities.

The child learns their place in an ordered universe through interactions with parents attuned enough to help them make sense of their experience. When the child does not have sufficient impact on others, they cannot find themselves in the engagement. "The infant's perception of contingencies, in conjunction with an optimally contingent environment, organizes the infant's expectation that he can affect, and be affected by, the partner, a crucial origin of the experience of effectance" (Beebe et al., 2003, p. 826). Disruptions in the experience of contingency are profoundly disorganizing for both parent and child in ways that echo back and forth between them, resulting in incoherent narratives with far-reaching effects (Murray & Trevarthen, 1985). Holes in the family story make it difficult for parents to pass along to their children not only the particulars of their life story but, perhaps more importantly, the process of narration itself (Thorne, 2000), including one's ability to locate oneself within the values and meanings of the social structure (Fonagy & Allison, 2023).

The development of a coherent, elaborated sense of self is profoundly and integrally linked to the coconstruction of narratives between parent and child (Fivush, 2007). Identity becomes further consolidated in adolescence and young adulthood, but the early engagements between parent and child form the bedrock of all later development. Receptive, responsive engagement tells the child that they are valued and valuable—worth paying attention to—as their experience is recognized and elaborated on, first in nonverbal and then in verbal forms. The verbal elaboration is critical to the development of autobiographical memory, a fundamental aspect of identity (Fivush et al., 2011). The ability to discuss difficult or negative emotional experiences and also to recognize positive aspects of those events provides crucial reference points that not only aid in negotiating difficulties as they arise but also enhance the understanding of self and relationships.

THE IMPACT OF CULTURE

Children begin to develop ideas about what is to be valued or devalued very early on. These sensibilities are infused by cultural messages that may not be consciously recognized by those around them. Even at preschool age, children demonstrate a sensitivity to issues such as social structure, privilege, and status (Black-Gutman & Hickson, 1996). Histories of oppression also have an impact, haunting future generations precisely in relation to what remains unknown and is not worked through by the previous generations (Apprey, 2024). Most destructive, likely, is the impact of internal representations of negative stereotypes on the person themselves, particularly in light of evidence that exposure to racism exacerbates psychological trauma and increases the effects of posttraumatic stress disorder (Ford, 2008).

As identity is formed, cultural differences emerge in the ways autobiographical narratives are constructed between parent and child (Fivush et al., 2011). Likely, these cultural differences point to the values and skills required for adaptation within that cultural milieu. This variability can cause difficulties for the individual caught between two disparate cultures, particularly when the parents are not available to help the child recognize and sort through disparities as they arise (Charles, 2010, 2014). Gender differences also emerge, with girls' stories focusing on relational themes and boys' stories on autonomy-related themes. Such differences highlight the importance of sensitivity to learning how the individual constructs their inner world and relationships. Increasingly, gender itself has become more fluid, affording greater possibilities but also, perhaps, greater anxieties in establishing a sense of self (Watson, 2022), requiring greater sensitivity on the part of the clinician to the person's own relation to gender and gendered meanings (A. Cohen, 2024; Hammack & Manago, 2024).

Differences also arise in the gaps between the generations. Because cyberspace has afforded young people increasing opportunities for encounters with others, there are new possibilities for self-construction (Strenger, 2003). Although this *networked era* provides new opportunities for self-construction (J. L. Davis, 2014), the vastness of opportunity provided within this extended frame also creates new dilemmas for generations growing up without the safe containment of prescribed limits within which to make sense of self and other (Strenger, 2005). Tensions arise between what Katie Davis (2012) termed differing and, at times, conflicting *spheres of obligation* "to self, interpersonal relationships, online social norms, and broad community-level values—that function as implicit limits on self-multiplicity" (p. 634). Authenticity in self-definition emerges as a particular challenge in this era in which there may be multiple contexts in which identity is developed (Hammack & Manago, 2024).

Trauma and Cultural Loss

Beyond the possibilities and challenges afforded by social media, identity development can be complicated for those who are caught between cultures, particularly for those whose cultural ties have been disrupted (Charles, 2000b). Histories of trauma and disruption cause tensions for the developing child; those tensions are exacerbated by difficulties associated with disrupted mourning, which are compounded for those who have lost touch with the cultural legacies that facilitated mourning in previous generations. Unresolved intergenerational histories of trauma result in cultural burdens of rejection, denigration, and persecution that make it even more difficult to develop a healthy, resilient sense of self. This lack of resolution itself has an impact, at times imposing itself in the form of what Apprey (2024) termed a *toxic errand* that carries the frozen, traumatic history forward to be managed or metabolized by future generations. Indeed, trauma symptoms can be a form of memory, a link to a dispossessed past (Beneduce, 2016; Davoine & Gaudillière, 2004).

Many of the difficulties associated with cultural losses can be traced, in part, to feelings of shame that result from being discriminated against, devalued, and depicted in negative terms without recourse to the collective social knowledge, lore, and practices that might have moderated or attenuated these destructive forces (Atkinson, 2002; Charles, 2000b). These difficulties are exacerbated when identity needs associated with one's ethnic identity are at odds with those of the majority culture (Akhtar, 1995). Children growing up under such conditions can feel torn between two worlds, neither of which entirely fits, making it difficult to develop a healthy identity that integrates aspects of each culture (Brance et al., 2024; Charles, 2014; Tummala-Narra, 2020).

Self-esteem itself may be thought of as a culturally loaded construction. In the United States, autonomy is valued highly, whereas in many other parts of the world interdependent representations of self predominate. "Representations of self and other are inevitably tied to the social context, which is grounded in historically, culturally, and socially derived philosophical, religious, political, and legal systems" (Fryberg & Markus, 2003, p. 326). When there are cross-cultural ties with opposing underlying values, people struggle to integrate and make sense of conflicting aspects of cultural identifications (Tummala-Narra, 2020), a project that is complicated in our digital world (J. L. Davis, 2014; K. Davis, 2012).

Cultures develop master narratives "that contain abstracted information about the cultural standards that individuals should follow and use to position themselves while constructing/sharing an autobiographical narrative" (Fivush et al., 2011, p. 334). An unintegrated traumatic past can disrupt the transmission of the master narratives that might engender pride in one's ethnic identity. Studies have shown that a strong ethnic identity is associated with higher self-esteem when the individual also has a positive identification with the majority culture (Phinney, 1991). Resilience is enhanced when one can locate oneself with relative ease in one's family, social group, and the larger social matrix in which one is embedded (Adams et al., 2006). With increasing age, cultural identity seems to become even more important as the person builds their identity within the larger social context. It also becomes more precarious when particular aspects of self-identity are at odds with the culture of origin (Thibeault et al., 2018). The clinician needs to be open to the ways in which an individual locates themselves within the various aspects of identity that make up—and can undermine—identity (Belkin, 2021a, 2021b).

Intergenerational Transmission of Risk and Shame

In addition to the cultural factors that can impede ethnic pride and interfere with the ability to mourn and effectively work through traumatic experiences, familial factors also come into play (Charles, 2000b). Families pass along both strengths and deficits to their children, directly and indirectly. Through the process of *social referencing*, infants develop the capacity to learn about the objects around them by recognizing the adult's emotional reactions, whether positive or negative (Flavell, 2004). As noted in the previous chapter, nonverbal elements of communication are taken in directly from parent to child, including not only explicit meanings but also implicit, underlying cultural values (Fonagy & Allison, 2023). In this way, aversions or inhibitions of the parent may be passed along directly to the child without inviting reflection, but rather being experienced as "truth."

As we are learning more about what can be invisible from the perspective of someone whose identity is more fully ensconced with the majority culture, we are invited to be curious about factors that may initially be invisible because they are hidden. I think, for example, of a young woman whose family had immigrated to the United States from another culture. Jean, a young woman in her early thirties, was very successful in her chosen profession despite learning difficulties that at times obstructed her progress. Her internalized shame was so virulent that it was difficult to recognize. The main marker was the eating disorder that she had relatively successfully kept hidden. As described in Chapter 8, eating disorders tend to mark developmental difficulties that are often obscured by outward markers of success, such as high academic achievement. For Jean, the need/fear dilemma that was marked by her eating disorder also played out interpersonally. What was most difficult to recognize was the way in which her internalized shame for "being different" was playing out in all of her difficulties. As we began to recognize the cultural piece at play, her defenses relaxed, and she became better able to make use of her strong intellect in the service of reflecting on her internalized shame rather than merely trying to avoid it, helping her to build a more solid identity and stronger relationships.

The intergenerational transmission of risk in non–majority culture children not only creates social disadvantage but also jeopardizes the development of self-esteem by inhibiting experiences of mastery that might enable a child to engage with challenges more effectively and overcome them (Benzies et al., 2011). Experiences of mastery elicit pride, whereas failure elicits shame, which is evoked whenever our interest, concern, or curiosity is broken into suddenly or disappointed (Tomkins, 1982). Shame casts down our eyes, disrupting the interpersonal bond and impeding repair. Perhaps more insidiously, it also amplifies all emotion, inhibiting our cognitive capacities and leading to the development of scripts, that is, ideas about how the world works that are so powerful that they can preclude reflection or integration of new experience (Tomkins, 1978). When our natural curiosity has been punished, it can be easier to turn away rather than face a challenge, leaving us prey to whatever closed systems of meaning we have inherited.

The amplification of affect makes it difficult to sustain curiosity in the face of novelty, the very curiosity we need to take the types of risks required for new learning to occur. Learning to persist even in the face of challenges builds resilience and results in the experiences of mastery that not only build positive self-regard but also help develop our metacognitive capacities (Fonagy et al., 2002; Lysaker, Dimaggio, et al., 2010; Lysaker, Erickson, et al., 2010; Lysaker et al., 2011). Shame also interferes with the development of healthy social relationships—essential to the development of self-esteem in childhood—by inhibiting our ability to look outward. Being able to look both inward and outward affords the perspective needed to make sense of self in relation to others, the core constituent of metacognition and reflective function. Increasingly, we can recognize ways in which negative effects of colonization, misogyny, and ethnic distrust persist across the generations and create shame on all sides, making it difficult to work through these tensions and to overcome their effects.

Children who are born in the United States to immigrant parents can face complex challenges in building a solid and coherent identity. For example, I worked with one man in early adulthood whose parents had immigrated from Southeast Asia. He thought of himself as "American" and resented some of his parents' impositions that seemed out of touch with his perceived developmental needs. His alienation from his parents' world left him feeling uncertain, unstable, and vulnerable to attack. Despite his conscious affiliations, in his dreams we could see the profound impact of his familial culture on him (see Charles, 2010, for more details). In the psychotherapy, learning to recognize his own ties to that culture, and their meanings for him, helped him to integrate his American self with his Indian self, consolidating a more solid and resilient identity through which to build deeper and more satisfying relationships with others as well.

SUPPORTING POSITIVE IDENTITY DEVELOPMENT

If part of the journey into adulthood is to slay whatever "beast" stands in the path of self-knowledge (Campbell, 1949), those who carry a burden of self-denigration have a particularly difficult challenge. We all must be wary of our willingness to yield to the authority of others if we are to encounter ourselves in ways that invite enrichment of our innate capacities rather than the sense that we must be other than ourselves to be valued. Particularly for those who have been neglected or maltreated and are hyperresponsive to threat, treatments that focus primarily on behavior change may encourage compliance rather than resilience (Gunnar & Fisher, 2006). More effective are treatments that recognize that "development, in itself, contains the power for growth and change" and so attempt to harness the force of the developmental thrust present during early childhood and adolescence to facilitate development that has gone awry (Schmidt Neven, 2005, p. 190).

Compliance keeps the focus on others, thereby lodging knowledge and the power to change outside of oneself. Such a position encourages dependency on others rather than learning to more effectively recognize and respond to internal cues. Maintaining contact with one's own perceptions, thoughts, and feelings can be a particular challenge for traumatized individuals, who are more likely than others to dissociate under pressure and lose touch with their experience. For the clinician, it is important to appreciate how fundamentally our cognitive capacities are tied to the self-regulation of emotions that allows us to stay present in our experience and work through challenges as they arise. That perspective helps us appreciate that, whatever the ostensible "problem" the person presents with, underneath we will likely find failures in development that have not only affected the person's well-being but also their sense of identity. Failing to meet anticipated milestones results in shame, which becomes internalized as an internal deficit when the external causes are not apparent. In our work, it is often the person's relationship with themselves that is in most need of repair.

From that perspective, an important part of the clinician's job is to help the person to respectfully find themselves within their own life story as it has happened. In this way, milestones can be marked and either met or accommodated to. We often encounter individuals who have "had everything" and yet have failed to thrive. Inquiring more carefully into the story, we can discover places where there was a gap in learning that needs to be addressed. In this way, we can highlight the importance of support that provides a scaffolding for self-development rather than becomes a more permanent crutch, inviting a focus on mastering challenges rather than lamenting failures.

At times, identity development is foundered by parental deficits. As we saw with Olivia (introduced in Chapter 3), loving, well-intentioned parents may not have the internal resources to help build resilience in their children. Take, for example, Lina, a bright, creative young woman who founders at the point of leaving home (see Chapter 5 for an explication of this case). Adored by her doting but narcissistic father, Lina finds herself lost when his sudden death leaves her alone with her highly limited mother. She finds herself adrift alongside the mother, who is too lost herself to provide any anchors for the daughter. Lina seeks residential treatment, looking to find herself but unable to look within. Rather, she looks to external markers of value as a way of perhaps locating herself. In these efforts, we can find her in the dilemma Strenger (2005) described, in which the self that was insufficiently constituted in the parent–child relationships is sought within one's own generation.

In our work together, Lina became preoccupied by finding the "right clothes" that would portray her in a way that could launch her into the world in a way that felt satisfying. I suggested that it seemed impossible to find the right image from the outside. Rather, she might need to learn—from the inside—what she likes so that she can have a sense of what clothes might suit her own sensibilities. Initially frustrated by my words, over the course of many months together, Lina finally began to recognize that there was no way to discover herself from the outside in. Rather, she needed to learn to pay attention to her own likes and dislikes and take them seriously. In her dilemma, we can recognize the problem Strenger (2005) marked as a shift from an identity established in relation to parents one can admire, emulate, learn from and be recognized by to a sense that one must find oneself in relation to the external world without being anchored in one's own history. In adolescence, in particular, there is the challenge of finding oneself with authenticity in relation to the various social contexts one inhabits (Rivera et al., 2019).

In addition to the problem of insufficient parenting and the challenges of disparate social demands in cultural contexts in which loss and strain are prominent features, children are faced with noncontingencies that impede meaning-making and effective action, making it important to recognize when our offerings are treated with suspicion or disinterest. As an example, take Adam, a young man in his early twenties whose parents delighted in his accomplishments but were insufficiently available to help him negotiate obstacles as they arose. Preoccupied by their own troubles, they were not even useful models for managing adult activities, such as cooking, driving, or handling money. School provided an environment with achievable milestones but, when school ended, Adam found himself unable to manage the basic tasks of adulthood. His escalating frustration and distress were read as signs of "mental illness," and he was offered psychotherapy, which afforded him some of the relational holding he longed for but at the price of further blows to his fragile sense of identity.

In our work together, I offered Adam a story of a precocious child who had not been offered the assistance he needed, leading him to jump past obstacles rather than meet challenges as they arose. When we first met, learning seemed both impossible and humiliating. The initial challenge was for Adam to learn to tolerate his frustration sufficiently that he could find his own desire to push past it rather than experience the need to grow up as something imposed on him by others. Building frustration tolerance is often the first step in working with those who have not learned it. Recognizing that there is a skill that must be built—rather than an inherent deficit to be hidden—is a prerequisite for developing a more positive identity.

Much as we see with Adam, a developmental model invites interventions that assist the person to better negotiate difficulties and make sense of the contingencies faced in their environment. Recalling that implicit knowledge is not easily recognized or communicated in words, it is important in work with traumatized individuals to be able to hear the story being told through the symptoms and to witness and recognize aspects of those stories as we encounter them. In this way, the person is not left so alone with their trouble, and the experiences that have been left unsymbolized can be brought into words. Actively seeking out the potential for engagement and communication is particularly important for those whose lives have been affected by loss, given that the debilitating effects of trauma can otherwise be mistaken for incapacities. When symptoms are misconstrued as deficits, a terrible injustice is done that further impedes learning and healthy identity development.

Clinicians also, however, need to recognize the importance of the primary bonds between parent and child and the hazards of interfering with those bonds. We want the person to understand what has happened to them—but not in a way that blames the parents or further disrupts family ties. Having in mind that intergenerational trauma is transmitted helps us recognize that parents can have good intentions without necessarily being able to act on them effectively. That awareness helps us recognize each person's distress with respect as we hear the larger story in which the family members are all caught. Crucial here is the capacity to hold each person responsible for their behaviors without denigrating them. Given that shame is integral to these struggles, this distinction is critically important. We must remember that we each inevitably will—and also need to be able to—identify with each parent. Being able to find the good along with the bad in parents is essential to our well-being.

CONCLUSION

With those for whom identity development has been waylaid by relational trauma, we hope to show that something more is possible. As in the clinical work described here, we hope that our faith that real change might be possible, even if difficult, can help regenerate the capacity for engagement, interest, and curiosity so important to learning and to the development of self-knowledge. Identity development not only depends on interpersonal engagements but also on how meaning is made from these encounters. Being able to read one's own feelings in relation to the feelings and actions of others is a crucial part of this learning process, helping to build the experiences of mastery so crucial for facing new challenges.

Thus far, we have focused on how identity develops and how the therapist can play a critical role in providing an environment that challenges the person in ways that help further the reflective capacities—and the experiences of mastery—that are essential to ongoing, adaptive identity development. Beginning with Chapter 5, we explore how therapists can accomplish this by working with transference and countertransference dynamics as they play out in the consulting room. These efforts help us develop formulations that can be offered back and worked with collaboratively through the type of interpretive—or reconstructive—process that is discussed in Chapter 6.

PART II INTERPRETING TRANSFERENCE AND COUNTERTRANSFERENCE

5 TRANSFERENCE AND COUNTERTRANSFERENCE

In this chapter, I consider how to make use of transference and countertransference, central concepts that inform our understanding of the psychoanalytic process and also our technique. Although ideas about transference and countertransference have evolved over time, they remain useful grounding points in the clinical work, reminding us of the power of psychic reality in formulating meanings and further experience. Ideas about transference have evolved from Freud's (1912/1958a) early recognition that his patients were carrying past experience into the present in ways that interfered with their lives. His initial model of transference was of a stereotype plate that evolves and repeats itself, including in relation to the analyst. He saw transference as endemic in human relations and useful in developing a therapeutic relationship—but also inviting negative anticipations and resistance.

In his original model, Freud viewed transference as an obstacle to development, and interpretation became a means for making these patterns of relationship visible to break through the repetition and allow for more adaptive living. Freud originally saw *counter*transference as a toxic infiltration to be avoided by undergoing "a psycho-analytic purification" (Freud, 1912/1958c, p. 116). Ideas about the relationships between transference

https://doi.org/10.1037/0000455-006
Echoes of Trauma: Meaning and Identity in Psychoanalysis, by M. Charles

and countertransference have evolved over time, offering different vantage points. Later views saw countertransference as affording potentially useful data to the psychoanalyst, beginning with Heimann's (1950) thesis that "the analyst's emotional response to his patient is one of the most important tools for his work. The analyst's counter-transference is an instrument of research into the patient's unconscious" (p. 81).

A personal analysis helps the clinician develop their own self-reflectivity, learning to recognize their own internal signals in ways that can make their offerings more useful and can inform their ideas about the other person's internal workings and transferences as well, inviting, perhaps, a more empathic or insightful engagement. Given that transference (and trauma) repeat, it is useful to be able to reflect on an encounter rather than reactively repeat in ways that might be retraumatizing. Moving from the position of receiving the force of the other person's affect to reflecting on what internal forces might be at play inside them helps us to set in motion our own reflective functions in moments of strain.

Although views of transference and countertransference have changed over time, *transference* remains one of the most crucial concepts in the psychoanalytic therapist's arsenal. This concept highlights the fact that we all act in the world based on our ideas of people. When all goes well, our ideas evolve in relation to our experience as we bump into data that alert us that we are missing something. As we have seen in previous chapters, however, trauma and neglect interfere with our resilience in the face of novelty, impeding our ability to learn from our experience and adapt to change. *Countertransference* is the term used to mark the therapist's embodied experience with the person they are working with; that experience provides data at the nonverbal level. Recognizing the importance of these data helps the clinician to ride the emotional waves and try to make sense of what is being experienced in light of what they know about themselves and the other person. The focus of this chapter is on transference and countertransference as technical tools; I will then turn to interpretation in the next chapter, in which I explore how we develop our formulations and make use of them. After looking at these three concepts in turn in Part II, we then consider their clinical utility in relation to particular symptom pictures presented in Part III.

TRANSFERENCE

In contrast to Freud's approach to transference as something to be explained, explored, and perhaps dispelled, for Kleinians, transference is endemic, but there is still the idea that we might discover the reality that underlies it.

Said Klein (1952), "It is only by analyzing the transference situation to its depth that we are able to discover the past both in its realistic and phantastic aspects" (p. 437). Kleinians recognize the complexity of the transference/countertransference matrix as a crucial information source and encourage an active participation in whatever is playing out in the intersubjective field (Joseph, 1985). In their view, however, the analyst's knowledge is privileged over that of the analysand rather than merely affording another perspective. If our intent is to encourage the person's ability to rely on their own knowledge of self and other, positioning oneself as the authority in this way is problematic.

On the more positive end, however, the active participation encouraged by Kleinians is in alignment with what we know about mirror neurons and their direct impact on behavior (Gallese, 2005). Levenson (2009), for example, recognized how imitation can mark meanings such that "psychoanalytic insight may be first experienced and *then* formulated; that the direction of learning may be, not from the head to the body, but quite the opposite—a matter of what is said about what is experienced" (p. 174). Opposing the Lacanian notion that one cannot know the experience of another, findings regarding mirror neurons have suggested that empathy is based precisely on having experienced "to some . . . degree what the patient experiences [and that] mirroring or imitation" may be the medium of exchange (Levenson, 2009 p. 176). Respect for our less conscious, nonverbal, implicit knowledge is crucial to adaptive meaning-making.

In parallel to these ideas, albeit in a different language, Lacan (1964/1977e) suggested that "the transference is the enactment of the reality of the unconscious" (p. 146). Like all products of the unconscious, the "transference both misleads and deceives by presenting truth in the form of lies" (Patsalides & Patsalides, 2001, p. 217). Appreciating the power of ambivalence is useful when our attempts at self-discovery are subverted by what Bion (1977) called our *willful blindness*, our tendency to close our eyes at critical moments. Although this blindness can obscure needed truths, it also protects us from being overwhelmed by more than we can manage. In this way, psychoanalytic work allows for the titration of truth by accepting it without imposing it, and analysts must learn to tolerate the analysand's trajectory rather than to more actively attend to our own suffering, allowing our reflective efforts to attenuate the tension.

Historical Views of Transference

Early on, Freud began to recognize that there was a carrying over or transference of feelings from important early relationships to persons in the present

(Breuer & Freud, 1895/1955). It was not until the case of Dora, however, that he began to describe the phenomena more directly, suggesting that relational elements from the past were recreated in the relationship with the analyst, providing important data. He said of transferences:

> They are new editions of facsimiles of the impulses and fantasies which are aroused and made conscious during the progress of the analysis: but they have this peculiarity, which is characteristic for their species, that they replace some earlier person by the person of the physician. To put it another way: a whole series of psychological experiences are revived, not as belonging to the past, but as applying to the person of the physician at the present moment. (Freud, 1905/1953a, p. 116)

Freud recognized the positive aspects of the transference that help establish a working treatment relationship. By 1910, he suggested that analyzing the transference was the only means to a cure, but he also recognized resistances. In "The Dynamics of Transference," Freud (1912/1958a) offered this formulation:

> Transference to the doctor is suitable for resistance to the treatment only insofar as it is a negative transference or a positive transference of repressed erotic impulses. If we "remove" the transference by making it conscious, we are detaching only these two components of the emotional act from the person of the doctor; the other component which is admissible to consciousness and unobjectionable persists and is the vehicle of success in psychoanalysis exactly as it is in other methods of treatment. (p. 105)

In 1914, Freud (1914/1958d) referred to transference in terms of a repetition compulsion through which the analyst can recognize resistances within the analysand as the past plays out in the present. Klein (1952) extended Freud's views to note that transference originates in the earliest experiences of self with other that form the bedrock of meaning and being, as we have been discussing, making a focus on pre-oedipal experiences essential to the working-through. From a contemporary perspective, Levenson (2009) joined Klein in this recognition of the ways in which the transference marks patterns of meaning that may never have been conscious and yet have a profound impact. He suggested that transference is not merely a resistance to change, but "rather some *mysterious, inherent, correlate of the inquiry*—. . . a natural aspect of cognitive processes, not an artifact of anxiety or defense" (Levenson, 2009, p. 171). The person's "flow of consciousness [tends] . . . to play out or *mirror* what is being said" (Levenson, 2009, p. 171). In the consulting room, there is always a replaying, an enactment patterned on both parties' experience. What we say is based on our own experience from contact with the world of the other person that is modified by what we receive back.

To paraphrase Kafka (1919/1971), the learning accrues over time; the meanings imprint themselves on us, and we come to know them through our bodies.

Although spoken in a different dialect, Levenson's ideas are consistent with Lacan's (1964/1977e) suggestion that the transference in psychoanalysis is a function of the analyst's desire. To the extent that we are interested in the unconscious alienation at the core of human suffering, we invite the person's interest in that project, leading them to notice and inquire into their conflicting or unrecognized motives. Lacan contended that people often seek treatment hoping for a new and more gratifying false self rather than grappling with the alienation that supports the illusion. The challenge, then, is to facilitate a confrontation within which the person "feels a desire to say precisely that which he feels pressure not to say" (Friedlander, 1991, p. 129).

For Lacan (1954–1955/1988), explanations are corrupt, keeping us at the surface of meanings rather than searching for messages from the unconscious, Laplanche's (1997) *enigmatic meanings* that remain to be deciphered if we can be open to them. This is also the realm of Levenson's (2009) *mystification*: "the gap between what is said and what is shown" (p. 173). As we have seen, this inquiry is complicated for those without the type of "good enough" early environment described by Winnicott (1971). As Fonagy and his colleagues (2002) put it: "Suboptimal early experiences of care affect later development by undermining [our] capacity to process or interpret information" (p. 7), leaving us at the mercy of others who might mistranslate for us rather than leaving us space to discover ourselves. Paradoxically, most people come to analysis desperately hoping for such a mistranslation to counter shame-infused constructions of identity with absolution rather than with the recognition that might transform them. However, as M. Feldman (1993) showed, overt reassurance is seldom helpful because it speaks in the wrong register and fails to address the certainties underlying our presumptions.

For me, the best model for thinking about transference is found in Lacan's (1974–1975, 1975–1976/2016) ideas about the *sinthome*, his recognition of the profound particularity of each person's experience. That particularity, and the pervasiveness of perspective, is what we hope to better elucidate through the psychoanalytic process while also needing to recognize our perspective as well. We can try to become more conversant with our own modes of thought and defense, but we can never entirely get out from under them. Paradoxically, we can never fully know the other, but our best approximation comes through an immersion in self-experience as it occurs in relation to our encounters with them.

Case Illustrations

The disruptions in early development described in this volume have important ramifications for the transference and how we make use of what we learn through it. We recognize that problems in early attachment relationships make it difficult to trust in the possibility of deep engagement but also increase the hunger for them, often resulting in anxiously avoidant or even aggressively counterphobic dependencies. Take, for example, the case of Val, a young woman in her very early twenties, who arrived for treatment defensively contemptuous and counterdependent (see Chapter 12 for an explication of this case). I found myself caught between the contemptuous father, whose interpretations were "too abstract" and made her feel small, and the pathetic mother, whose empathy invited her contempt. Insisting that I might be human and also have something worthwhile to offer became an important touchstone in our work together. With individuals with such intense narcissistic vulnerabilities, knowing something more than they know is itself humiliating, making it difficult to add anything of value without the offering being experienced as an assaultive intrusion.

Taking the transference seriously rather than merely trying to avoid or manage it helps us think about whether to lean in or pull back. It is easy to feel empathy toward the other person's distress and lean toward them. But when parental care has felt narcissistic, needy, and smothering, empathic attunement needs to be conditioned by an awareness of the actual transference dynamics for that person. In such moments, speaking to the dilemma—without trying to "empathically" resolve it—can help mark it in ways in which the person can tolerate us seeing where they are caught so that they might, perhaps, recognize the problem in our presence rather than merely feel caught in something they want to get out of.

Think, for example, of Adam, the young man we first encountered in Chapter 4, who was unable to manage the basic tasks of adulthood. His experience of mother was one of an engulfing desire that left her always disappointed, whereas the father seemed satisfied by the very engagements that left Adam feeling dissatisfied. In the transference, my attempts to help him to locate his own desire were felt to be either a maternal abandonment or a paternal fetishization. In either case, he was left unseen, frustrated, and alienated. Anger seemed too dangerous to imagine, leaving him feeling sad and empty of any feelings of vitality or even of a mind through which to think about his troubles. We wish we could refuse these impossible transferences, but refusing them merely exacerbates the problem, and reassurance easily feels false and pushes the data needing attention even further afield (M. Feldman, 1993).

Instead, empathically leaning in and recognizing how the person is caught at least recognizes the dilemma that we cannot solve for them but perhaps can help them to bear. *Taking the transference* in this way is an important precondition for being able to talk about it (Mitrani, 2001) as we shift from a focus on our own discomfort to attend to the reality of the other person's experience in the moment. In this regard, we should be wary of our desire to "explain ourselves" and reflect on these urges before speaking. Usually, we can recognize that our self-interest has momentarily obscured the other person and *their* experience from view. Our discomfort, however, can also provide important data regarding the person and the characters in their object world as we will explore in the next section.

COUNTERTRANSFERENCE

Shifting our focus from the other person's transference to our own, we can see how Freud's (1912/1958c) original idea of countertransference as a problem that could be avoided was countered in the early 1950s by analysts who recognized both its ubiquity and therapeutic potential. Tower (1956), for example, stressed that, as human beings, analysts also have their own transferences, evolving from their own personal experiences. The challenge, then, is to make use of what we have learned about ourselves in relation to others so that our countertransference might be not a hazard, but rather a primary "vehicle for the analyst's emotional understanding of the transference" (Tower, 1956, p. 252).

That idea of making use of the countertransference forms the cornerstone of the contemporary Kleinian practice that reminds us to pay close attention to patterns of process, nuance, and emotional meanings as they play out in the work (Charles, 2018). These ideas have also been incorporated into many other strands of contemporary practice in line with the greater recognition of the nonverbal communications underlying all human meanings. Notably, the term *countertransference* itself threatens to take our attention away from the ubiquitous nature of transference as a universal process through which current experience is parsed in relation to past experience.

Betty Joseph (1985) pointed to this ubiquity in her term *total transference*, which marks her conviction that the other person's internal world is revealed in the moment-by-moment experiences that inform our ideas about their object world to the extent that we can be sufficiently present to use our own affect as signals to guide our understanding. Particularly when working with those for whom early trauma and neglect have interfered with their ability to decode affective signals, the analyst's attention to and verbal recognition of these messages are crucial to the development of those capacities in the analysand.

As an example, let us return to my work with Olivia, the young woman who had become manic, deluged by signals she could neither decode nor manage, whose case we explored in Chapter 3. The story, as we put it together, was one of having had disruptions in her family of origin that left neither parent sufficiently available to help her recognize and manage her feelings. This left Olivia feeling unknown and unknowable. She sensed her parents' devotion to her, but, unable to engage actively in conversation, she turned toward offering them productions in the hope of receiving the elusive something she was longing for. In adolescence, this elusive pull led her into enmeshed relationships that never quite filled her needs, resulting in increasing confusion regarding how to make meaning from her experience. The treatment consisted of attending to shifts in her affect and remarking on them, assuming that they were part of a story that would make sense as we began to put the pieces together.

Such work requires a profound depth of being-with as Olivia leans into the presence she has longed for but then braces herself for the abrupt and terrible disruption at the end of the hour. Engaging deeply can obscure the line between self and other, which can be uncomfortable for the clinician, too, as we come up against both the too-much of the immersion and then the sense of betrayal—as though a promise has been broken—when the hour ends. This immersion, however, is also useful and most likely essential in our work with those dealing with traumatic experience or early disruptions, who may not consciously know what they are contending with and have to experience aspects of the trouble with someone who believes that their experience has meaning. Bumping into one another in this way provides opportunities to experience the rupture and repair so crucial to the development of resilient relationships. As Kernberg (1965) reminded us, intense countertransference reactions with those who present with severe disturbance "may at times give the most meaningful understanding of what is central in the patient's chaotic expression" (p. 40).

Modern Views of Countertransference

Racker (2007) has helped us orient in this strange universe by distinguishing between *concordant* identifications that arise through our empathic attempts to understand from the other's perspective and *complementary* identifications in which the analyst is positioned as a projection of an internal object.

The concordant identification invites a sense of empathic knowing, whereas the complementary identification invites a sense of alienation that provides relational data. Together, they offer information regarding the person's position in their object world.

Tracking meanings as they emerge rather than merely reacting to them invites greater reflection, but there is always a tension, contended Hinshelwood (1999), between emotional freezing or being overly human and seduced out of role. We are then left with the problem, in Brenman Pick's (1985) words, of "walking the tightrope between experiencing disturbance and responding with interpretation that does *not contain* [the] disturbing anxiety" (p. 157). With those like Olivia who are hungry for symbiotic engagement, the challenge is to recognize the intensity of the problem—for the person themselves—of needing to manage the disturbance. Technically, this often means marking the problem with words rather than merely trying to avoid or repair the distress. For Olivia, my statement that real change can feel catastrophic meets her sensed experience and is relieving, affording a mantra she can play in her mind in my absence.

Recent conceptualizations have expanded beyond even the more inclusive notions of countertransference. Parsons (2007), for example, suggested that the internal setting in the mind of the analyst may be more important than the external setting, challenging us to protect our ability to free associate even beyond our ideas of what is and is not "right." This is also the territory inhabited by Bionian field theorists, who have recognized the importance of providing a space in which analyst and analysand can increasingly dream (Civitarese, 2005; Ferro, 2009) in the sense that Winnicott (1971) used the term: the dreaming that potentiates possibilities. It can feel odd or illicit to be "daydreaming" in another person's presence, and yet, if we can link the daydream to the person's material, we often find that we have caught something with our unconscious mind that is profoundly relevant and even potentially enlightening.

Psychoanalysts talk a great deal about the unconscious, and yet we can behave as though we do not actually respect its power or value. When ideas regarding psychoanalysis become superego impositions rather than useful parameters, we need to try to free ourselves up to consider what actually matters in the work and to hear the possibilities of meaning in what is being said rather than abstracting meaning from it. Speaking from what we are hearing leaves us closer in, much in the spirit of what Mitrani (2001) called *taking the transference*, allowing ourselves to be used by the other person as they play out a past that may not be accessible to conscious thought except through the enactment. Speaking *from* our experience—rather than *about* it—

lends an air of authenticity and models what we hope to invite from the other person: to be more fully present and speak authentically from their current experience.

When working with those for whom traumatic experience occurred too early or too assaultively to be encoded into verbal memory, we often register important truths through the countertransference as we participate in enactments and pick up on nonverbal signals that the person themselves cannot yet decode. Within the context of an attentive, attuned relationship, meanings can be built. Taking seriously what we are learning about mirror neurons and embodied simulation, we can see how, in the countertransference, we take in crucial information about the other person's world, much as they do ours (Gallese, 2009). This interactive prosody makes our most important interventions, not our ostensibly brilliant interpretations, but rather the effort we put into understanding whatever eludes our comprehension.

In this way, psychoanalysis provides a model of engagement with the unknown that presumes that meaning is to be found beyond the "I don't know" that can otherwise seamlessly cover over whatever facts are yet to be revealed. To emphasize: clinical work is at its best when the person seeking assistance is able to emulate the method the clinician undergoes in trying to understand whatever eludes them. Most crucial to pass along is the reflective process that Freud offered, and our most valuable information with those whose development has been waylaid by trauma may be obtained through the countertransference.

Through our respect for the meanings offered in that matrix, we can begin to build the type of *holding environment* necessary to build the capacities for symbolization and for the playing with possible meanings that allows identity to be built (Winnicott, 1971). A fundamental tenet in building this holding environment is an utter respect for the individual. Such a stance requires trying to understand the factors that have brought them into the consulting room and recognizing the symptoms as meaning structures only translatable through a deeper understanding of the contextual factors that gave rise to them. Meanings are inevitably personal; thus, my perspective slants away from the language of psychopathology and into the language of development, distress, and adaptation, hoping that my intense focus will help the other person to turn their own focus inward—past whatever resistances are encountered—toward a deeper search for meanings increasingly marked by an internal sense of truth. I try to ground this search in my own respect for whatever data I am able to pick up through the countertransference as I learn more about how to parse this information in light of what I am learning about the other person.

I recognize that multiple communications are always being enacted at various levels. In my work with those for whom trauma or neglect has impeded the elaboration of that internal sense of truth and, with it, of self-development, I am particularly focused on trying to attune myself to those rhythms of meaning as they manifest themselves and to use whatever information I take in in ways that might be useful to the analysand, most particularly to demonstrate that very effort as an endorsement of their own efforts toward self-understanding.

Recognizing that each person is unique and so must discover themselves for themselves helps me tolerate not knowing where we are going or what we are doing. That tolerance helps the other person find their own equilibrium and begin to make their own meanings in relation to someone who believes that they can indeed find answers within themselves. In that way, a process might unfold in which they are better able to make use of internal and external signals as they encounter them: to recognize patterns, locate desires, and make choices.

There are key conceptualizations from Lacan that I find particularly useful in helping me tolerate the not-knowing that enables those I work with to find their own creative edge rather than to merely encounter another "expert" who loses them in the process of finding them. Lacan's (1964/1977e) emphasis on the subject of the inquiry helps me keep my eye on the prize, so to speak, in line with Bion's (1977) endorsement of a "truth instinct" that might guide our efforts if we can steer by it.

Taking seriously Lacan's (1964/1977e) ideas about the *subject caught by the desire of the other*—that we all tend to get lost in the presumption that someone else is in charge of our value—I work hard to locate the person who has lost themselves, to invite them to take themselves seriously enough to bring their fears, hopes, and passions into the room. I also appreciate Lacan's recognition of the gaps, the ellipses, such that what most needs our attention is often what is missing. My sense is that Lacan's focus on the *oblique angle*, the view from the side, the picture in which our gaze is caught but missing, are metaphors that speak to our position as supplicants—come to receive a knowledge that is barred precisely because we seek it directly—to *replace* a lack rather than to *illuminate* it (see Chapter 12). The challenge for the clinician, then, is to make offerings sufficiently respectful of the limits of what anyone might know about another person that they further the reflective capacity of the person seeking treatment rather than pretend they can take the place of it. From this perspective, our job is not to "fix" someone or something, or to provide a cure, but rather to encourage the person to continue to develop beyond the places where they have become caught.

Lacan's work is paradoxical in that he stood as "The Master" while also taking a stand for becoming one's own Master. Opposing the more normative view in which his early work was cast, in his later years Lacan (1974–1975, 1975–1976/2016) developed a model that focused on ways in which idiosyncratic meanings are "knotted" together for an individual such that we can only find the key to the person's mysteries by paying close attention to those meanings as they manifest in the material. Much as we have found in Winnicott (1971), helping others to locate themselves—and take themselves seriously—such that they can be more creative in their lives and engagements seems to be at the core of the psychotherapy process, as I understand it.

Both Bion and Lacan stressed that our most important truths are often hiding in plain sight, that what is needed is to dim the stark light of reason or theory sufficiently to be able to allow the person before us to emerge. When trauma has impeded development, the child carries the marks of that trauma as a symptom, a sleight of hand that marks the problem in disguise. In psychoanalysis, we hope to be sufficiently respectful of the need for disguise that we can provide a space in which the person can find their own truths in their own ways.

As we have seen, interpersonal learning requires sufficient space to engage with others as Winnicott (1971) described it: to play. When trauma and neglect have impeded the development of sufficient separateness to engage with another person playfully, bumps can feel shameful, and fear can inhibit further engagement. Under such circumstances, interactions can become routinized and constricted, impeding the person's ability to learn from their experience. The clinical work, then, depends on developing sufficient interpersonal trust that the person might develop the *epistemic trust* Fonagy and Allison (2014) highlighted as essential to building their metacognitive capacities. This trust affords the type of safety needed to begin to play with others and with ideas.

The Role of Play

Long ago, Winnicott noted the difference between a type of play that was ruminative and obsessive, one that destroyed reality, and a type of play that was creative and fruitful. He described this difference in terms of a type of empty, ruminative, repetitive fantasying that goes nowhere versus a dream that has creative potential because it has "*poetry in it*, that is to say, layer upon layer of meaning related to past, present, and future, and to inner and outer, and always fundamentally about [one]self" (Winnicott, 1971, p. 35).

Play can be impeded by fear. At some level, the fear of difference is a fear of being seen. Early parental failures become internalized as an essential inherent internal badness. Whatever we are avoiding seems to lurk at every turn. When what we are avoiding is a confrontation with the self, the danger does lurk at every turn; we are always in danger of being caught being ourselves. I recall that pivotal moment when I recognized that I was seeing in a woman's face the mirror of what she had seen in her mother's. Reflecting this impression to her helped to break through the certainty that she was the vile repugnant creature her mother seemed to be seeing (see Chapter 6 in Charles, 2004). Such moments help us appreciate the importance of trying to be a mirror into which the person can peer without turning to stone or being annihilated, a mirror that can be truly reflective. The possibility of reflection that enables the disruption of destructive internal truths requires a psychoanalysis that is creative enough to offer alternate truths in successive doses that can be metabolized. Staying close to the person so we can learn their language and see the world through their eyes, as much as possible, is essential for this careful work that is guided by the signals we receive through the countertransference.

As the clinician registers the distress through the nonverbal channels, trying to hear the story being told and to see through the other person's eyes, we are offering a model of being-with another that likely is a new experience, one that is essential for creative development to occur. The ability to register in another person's heart, mind, and being—without getting lost or losing the other person—seems to be at the core of self-development and therefore of the capacity to be creative, as illustrated in the case that follows shortly.

Developing the Capacity to Play in the Consulting Room

Winnicott (1971) wrote that one of the preconditions for becoming a separate self was to be able to use another person. There is something about being able to push the parent away, dismiss them from our mind and universe—and then find them still standing—that is important for both self-development and the capacity to play. We may recognize this truth in principle and yet may also lose sight of ways in which our own need to be clever or useful may inhibit the nascent development of reflective thought in the other person. Traversing this territory requires sufficient attention to the countertransference as it plays out moment by moment that we can catch a shift and inquire into it with care, interest, respect, and curiosity. In that way, our careful tracking insists that it is the other person's experience that is most important, reminding us to be a humble fellow traveler rather than imposing ourselves as a "valuable" guide.

Playfulness is at the core of the fundamental rule, and yet "free association" is never truly free and can represent an impossible demand for those who are massively ungrounded in their internal experience. If there is no safety in relationship, then, as social beings, our survival is too precarious, and whatever internal capacities we might have, there is no room for play. I see this, for example, in Lina, a young woman in her twenties whom I referred to in Chapters 3 and 4. Lina wanted to become a writer but discovered that once she had written the story that needed to be told, there was nothing more to say. Her eventual collapse helped us recognize that her early life had given her insufficient grounding on which to build a self.

When, early in our work together, she tried to talk with her mother, Lina could see the mother's inability, despite her good intentions, to truly be available to her daughter. Rather, at any hint of need, the mother collapsed and became preoccupied with her own well-being. Encountering this utter unavailability helped Lina to understand the story I was telling her of a feral child who, despite the love and adoration of her parents, was never given the wherewithal to survive and thrive in the interpersonal world. The creative capacities that eluded her needed to wait as she developed a way of understanding self and relationship. She tried to hold on to my faith in such an outcome because she had no way of imagining it (Charles, 2003).

Much of our work together entailed finding sufficient safety in the consulting room to be able to lay aside her mask and focus on a process of self-discovery that included mourning the terrible years in which she had been so utterly lost. Encountering and facing the gaps within self and experience required courage and fortitude as she faced her shame and her fear. Through these efforts, she began to build the epistemic trust so crucial to development, including the capacity to play (Fonagy & Allison, 2014).

Lina's innate creative drive helped her make use of her intelligence and curiosity despite her shame over feeling so young in relation to her actual age. Finding a way to enjoy trying various aspects of identity on for size can be a challenge when we would seem to be past the age for "dress-up" and the types of compelling identifications usually associated with early adolescence or even childhood. In such work, the analyst's ability to hold lightly the paradox of being both child and adult can help the person tolerate the disjunction and perhaps be playful within the spaces thus afforded.

Playing With Metaphors

Because of the difficulty of holding hope and also of communicating experience that is largely ineffable and beyond words, metaphors are profoundly important in working with people whose development has been impeded by trauma. Metaphors breathe life into the work because they are, of essence, playful: They cannot be taken in directly, but rather must be *played with*. The analyst can lead the way by recognizing and trying to make use of the person's own metaphors. Rather than imposing or insisting on our metaphors, being able to catch the metaphors as they emerge in the work helps to mark them rather than just let them go by.

People often do not recognize the value of the particular ways in which they invest and invoke meaning, and yet the clinician knows that this is precisely the territory that must be mined so that they can find their own truths. To counter this confusion, we insist that their metaphors have meaning by making meaning from them, thereby taking our part in creating the possibility of playing with them together. We hope to mark the potentiality of meaning in even the most concrete and unwieldy metaphors in ways that will enable those meanings to unfold.

One metaphor that emerged in my work with Lina was that of windows and doors. She had been talking about needing to get through the window, which had brought up the question of why she thought of a window rather than a door. As Lina considers this question, she can recognize that windows are difficult to get in or out of with attendant hazards. But, she says, that is precisely how she envisions herself, staring out a window at a life that is not hers. "Here I am," she says, "looking out the fucking window." She can recognize that the window that might have opened onto possibilities has, for her, become a prison. "If you go out the window, you die," she says. "I've been living in a hallucination of what's outside the window. I made up life. I made up the truth. But this is where I am. And it hurts."

She continues,

> I was just the mannequin I didn't use because I was in the wrong location. It would be weird to dress me up because I'm so used to dressing someone else up. I gave up, was the thing. I didn't try to be pretty or cool. I just defected. I followed cool people around like a stray dog, protecting myself from this sorrow I feel. I'm very wounded by the fact that I couldn't compete. It would be nice to just be myself, and just dress how I want to dress, however. It's all I have. I have spent my life looking outside but it's the interior. The interior is all I have. I went home and took a shower and washed my fucking hair. I just did it. I washed my fucking hair.

When we reached this point in the treatment, we could also recognize that this trope of the window that affords an image of possibility but no path for entry was presaged in Lina's dreams as she reported them very early in the treatment. Early dreams invite the clinician into the person's fantasy world, the locus of the more primary hopes, fears, and relational meanings, and therefore the potential space of the analytic process itself. That potential space may be, as was true in my work with Lina, largely potential without much room for creative engagement—with the illusion of insight or reflective thought but without any of its layering. Of one dream, for example, Lina says,

> I am trying to get people to the beach. I can look down at it, but the pathway is under construction. It is demolished, but the workers are there. I can see the ocean; I can see the beach, but I'm overlooking it.

I find myself playing with this word "overlooking" but recognize that I am largely alone in that play. I am free to wonder in what ways Lina is *over*looking—looking past details that might need to be put into place to successfully accomplish the journey she hopes to undertake—but, for Lina at this point, the overlooking is a condition of existence rather than a possibility that can be played with. In such moments, it is important for the clinician to recognize the constraints the person is working under rather than try to force something that is not possible. Our feelings in the countertransference offer a useful guide as we track the person's responsiveness in the moment.

Lina describes the feeling in the dream as "stressful. There is a gap between that child self and my rational self," she says. Although Lina is aware in this moment that the move toward intellectualization enhances a gap she stumbles over, many months go by before she can tolerate taking conscious steps to attenuate that gap. The pain of reconnection with her "child" self, her affectively-engaged self, is profound. At this point, standing back from the emotion and remaining in the realm of cognition, we can talk about the pain in terms of something she previously needed to attenuate directly through medication to survive but that she may now need to tolerate sufficiently to work through to more truly live. From this affective distance, Lina speaks about having had "the fight taken out of me. The idea that it's not going to matter. It'll be taken away, compromised. It won't be mine." "The storm has passed," she says, "and the ship has run aground on a landscape of featureless monotony."

My countertransference in this moment is in line with her description of the terrain in which we have become mired. During this early time of our work together, my experience is of such a featureless monotony that I have no anchoring points through which to fix the events she depicts into any sort of coherent narrative, resulting in sleepiness on my part and Lina's experience of not being heard. "I told you that," she would say. I would feel embarrassed and ashamed but would also come forward to meet her by recognizing that very difficulty in putting together the narrative of her life as something likely meaningful and worth our considering. I take a stand in relation to my feelings in the moment and say, "I find it difficult to have a sense of where you are emotionally. That makes it hard for me to have a sense of how to locate *you* in this story you are telling."

Placing priority on the affective aspects of meaning counters Lina's desire to have the words say it all. For Lina, affect has become a terrible storm/nightmare that has made both thought and action impossible. Attenuating the affect through medication and dialectical behavior therapy has made it possible for her to think once again. But she is too out of touch with her feelings to be able to make use of them, leaving the landscape empty and monotonous and, worse still, leaving her feeling empty—"concave," as she puts it—uncannily or intentionally using my metaphor in the words of an early paper I had written on the experience of emptiness in women (Charles, 2000a).

In sharing these metaphors, personalized by our unique individual experience and also by our moments together, we begin to build a language that is increasingly embodied as she recognizes both the absence and her desire to fill it without leaving herself behind. We struggle together with the price of increased affective engagement so that she can locate herself in the struggle between the too-much and too-little of mind and body and get her bearings and find her own equilibrium. I do not have the answers; I can only recognize, respect, and insist on the legitimacy of the questions and her efforts to find her own answers to them. I can participate with her in this enterprise of meaning-making, trying to dream through the sessions along with her in the fashion described by the Bionian field theorists Ferro (2009) and Civitarese (2005; see Chapter 13 for an explication of Bionian field theory).

Metaphors become important transitional objects and markers of meaning in conceptual space for both individuals in the consulting room, helping us to stand on unsteady ground (Katz, 2013). Such a stance is most urgent with those for whom early developmental failures and trauma have interfered with their ability to establish a coherent and stable identity. With such individuals, respect for our own countertransference feelings helps to provide the type of attuned and attentive tracking through which the narrative of self-identity is developed as they learn to attend more respectfully and with greater nuance to the subtleties of their own internal experience.

Building a Safe Playing Field

We hope to invite greater playfulness into our work, but play can only be free and creative to the extent that one can trust that there is an environment sufficiently safe and reliable on which to land. Taking a stand regarding the possibility of meaning-making and trying to offer missing pieces as they emerge in the work without imposing or demanding any particular meaning help the person build a coherent narrative in which the fragments that could not be assimilated can come together into a more coherent form, guided by their own internal sense of truth.

Paying attention respectfully to our countertransference feelings helps us remain in touch with our primary process even as we more actively reflect on possible meanings in the secondary realm. As we interplay over time, building meanings at the intersection of primary and secondary process, being able to work in realms without words can be extremely useful to those seeking assistance, helping to afford a grounding in primary sensory experience. Much as clinicians need to be able to tune their sensibilities, their *instruments*, if you will; so, too, each person must become familiar with their own.

Lina begins to wander down to the shop, where she plays at drawing. Lina—whose perfectionism and attention to values endorsed from the other side of the window make it difficult for her to discover her own—begins to imagine being able to surmount the impasse by doing "bad art." This is likely a brilliant move on her part. We call it the *talking cure*, but, as with Lina, talk can cover over the work remaining to be accomplished beneath the veneer of words that seem to be so well put together. Allowing that veneer to slip enables Lina to encounter more of herself—and with it, her pain—through which process she begins to come alive sufficiently to feel anything at all beyond the abject and nameless pain she was suffering when we first met. She worries that she is getting worse but also has the sense that she is getting better. "You've been numb," I say. "And it hurts to come back to life."

Much as Winnicott (1971) noted in descriptions of his work with a young adolescent, truly being present with one's deepest uncertainties can be so painful that it presents both analyst and analysand with an utterness that feels unendurable. At times, Lina pushes herself beyond her limits into a space in which she can only scream, cry, rend her clothing, or throw things. In one such moment, she takes me to task for wasting her sessions, at times, by trying desperately to ease her distress. I acknowledge with humility my complicity in these enactments and tell her that I recognize that the last time she was in such an unendurable space was also the time when she held the space by recognizing its value. In the current moment, as she tells me with anguish that she cannot live, that she is trapped with no hope or possibility, I remind her that this is familiar territory. This seems to be the way she corners *herself* to force herself to confront what she otherwise so effectively avoids. We can see her using the same defenses that keep pushing people away. She hates being hated, and her anguish is like a violent force field that pushes everyone away, leaving her profoundly and terribly alone. The challenge seems to be to recognize her part in this without turning the icy shards of hostility on herself. This is a challenge she must be able to face.

Lina tells me that in her dreams, her father is alive and she is back in her home state with people she had hoped could be friends. She then awakens each morning to this terrible isolation, feeling as though anywhere she turns, the space will become empty. I enter empathically into her reverie and relate to her the images as they come to me, first as though people split into fragments of mercury that disperse as she approaches. This seems off target, and I wonder if it is more as though she is inevitably at the wrong end of the magnet, repelling anyone who comes near. Moving together into her dream space seems to help keep us in the right place, in the analytic space, where we can encounter the distress and stay alive within it together. From this position, she seems able to use the same defenses that push people away but without holding herself to blame. Seeing her part without reverting to her stance of inevitable internal badness, she can keep her mind active and perhaps choose to do it differently. There is the possibility of speaking to others to try to bridge the gap rather than maintaining it by using them as vehicles for discharge and despair.

I remind her that she has found in her own mother one who is good-enough despite her mother's very real limits and that she, Lina, was profoundly instrumental in allowing the mother to become good-enough. I suggest that if she can accept limits, she can likely build possibilities both creatively and relationally. Most crucial for us—and for her own development—is that she can hate me for my limits, so she doesn't have to displace that hatred and despair onto others. I acknowledge the difficulty she is in, that, much as must have occurred with her mother during childhood, she can sense my reluctance to be hated but that accommodating to my need rather than her own leaves her unable to move on. Accommodating to my desire rather than being present with her own keeps her from going places she needs to go, keeps her from sounding the depths of her own despair and recognizing that the dark sludge she feels pulling her seemingly into nothingness and death is not madness, but rather recognition of all that has truly been dark but need not be entirely that. It is fear that has her in its deadly grip, not truth.

Beyond the darkness of the distress, there still exists all of her extraordinary potential as a human being. And so, I tell her that despite our mutual reluctance to enter this darkness, we can survive it—together. Loving and hating me provides some real ground on which we both can stand, from which place she can perhaps discover the potential she carries in ways that are enlivening and fulfilling.

CONCLUSION

In this chapter, I considered ways in which the concepts of transference and countertransference can inform our clinical work. These ideas are particularly useful to have in mind when working with individuals whose maturation has been constricted by trauma or neglect and who have not developed the capacity to learn through playful interactions with others. In the following chapter, I turn to interpretation. *Interpretation* has become the term used to describe how we offer our formulations to the other person for their consideration. Although interpretation has become the accepted goal in psychoanalytic work, Freud recognized as early as 1937 (Freud, 1937/1964) that when trauma was involved, construction—or reconstruction—may be the primary goal. These considerations may assist us in our efforts to provide offerings that invite curiosity and reflection rather than merely provide data that might further close down the reflective space we are hoping to build in the consulting room.

6 INTERPRETATION

We come now to the problem of *interpretation*, offering back to the person what we have learned in our encounters with them thus far as we try to break through repetitive patterns of behavior by making them visible. As noted in the previous chapter, although interpretation has come to be seen as the prize of psychoanalytic work, Freud (1937/1964) noted early on that the more essential effort is put into construction, particularly with those for whom trauma has impeded memory. Freud suggested that *construction* is a more apt term for the work of the analyst: "Interpretation applies to something that one does to some single element of the material, such as an association or a parapraxis. But it is a 'construction' when one lays before the subject of the analysis a piece of his early history that he has forgotten" (Freud, 1937/1964, p. 261). With this caveat in mind, in this chapter, I trace the use of the term *interpretation* and offer clinical illustrations.

THE CONCEPT

From a classical perspective, interpretation makes use of the transference to recognize the interplay of wish, defense, and guilt. In Arlow's (1987) words, "Treatment, then, becomes a matter not of recollecting and purging one's self

https://doi.org/10.1037/0000455-007
Echoes of Trauma: Meaning and Identity in Psychoanalysis, by M. Charles

of a noxious memory from the past; it becomes instead a matter of knowing and mastering a persistently disturbing influence in the present" (p. 75). Rather than bringing the unconscious to light, the goal is to encourage insight by attending to the "conflictual compromise formations . . . [that show] the evolving pattern of the dynamic conflict" (Arlow, 1987, pp. 85–86). Focusing on the underlying conflict helps keep visible the transference to authority, marking when a shift may be in compliance with projections regarding the analyst's desire rather than showing actual insight or reflective capacity. We must also be wary of our own investments in whatever "truths" we carry. The idea that we already have the answers interferes with our ability to learn, encouraging us to keep in mind Bion's (1967a) admonition to avoid memory or desire in the clinical encounter.

Arlow (1987) opposed ideas regarding Strachey's (1969) *mutative* interpretation that presumes to offer a truth to help the ego attain mastery, suggesting that a useful interpretation may emerge in the form of a sound or a single word that punctuates and impacts the person's productions. Lacanian views also have endorsed the value of punctuation, through repeating words or ending a session on a moment of potential insight but shifting the focus toward disruption rather than education. This disruption includes attention to the transference to authority so that the interpretation might potentiate "self-recognition by allowing a transference to develop and then systematically differentiating [one]self from the Other" (Friedlander, 1991, p. 118).

In this way, the Lacanian perspective moves toward breaking into the person's presumptions regarding the analyst's privileged knowledge and encouraging them to focus on what they might know from their own experience. Contrast this perspective to traditional views that might encourage confrontation or relational perspectives that encourage self-disclosure. The disruption is aimed toward highlighting "the nonsense, the Other sense in what is being said, to get to the structure, to the saying and the main signifiers of the subject" (García Salas, 2018, p. 42). The goal is not to speak "*about* [emphasis added] the truth but instead, making the truth present in the session" by exposing the misunderstanding revealed in the person's speech (García Salas, 2018, p. 37). To accomplish this task, the analyst must be willing to take seriously the fact of our own desire as it manifests within the work so we can think about our own contributions rather than use the idea of countertransference as a means of excusing ourselves from responsibility (Wilson, 2013).

Bion (1967a, 1980), too, warned against our memory and desire and the hazard of inviting adaption to the analyst rather than encouraging people to become themselves. In his clinical seminars, Bion actively disrupted presumed meanings that hid behind another's authority; he encouraged analysts to use their own experience to guide them. He stressed that psychoanalysis requires a refinement of attention, building the capacity to think rather than accumulate knowledge (Bion, 1977). The Lacanian view went even further, opposing ideas about cure, healing, or even adaptation to reality in favor of showing how the psyche "assists in the construction of that very reality" (Lacan, 1958/1977a, p. 236.) From this perspective, the function of interpretation is *revelation*: It "must introduce . . . something that suddenly makes translation possible," (p. 233) that enables the analysand to speak for themselves about what had been suppressed.

Perhaps most essential for the clinician is to hear. I may not understand what I am hearing but that is not the essential thing. In the not-understanding, we point to something elusive that needs further inquiry. "The analyst gives his presence, but I believe that this presence is first of all simply the implication of his listening," said Lacan (1958/1977a, p. 255). In hearing without speaking, we frustrate the part of the person who is looking for an answer to override their own. Inhibiting reactive speech can keep us from behaving as though something makes sense that does not. In allowing ourselves space to not understand, we invite the person to think more reflectively about what they are saying. We can also actively inquire into the gap, wondering aloud about what we are stumbling over.

For Lacan, interpretation is aimed toward revealing the subject's masked desire, which then restores the meanings of the symptoms. Even in Freud's (1895/1955d) earliest work on technique, we see references to an *other* within the self: the unconscious speaking through the symptom. From this framework, the Other supposed to know is neither the analyst nor the analysand but the unconscious of the analysand. The analyst knows not the unknown knowledge but only how it hides and reveals itself. We know where to look, and our interpretations aim toward encouraging the person to discover who they are addressing and to what end (Lacan, 1954–1955/1988). Lacan's (1964/1977e) *oblique angle* reminds us to watch the performance from the side so that we can address the fact of it rather than merely be saturated by it (see Chapter 12 for further discussion of the oblique angle). As Winnicott (1971) encouraged, it is better not to interfere with the person's creative engagement, but rather leave them to struggle with their own questions of what they are up to.

From a Lacanian perspective, the purpose is not to point out the fact of the transference, but rather to analyze what is being projected from within the transference as a way of inviting a consideration of whatever is being played out (Lacan, 1964/1977e). In this way, the interpretation points back toward the unconscious as knowable through its acts. We are in the realm of Freud's (1895/1966) *Nachträglichkeit*, the afterwardness through which a new perspective might be attained (see Chapter 14 for a discussion of psychic time).

Interpretation aims to stand between enigma and knowledge so that it can reverberate in the analysand because it is not immediately comprehensible. The interpretation that cannot be easily contained echoes, inviting meaning-making. To this end, disruption of accepted meanings can be more useful than any attempt to convey "knowledge" (Patsalides & Patsalides, 2001). We are not so much constructing or finding the real meaning, but rather deconstructing—in Bion's (1962) terms *unsaturating*—the accumulated meanings so we might decipher what lies behind them (García Salas, 2018).

The question of interpretation invites us to consider how best to offer what we have learned to the person in ways that might invite them to actually think about what we—and they—are saying. Interpretations are most useful when they meet both the reason and the affect. If the affect is too intense, the reason falters; without affect, the speech is empty. We need the right balance for meanings to be considered in relation to experience, which means paying attention to building reflective space within the treatment. In contrast to perspectives that focus on transference interpretations, particularly in work with those without a sturdy internal foundation, it can be important to respect the value of the displacement for those needing that safety.

The problem of providing conditions of sufficient safety that meaning might be made and development proceed is the challenge Winnicott (1955) pointed to in considering how to work with undeveloped aspects of self that are present in us all. In such cases, Mitrani (2001) stressed the importance of taking the transference and keeping our interpretations in close relationship to what seems most immediate in the moment, maintaining contact with elements of the person that seem most in need of elaboration, including "vulnerable, embryonic . . . aspects . . . not yet fully formed" (p. 1100).

THE CLINICAL CONTEXT

Interpretation has become the catchall term for how we make use of the information obtained through the transference/countertransference matrix described in the previous chapter. When working with those impacted by trauma or neglect, it is particularly useful to have in mind Freud's (1937/1964) distinction between the work of remembering and the analyst's need to construct meanings, not only from what has been repressed but also from what may never have been consciously known. These are the echoes of experience that lie in the realm of the embodied memories often found in individuals suffering from complex trauma. It is also useful to keep in mind the shift in Freud from seeing the function of interpretation as merely making the unconscious conscious to involving the person in a process in which affect and representation can come together to afford greater insight. "If the interpretation is too premature or too deep-rooted," suggested Sirois (2012), "it will be taken by the patient to be either, on the conscious level, an item of information or, on the unconscious level, a gratification or an intrusion" (p. 1383).

Because we can never know precisely how someone will take in an interpretation, de M'Uzan (2019) stressed the importance of spontaneity and ambiguity. *Spontaneity* allows the impact of the unconscious aspects driving the current moment to affect the analyst's speech, and the *ambiguity* invites the analysand to make their own meaning. In this way, the interpretation points to Bion's (1977) particular use of the term *passion* in recognition of the primacy of the nonverbal in meaning-making between persons such that the truth of the lived moment can resonate in ways that carry forward into future moments of engagement. From this framework, passion marks something important even beyond our ability to precisely communicate it.

Interpretations can serve diverse functions depending on the status of the treatment. For those not fully engaged in an analytic process, Sirois (2012) suggested a category of *preliminary interpretations* that is aimed toward either monitoring and managing anxiety, preserving the setting, or facilitating free association. Most useful are preliminary interpretations that aim toward the vitality of the present moment without overwhelming either the emotions or the intellect. Finding the most accessible point of entry requires our sensitivity to the person's state in the moment. In this regard, Loewenstein (1956) detailed three functions of speech—representation, communication, and expression—in relation to which Sirois (2012) detailed three modalities of interpretation: those that enlighten, those that "say" something, and those that "touch."

Interpretations that *enlighten* mark an evolving conceptualization that feels revelatory when it finally emerges. The *metaphor* allows the ambiguity to remain intact, open to further consideration, evolution, and interpretation. In contrast, interpretations that *say* something communicate directly to the person factors that seem to be at stake affecting the treatment, allowing something hidden to become more visible or putting an underlying fantasy into words. The interpretation that *touches* "bears witness to the analyst's *presence* with the analysand" by empathically marking the person's state of mind (Sirois, 2012, p. 1392). This type of interpretation facilitates symbolization by recognizing a feeling, to "put words on it and give it some functional meaning" (Sirois, 2012, p. 1392). I think that Sirois's interpretations that touch fall into the same realm as Bion's passion.

Beyond this discriminative value at the nonverbal level, there is also the more active meaning-making promoted. According to Sirois, to be most useful, "an interpretation should act *as if it were a metaphor*" (Sirois, 2012, p. 1398). "Aimed at the Preconscious, it should bind rather than explain, it must be concise and spontaneous, . . . relatively ambiguous, and it should act like a perception following a clear sensory path" (Sirois, 2012, p. 1398). Whatever form it takes, the interpretation that functions as a metaphor holds the power and vitality of images and speech together. Interpretations that enlighten "operate on various levels simultaneously—they are meanings, signs and references that imitate human activity and, in so doing, imitate what motivates it" (Sirois, 2012, p. 1399).

DREAMING THE SESSION

Concepts such as Bion's (1992) notion of *dreaming the session* can help free up our unconscious mind and also attenuate the affective intensity that can obscure meanings. Bion used the term *dreaming* to mark an associative engagement with material that marks a deeper level of engagement and integration rather than merely taking in facts. This is a position from which we might be able to be sufficiently playful to be able to consider how our unconscious stirrings may relate to the unconscious of the other person. Profoundly being-with without becoming lost can be a challenge, and I would argue that, at times, we need to become lost for important meanings to take hold. This stance is in line with Parsons's (2007) idea that evoking the unconscious does not necessarily mean bringing material to light, but rather "the analytic situation may also evoke capacities, and functions, in the analyst's psyche, of which he was not previously aware" (p. 1453).

From this perspective, our openness to experience is more important than any knowledge we might reach for and is in line with Bion's (1967a) admonitions regarding abstaining from memory or desire. Being as fully present as we can enables us to find the parts of ourselves that are touched by the other person's tragedies and to speak from profound empathic resonance rather than a more shallow surface meaning. To be present to another's pain, said Parsons (2007), we need to be as alive as we can, and we need to learn to allow our offerings to be empowered and legitimized by the vitality—and authority—of the lived moment.

Parsons's ideas are in line with Shapira-Berman's (2022) suggestion that what is most transformative in psychoanalysis is not the interpretation per se, but rather the analyst's transformative act. When people look back on their analyses, what has been most crucial is often an act rather than a statement. There is likely something about the spontaneity of the act that marks its meaning and its truth value (Symington, 1983). Shapira-Berman embedded her ideas in the early childhood literature, noting that there is a compelling truth to nonverbal meanings that we experience at a more profound level than words. Experiencing something together registers at a deep, embodied level, the level of Winnicott's (1971) playing as doing. For Winnicott, when there is no play, interpretations are not useful. "*This playing has to be spontaneous and not compliant or acquiescent*," he said, "if psychotherapy is to be done" (Winnicott, 1971, p. 51).

In this realm of play and being-with, there is the possibility of one unconscious communicating with another. Given that much of what drives us is known implicitly and not explicitly, we need to trust and build our ability to be-with another person and attend to our internal experience reflectively with interest and curiosity and without the irritable reaching after fact and reason that Keats (1899) and Bion (1970) warned against. Moving into this creative space, suggested Winnicott (1971), invites the person to encounter their own truths—from their own experience—and reflect on them within the potential space that the analytic environment can provide.

CLINICAL ILLUSTRATIONS

For example, a seasoned clinician consulted me about an odd experience in her work with a woman who is a survivor of incest with ambivalent feelings over having been made special but also used by her parents. There is an uncanny now-you-see-it, now-you-don't quality to the work such that the clinician is never quite sure how conscious the memory of the abuse might be in a given moment. Initially, the work was almost impossible. The woman barely spoke, and most present was her suffering. The analyst easily suffered from her own failure to relieve the suffering, but thinking about her own distress helped her tolerate the discomfort as the woman began to find her way into the room.

Over slow, excruciating time, the woman became more engaged, spoke more freely, and even began to bring in dreams. At times, it was only through consultation that this analyst could even mark progress, particularly as the suffering became more intense. Without that touchstone outside the dyad, it could feel to the analyst as though, in failing to relieve the suffering, she was the source of it.

Recently, the analyst told me about an incident that unnerved her. There had been two difficult sessions, and then, during the next session, she began to feel very ill and could not even stay in the room. She did something she had never done before: excused herself in the middle of the session to go to the bathroom. She washed her face with cold water and felt better. She was so caught by the intensity of her sudden illness and feelings of failure that it was hard for her to think about the powerful transference/countertransference dynamic at play.

As we linked together the threads of the woman's dreams with the recent sessions, the analyst could see that, in her willingness to be profoundly present, she was being invited to feel something of the impossible feelings facing the woman as a child that likely led the woman to dissociate. We could conjecture that the feelings this woman could not feel were still present in the room, and the only one remaining to feel them was the analyst.

Inviting the analyst to feel these feelings so profoundly was a way of registering their truth. The interchange that had not happened in childhood—of parents recognizing, facing, and living through impossible feelings with the child—was occurring in the consulting room. Our conversations helped the analyst more fully register those meanings and be empathically connected once again rather than feel so lost and ashamed of feelings that likely would drive anyone out of the room. Living through the feelings provided a statement of hope because they were lived out with the woman in real time.

As we see in this vignette, recognizing the value and validity of inchoate or bodily feeling-memories can be pivotal in our work with traumatized individuals who may have no other way of communicating—even to themselves—what they are contending with, a subject I explore more fully in the following chapter. When there is no storyline, our determined respect for the work being done to make sense of what is coming into being provides us room to catch hold of the meanings, put them into words, and begin to develop a narrative.

The language of trauma can be off-putting, inviting alienating attributions often in the form of dehumanizing, diagnostic jargon. We must fight against our own resistance and allow ourselves to be drawn in and pull toward greater coherence rather than to leave the person seeking assistance further alienated, floundering, and alone.

In working with people at this level, it is useful to have in mind the primary nonverbal communications that are always at play but, as we age, tend to be overridden with ideas about the way things should be, ideas that can invite us to think our way past meanings we might need to register more fully. For example, if that analyst had decided she was merely ill, the information being communicated in the sessions would have been lost. Meanings become meaningless in the presence of someone who fails to register them, whereas if we take seriously what we can learn from Sirois (2012), we might offer containment through an interpretation that touches—that meets the emotional intensity of the moment sufficiently to make reflection possible.

With people who experienced insufficient containment from their parents, the analyst must tolerate being experienced as the insufficient object in the transference while also working to hold meanings in mind as they evolve in the reciprocal process of knowing and not-knowing that allows those meanings to transform. That process requires our ability to recognize our own resistances and work with them as they arise so that whatever is unresolved in us is not so blindly obstructing the development of the person needing containment.

In line with Sirois's (2012) notions of interpretations that *touch*, both Bion (1977) and Winnicott (1971) used maternal metaphors to describe this crucial containing or holding function achieved in part through the analyst's *reverie*, our ability to absorb and metabolize the material as it emerges and to engage in fantasies in relation to it. Meeting people where they are, through our own affective attunement, helps them tolerate the present moment sufficiently to provide grounding for further growth.

Kleinian theory rests on the assumption that primary experiences must be metabolized to be useful as symbols through which the experience can be managed (Charles, 2018). When the child's attempts to master anxiety have not been effective, relational needs can be impossibly tantalizing, leading to splits between the desire for a good object and experiencing people as impossibly bad because they are not good enough. The lack of ego strength or object permanency lends itself—in the transference—to intense affective storms.

Take, for example, Val, the bright young woman first referred to in Chapter 5 (see Chapter 12 for an explication of this case) who came to a standstill in her late teens, caught between the devalued mother who is available but emotionally remote and the idealized father who is rarely present but can be affectively engaged. Neither parent was sufficiently useful as an object with whom to test herself and grow.

Val's identification with her contemptuous father left her critical and deprecating toward her own emotions, and she worked diligently to discover what she might be missing but disdainfully rejected what was offered. In the transference, I became the "stupid mother" immobilized by Val's contempt.

To meet her, I had to tolerate this countertransference experience and know that I also might have something useful to offer if Val could listen without rejecting all my words out of hand. This stance enabled me to find my empathy while also retaining my reflectivity. Recognizing the hazards of my empathic resonance and my reflective eye, I tried to offer interpretations that *spoke*, marking the dilemma without invoking too much affect, or reflection that felt like judgment.

Kleinians try to stay with the experience as it emerges in the consulting room to find Bion's (1977) passion, the inner truth that leads us toward the point of difficulty rather than away. When I managed to keep my bearings, although Val may have become enraged and reactive at what she experienced as my contempt and lack of empathy, she also was relieved by her inability to destroy me. In such moments, we can re-find one another and continue—as Val worked toward what Winnicott termed *the use of an object* (see Winnicott, 1971, pp. 86–94).

The term *projective identification* marks ways in which difficult feelings, such as anger or contempt, that cannot be recognized inside oneself can seem to be coming from outside (Joseph, 1997). For the analyst, recognizing the communicative aspects and reflecting on what is being denied and displaced helps us speak to the pattern being played out rather than merely reacting to it (M. Feldman, 1997; Joseph, 1997), or accommodating (M. Feldman, 1993) or even blaming the person for being manipulative or aggressive. When people feel powerless, their communications of need are impacted.

For many people, tolerating not-knowing enough to be curious is itself a challenge. For example, take Nikolai, a man in his early fifties caught between his sense that I might know something important and his fear that this knowledge will demean him (see Chapter 12 for an explication of this case). When I remarked on his tendency to already have the answers, Nikolai, with little interest in anything I might add, showed apparent interest while hearing nothing. Any difference became a sign of my not understanding, resulting in further attempts to explain his position. If I persisted, he was either dismissive or tolerated the intrusion but then returned with renewed grievances regarding my failure to understand or to offer relief.

In the transference, I was the impossible mother who overrides his sensibilities and denies his manhood, putting him in the position of the impotent father. From a developmental perspective, we see him caught in a shame–rage cycle in which the recognition of another person's knowledge is almost impossible to bear (Kealy et al., 2023). Taking a Kleinian perspective, I used my feelings as a frame through which to interpret my ideas, speaking to his dilemma in being confronted with the limits of what he knows. Shamed as a child for whatever he could not understand, Nikolai now pulls out of relationships as a way of not having to face humiliation but then finds himself terribly alone. He is so certain of his deficiency that being seen is shameful. His envy and shame invite him to fend off potentially useful information rather than take it in.

With M. Feldman's (1993) ideas regarding the perils of reassurance in mind, I knew that I must confront the defensive aggression rather than accommodate to it. I said to Nikolai that I think he has the idea that if he could just "say it right" then things would change, but I think that the root of the problem lies in his intolerance of anyone else having something he does not. This intolerance of otherness makes learning from another person impossible, and yet it is likely what he cannot see and cannot describe that he needs to learn something about. This interpretation says something about the dynamics playing out.

Even beyond the perverse dynamics we can find ourselves embroiled in with narcissistic individuals, when working with those who have been traumatized, we can find ourselves in even more challenging situations. For example, I worked with Tina, a young woman in her twenties, who experienced such massive failures that, at age 14, she gave up and hid out in substance use and video games until her alienation drove her into psychosis (see Chapter 7 for an explication of this case). That experience marked a limiting edge, pushing Tina to seek treatment. Her strident declarations regarding her commitment to treatment felt repetitive and irritating, suggesting that there were two levels of communication occurring.

We cannot help but be ourselves, and soon Tina was using substances to ease distressing feelings and justifying her actions—and her deceit—by blaming me for not easing her distress, forcing her to take matters into her own hands. As people increasingly suspected that she was both using and lying, the pressure mounted, and eventually, she acknowledged her actions. Once again, however, she hoped she might hide sufficiently well to not have to face the consequences. We are, once again, in that odd territory of peekaboo as though if the person does not look, we will not see them. Think how young this position is!

With Tina, I had to work very hard to reflect on my intense countertransference so that I could recognize how desperately she was fending off assumptions about her lack of value and fears that she would be despised and dismissed as worthless and beneath contempt. Her devalued sense of self was so strong that she invited precisely that reaction from others. Working diligently to imagine what it might be like to be her helped me move past that complementary countertransference and empathize with how desperately lonely and valueless she was feeling. Speaking from that more empathic place helped provide a bridge, affording more room to interpret what I saw in ways she might be able to reflect on rather than fend off.

That is the narrow margin we often work in: where people come to learn precisely what they most virulently fend off encountering. How we offer such painful information in ways that are not too aversive to be thought about is an ongoing challenge. For Tina, speaking at the level of metaphor afforded a safe transitional space between the intensity of the affect and the harsh light of reason. My interpretation that *there could be no treatment without truth* became something she could hold on to and, at times, use as a navigational tool despite her ongoing evasive efforts. We will encounter Tina again in the next chapter.

CONCLUSION

I often find myself making use of Kleinian and object relations theories to make sense of the chaos of the feelings that can arise during the session. But then my mind goes back to the primary texts of Freud that invite us to discover the strands of meaning within the disparate threads we are offered. Tracking very closely the material being offered and the person's relation to feeling and meaning in the moment, we can think about Bion's (1977) passion and Sirois's (2012) levels of interpretation and move toward or away from the affect as we try to offer an interpretation that holds both and leaves sufficient space to reverberate.

I also make use of Lacan's and Bion's ideas of disrupting set meanings to be able to look beneath the mask and find the something more that the person is both needing and hiding from. Taking ourselves seriously as receptacles of both verbal and nonverbal meanings and recognizing the ambivalence always at the core of interpersonal relations, I try to sit open to the question of what this person needs to find within themselves to be relieved from the struggle of running away from it.

Whatever we term it, I think of Bion's truth instinct and try to remain open to whatever truths and lies might reveal themselves so that I might find a path of integrity as the work proceeds. In being true to ourselves, if nothing else, through our mirror neurons, we chart a path that speaks truth to the other without imposing our particular truth on them. In this way, we join with García Salas (2018), who said the following:

> Interpretation then would show these two levels, show the structural misunderstanding which the subject is part of, and capture him at the place where

> he does not recognize himself, where the truth speaks and not where he is trying to speak about the truth. (p. 42)

In Part II, I outlined transference, countertransference, and interpretation (and construction!) as the essential conceptual tools we bring to the clinical encounter. These tools assist us in our efforts to engage with authenticity in our encounters, in this way adding legitimacy and potency to our offerings. In the following chapter, I consider how we make use of these tools in application to particular clinical symptoms and syndromes.

PART III UNDERSTANDING SPECIFIC SYMPTOMS

7 SOMATIZATION

In the next several chapters, I focus on applying what we have learned to particular types of difficulties we encounter in the consulting room. Although the symptoms are diverse, somatization, eating disorders, character disorders, and even psychosis can all be traced back to the types of developmental problems we have been discussing. Recognizing the underlying type of defense and the deficits helps us meet the person where they are so they might build their own internal resources rather than assume they somehow have to be "fixed" or "managed." This type of clinical work takes a stand for the importance of learning as the path toward greater resilience and a better quality of life.

We begin here with somatization. As we have touched on in previous chapters, early adversity can result in deficits in the capacity to symbolize, to formulate feelings into words. People who present with somatic complaints that cannot be resolved medically often find their way, somewhat ambivalently, into our consulting rooms. Such persons present difficulties relationally

---

Portions of this chapter have been adapted from "Somatization and Symbolization," by M. Charles, 2024, *American Journal of Psychoanalysis*, *84*, pp. 57–78 (https://doi.org/10.1057/s11231-024-09441-1). Copyright 2024 by Springer Nature. Adapted with permission.

https://doi.org/10.1037/0000455-008
Echoes of Trauma: Meaning and Identity in Psychoanalysis, by M. Charles

and technically: relationally because our attempts to understand their difficulties in psychological terms can feel out of touch with their actual needs and technically because of the need to shift focus from the physical to the psychic. There have been many attempts to conceptualize somatic complaints. In this chapter, let us first look at some of the major threads that have emerged from these efforts and then consider how we might apply these ideas in the consulting room.

CONCEPTUALIZING SOMATIC COMPLAINTS

Marty et al. (1963) characterized psychosomatic difficulties in terms of a lack of manifest affect in speech and relationships, impoverished use of language, and the prevalence of bodily expressions. In contrast, Kleinians locate the deficits in a mother–child bond that did not facilitate the translation of primary sensory experience into words (Klein, 1957/1975). From McDougall's (1974) perspective, the relational challenges stem from the relative isolation of the psychosomatic position, which lends an air of "invincibility that invades the analytic situation" (p. 458). Relentless attacks on linking thoughts with feelings can make an upsurge of emotion feel "like a 'crazy' intrusion" into the mind—and the body—of the analyst. Under such conditions, suggested McDougall (1974), the analyst's ability to "bear the coming alive of archaic instinctual impulses, and consequent ego [disturbance]" is crucial to the treatment (pp. 458–459).

Although the two main approaches to psychosomatic illness focus, respectively, on deficit versus psychic conflict, each recognizes an alienation from psychic experience that is profound, resulting in difficulties organizing the basic mental functions through which symbolization and identity develop. The deficit model espoused by the Paris Psychosomatic School (Aisenstein, 2006) contends that to make the shift from concrete absorption in the body toward reflection, the person presenting psychosomatic complaints needs to be actively invited into an analytic process through conversation. For Aisenstein (2006), to interest such a person in thinking about the underlying issues, "one must think with him and involve him in the process" (p. 670). Recognizing our own mentalization as an active process that invites the other person into greater reflectivity is pivotal in a therapeutic practice geared toward learning and growth rather than fixing problems.

For Kleinians, unconscious fantasy is inseparable from the body so that psychosomatic phenomena are linked not only to concrete mental representations but also to early fantasies (Bronstein, 2011). From that perspective, trauma impedes symbolization such that the pain becomes the tie to the needed object, and the challenge is to establish meaningful contact with the person's internal world. As with the Paris Psychosomatic School (Aisenstein, 2006), the analyst serves a crucial function in being available to think about the bits of experience that the person cannot yet think about. Technically, however, although Kleinians advocate for engagement in an analytic process, the underlying presumptions are developmental, taking into account the person's relative ability to function symbolically, always open to ways in which meanings may be received within the body of the analyst (Ferro, 2009).

Bion's (1990) view, rather than focusing on unconscious fantasy, went deeper, positioning the body at the core of meaning so that "mind and mental functions emerge from sensory and emotional data rather than the other way around" (Carignani, 2012, p. 311). This perspective led to Ferrari's (2004) positioning of the body at the core of all meaning-making, suggesting that it is the person's relationship with their own body that is primary and relegating relationships with others to a subsidiary, containing function.

Carvalho (2012) noted that Ferrari's "direct relationship between body and mind is in contrast to the object relations model in which this relationship is mediated through the breast" (p. 413). For Ferrari (2004), mind, or rather *mental functions*, emerge from the body, which he termed the *concrete original object*, and symptoms speak through the *language registers* that evolve out of patterns of bodily experience. The clinician must learn to read these symptoms as messages from the body that remains "a concrete object, the reintegration of which into the analytic process enables the patient to open up to experience, change and life, even before opening up to thought" (Lombardi, 2008, p. 106).

As we have seen, Aulagnier (2001) extended these ideas further, suggesting that, underneath even the enigmatic messages described by Laplanche (1997), early infantile experiences of flesh on flesh, infused by the caregiver's pleasure or displeasure, form a template, a *pictogram*, on which all meanings become patterned. The pictogram is the representational system of what Aulagnier termed the *primal* process, the underbelly of all sensory experience and human meaning.

Aulagnier's (2001) view argued for the essential particularity of human meaning and experience. As we consider the ramifications for technique, Fischbein (2011) has invited us to focus not on differentiations among schools, but rather on distinctions between types of somatic complaints as in those for whom illness intervenes and disrupts development—as in the case of Emily (see Chapter 3 for an explication of this case)—and those for whom disruption itself results in somatic symptoms—as in the cases of Roy and Tina (presented later in this chapter). Similar to Winnicott's (1974) position regarding work with the sequelae of trauma—that we must provide the conceptual framework that enables a person to recognize that a feared event has already occurred—Fischbein has invited us to orient toward the experience that did not register sufficiently for meaning to be made. Technically, this position brings us back to a focus on the particularity of the person and their experience. If we believe that deficits happen in relation to what is and is not offered to the developing child, then we need to pay close attention to the meanings of symptoms, including bodily and affective experience that requires further attention for sense to be made (Charles, 2021b).

SOMATIZATION IN THE CLINICAL ENCOUNTER

Working with a person who somatizes is complicated because they are the one who can potentially know most about what is happening inside their body but have not developed sufficient discriminative capacity to make sense of what their body is telling them. To the contrary, there tends to be an absolute disrespect for their own embodied experience along with a fearful desire to get rid of the signals rather than to learn from them. The analyst's interest in the bodily experience, and our willingness to imagine it and speak to our imaginings as we orient to signs of it and hear the person speak about their own experience, provides a containing space in which reflection is both modeled and offered, helping to titrate the intensity of the distress.

Within that type of play space, conjectures can be made so that the two can consider how the bodily experience might be relevant to the life story as it has and has not evolved, in this way allowing possible meanings to emerge for further consideration. This is the type of transitional space described by Winnicott (1971) and more fully developed by Italian field theorists Ferro (2009) and Civitarese (2015), who made use of Bion's (1965) concept of *transformations in hallucinosis* as a marker for the type of reflective capacity required of us when working with individuals whose internal landscape is largely unelaborated. This term recognizes that delusional material also has some grounding in physical reality, making it important for the clinician to find their own grounding when working with unmentalized material. In such cases, our efforts to populate the landscapes of the sessions with affectively infused images and characters are crucial.

With those who somatize, anxiety is often at the core of the trouble as presented. Many function in a concrete manner: They use words mechanically and are unable to integrate thoughts with feelings. Relationships tend to be similarly remote with no palpable emotional involvement. Bob, a man in his mid-fifties, for example, uses his intelligence in cogent and refined ways, but his constructions remain abstract, unlinked to his affect. He wards off attempts to meet him in a reciprocal discourse as though unable to tolerate, make sense of, or make use of anything that is "other." "Knowledge" becomes a defense against linking feeling with thinking, warding off the danger of contact with other's minds or feelings through obsessive, avoidant defenses (see Chapter 9 for an explication of this case and of obsessive defenses).

Despite his massive defenses, Bob seeks an analytic process through which his somatic complaints might help heal the split between feeling and thinking. Opposing any real learning, however, are his inhibited mental functions and concrete and factual ideation (Marty, 1968). Unable to reflect on his own mental world or that of others (Fischbein, 2011), Bob obsessively and relentlessly describes his particular variant of obsessive-compulsive disorder in which perceptions and sensations predominate. What appears to be reflective is merely descriptive, based on acquired knowledge, not embodied experience.

With people who are limited in their reflective capacities, I often find myself imagining and describing to them my fantasy of what might have led to symptoms that seem unfathomable. I look for the story underneath the story, hoping, in Sirois's (2012) sense, to *touch* them with an interpretation that makes sense because it gives form to feelings by empathically marking their state of mind. Take, for example, my work with Emily in which I needed to imagine her early experiences sufficiently to invite her interest in the possibility that those experiences might actually be meaningful.

THE RELATIONAL CONTEXT

My understanding of psychosomatic illness is that it is linked to disruptions in early development. Even when such troubles arise later in life, we find disruptions in the parent–child bond in the person's history. As we have seen, when children are offered a good-enough early environment, there is a normal progression from primary sensation to verbal language. Impediments to this process can result in the relatively impoverished capacities for self- and other reflection that have been linked to somatization and narcissistic difficulties (Neal et al., 2023).

Researchers have found that in families with multiple losses that have not been sufficiently grieved, the parents' defenses make them less available to their children for these types of attentive and attuned interactions. Cultural marginalization compounds these difficulties, adding layers of shame and internalized self-deprecation to the inhibitions against knowing self (e.g., Charles, 2014; Davids, 2011). Even with otherwise "good-enough" parents, the intergenerational transmission of trauma can leave the parent emotionally unavailable at times, leading to feelings that are untranslated and seemingly untranslatable.

In such cases, hypervigilance for the parent's well-being can short-circuit the child's developing self-understanding, resulting in relatively rigid and brittle defenses that are not well grounded in embodied experience. If not addressed, these types of developmental failures result in what we term schizoid, borderline, or narcissistic adaptations in adulthood. The narcissistic position is one of potential that cannot be realized because the bridge between self and other that would have enabled socioemotional development was insufficient. This deficit leaves the person pretending rather than being, with feelings that become problems instead of useful signals guiding adaptive action (see Chapter 10 for an explication of narcissistic defenses).

When feelings cannot be put into words, they remain as challenges to be managed or avoided. At the extreme, the strain of feelings that cannot be recognized and worked through leave them lodged in the body as symptoms that point to a problem but seem to point in the wrong direction. As we learn more about the complex intertwining of mind, emotion, and body, we are better able to decode these misplaced distress calls, to learn, as Ferrari (2004) suggested, to read the language registers that provide information regarding where the person is caught in relation to self and experience, whether that communication comes in the form of enactment, psychotic speech, or somatic complaint.

This perspective invites us to focus on the other person's body, including signs of affect, such as facial movements or behavioral gestures, to help the person recognize and take seriously embodied meanings. In trying to notice the language they are already using, we take a stand for the value and validity of their own experience, inviting them to take internal signals more seriously rather than merely as signs of trouble. In this way, we hope to help them attend more respectfully and speak more directly about their experience. Helpful in this project is our stance of validation of the essential worth of the person before us, marked by our interest and our respect. The truth of actual care speaks despite whatever noise impedes the message.

Paying attention to our own sensations affords us a reciprocal experience that might inform ideas as to what is happening inside them so that we might, in Bion's (1990) terms, introduce the person to themselves. Ferrari (2004) suggested offering *analytic propositions* rather than interpretations, recognizing the person as the source of truth rather than overriding their embodied knowings with our own ideas. That stance aligns with Winnicott's (1971) caution not to steal the person's accomplishment through our own imposition of meaning, and Lacan's (1964/1977e) warnings not to impose our own desire. Following Aulagnier (2001) and also Bion (1967b), I try to reconstruct in my own mind the conditions under which the current symptoms might make sense in relation to previous experience. In other words, I try to construct a story from the bits of what is known so that I can offer the construction to the person as scaffolding for their own evolving constructions.

CASE ILLUSTRATION: ROY

To help us think about how somatic complaints might be worked with in the consulting room, I offer two illustrations. The first example is a man in his late thirties who came to an impasse in his career, no longer able to perform the creative work that had been his greatest source of pleasure and satisfaction. Born into a household in which failures in their families of origin had left the parents impeded in their own emotional development, Roy was caught between his father's rageful outbursts and his mother's attempts to avoid or ameliorate them. In identification with the father, Roy was frightened of his own rageful aggression, and, in identification with the vulnerable mother, he was lost in a symbiotic enmeshment. Always highly sensitive, even in adulthood, Roy was hyperreactive to lights, sounds, and other sensations, in this way marking the too-much of the noise that made it difficult to make sense of the signals. His mother's failure to limit the father's affective storms left Roy dependent on her for care and attentive to her vulnerabilities. Not sufficiently developed himself to differentiate his own complicated feelings from his mother's vulnerabilities or his father's rages, he learned to withdraw and attend to other's needs as a way of managing his own shaky equilibrium and reassuring himself about his own goodness.

Bright and talented, Roy developed his creative capacities as a way of engaging with the social surround. He remained limited, however, in his affect tolerance, which resulted in increasing depressive withdrawals and somatization, exacerbated by his limited knowledge of the complexities of interpersonal engagements.

Roy's symptoms included muteness and somatic distress that he sensed was meaningful; at times he narrated the distress as he experienced it. He would describe "a tightness in my abdomen" or pause to notice "my throat just clenched." In this presentation, we see an attempt to bridge the gap in his development where meaning should have been made of his experience by an attuned other who was focused on him as the primary object of attention. Reciprocally, my curiosity about his experience of the physical symptom and how it related to what was happening in the moment became an important part of our work together, putting names to feelings and linking the feelings with experience-near meanings. Being able to be interested in the experiences as they occurred helped him reflect on them in the moment, attenuating the intensity that left him unable to speak or think, as had happened in his previous treatment. Recognizing the communicative efforts behind symptoms helps to soften them.

I began working with Roy after his psychoanalytic therapy for 3 years, 4 times a week, had broken down and he had become increasingly mute and unable to speak. The increasing frustration of his therapist only deepened the rift, but losing his male therapist was brutal because it mirrored his lost relationship with his father and increased his hopelessness at ever bridging that gap. He found in me, once again, an attuned mother, but, as with his own mother, he feared a symbiotic enmeshment in which he would become lost in my needs and vulnerabilities. Failing to find the deeply needed connection with a man left him dangerously and regressively adrift once again.

When we began working together, containment seemed to be the first challenge. I found him controlling. As I tried to make sense of what he was working at, I both leaned in with my attention and sat back from encroaching, trying to tolerate his silences while also inviting him to speak. I tried not to impose demands on him while also showing my interest in getting to know him and what he was hoping to accomplish with me. Initially, there were many silences as we tried to build a containing space in which Roy could speak from his own volition, where meanings were not predetermined, but rather could be considered.

Early sallies involved Roy's reporting moments of feeling misdefined and misunderstood or speaking about himself in a way that felt both alien and alienated. His attempts to "catch me up" left me feeling confused and insufficient as though he was trying to deposit meanings in me that I could not decode. I felt as though I had little room to think and as though communication might be dangerous, likely a concordant identification (Racker, 2007).

I tried to be respectful of his need for space but also to inquire into what seemed to be packaged meanings that he was carrying as unmetabolized wounds. One example was his attribution of aggression to himself, when his own experience was of desperately trying to defend himself. This seems to be the type of misrecognition Lacan (1964/1977e) warned of: inviting false reassurance rather than reflection. I found I needed to bump into the places where the sense of his speech eluded me so that we could consider what sense he was making of this experience. Our explorations brought up fears of identifying with his father and ways in which he felt held captive by each parent's needs and demands, making withdrawal the least offensive option. Hearing his previous therapist couch Roy's withdrawal as an aggressive attack had left Roy feeling paralyzed, caught in a terrible symmetrization of self with rageful father. His inability to assert his own embodied meanings left his aggression seeping everywhere. My recognition that he had been trying to spare his therapist helped Roy to think further about the impasse rather than merely feeling pinned by it.

Another important moment occurred when I went substantially over time—because my watch was not working—and this really threw him. It brought up terrors of maternal engulfment and the danger of having his desires satisfied, a recurrent preoccupation. We discussed the importance of being able to want something that he cannot have without the person's either succumbing, like his mother, or becoming angry, like his father. Finding a space where his desire can be recognized as his own, whether or not it can be filled, was crucial to his ability to make meaning from his internal experience. His distress also reaffirmed for me the containing function of reliable boundaries and limits.

Imagining directly satisfying his desires remained fraught. But as Roy became more reflective about the places where he gets caught, there was less silence and less somatization. He became less remote, more affectively engaged, and better able to make use of his own reflections. Instances of intense somatic experience provided opportunities for reflection rather than shutting it down, enabling us to integrate these moments into his increasingly complex and textured life story, a narrative that could move forward in his imagination and guide him in his interactions with others.

Looking back, I could see the impasse in Roy's previous therapy as related to his need for attention that was finely attuned to his needs of the moment. Important in moving us forward was a moment that was pivotal for him in our work but that I hardly registered at the time. Highly sensitive to noises and light, Roy was startled in a moment early on when my voice rose. I accommodated to his reaction, without really noticing, by reducing the volume of my voice and softening my tone. He referred to this moment repeatedly; it marked for him my willingness to accommodate to his needs and feelings rather than insisting on my own.

Whereas he and his previous therapist had found themselves in tangles over what had been defined as Roy's aggressive need for control, I assumed that we were working together to create an environment that felt sufficiently safe that he could do the work that was needing to be done. Not feeling in control invites indirect or strident efforts as the person works toward greater ease in asserting their own needs and feelings. Calling these efforts "manipulative" mislocates the trouble. In our work together, I found that Roy did not want me to indulge him, but rather wanted to be able to have his own desire, which required knowing that whatever limits and boundaries were in place, they would be held to. The ongoing negotiation of agreement between us regarding who is responsible for what enabled us to locate ourselves in relation to one another without becoming lost, as had played out in his symbiotic relationship with his mother and in his misattuned relationship with his previous therapist. There could be two minds to engage in the work at hand, each in touch with the signals that emerged in our bodies and with one another.

CASE ILLUSTRATION: TINA

In contrast to Roy, another young adult who was also unformed, unable to make use of her internal signals as signs to guide her, did not fare so well. Similarly distant from an angry father and symbiotically entwined with an attentive but dependent mother, Tina, a young woman in her twenties (introduced in Chapter 6), had become waylaid early on by learning difficulties that were not sufficiently differentiated to have enabled her to master the challenges she faced. Rather, her mother, in trying to "help" Tina, had so sheltered her from distress that she had, in effect, crippled her. Somatic complaints became a way to hold the world at bay.

When I first met her, Tina was committed to substance use as a way of managing her distress and had also become an accomplished liar. At the time, I told her that there could be no treatment without truth. She was eventually asked to leave the hospital because of her lying and substance use, and she went to a drug treatment center, determined to learn her lesson and return to work with me. That lesson, however, seemed to resist repeated trials of substance abuse treatment, and, some years later, Tina once again sought treatment with me.

Tina had spent the intervening years looking for the medical issue that might be the source of her distress. Forced to recognize that the underlying problems were not physical, she returned to the Austen Riggs Center. At admission, she maintained that she had abstained from all substances for the required 30 days. Although she had managed to abstain from alcohol use, she remained committed to cannabis as the one "medicine" that could relieve her distress. When confronted, she described cannabis as the one source of containment she could truly count on and was loathe to give it up.

I experienced Tina as desperate and unreachable, blaming anyone and everyone for her troubles. Her speech was a litany of complaints and reproach that could change direction in midstream at any sign of danger. No real contact seemed possible. This barrage seemed to serve as a relatively effective way of keeping hidden, and tensions began to emerge over different "truths" that could not be reconciled. Periodic moments of being caught in a lie resulted in trips to the local emergency room as her tendency to somatize under strain came to the fore. Unlike her relationship with her parents, however, her heightened distress did not result in our forgetting the problems at hand. Tina did not seem to be able to learn from her mistakes and eventually was discharged with encouragement to try to get hold of her substance use.

This end to her treatment was not surprising in relation to data from our metacognition project, which showed that commitment to substance abuse overrides whatever learning seems to be taking place in insight-oriented psychotherapy. Our investigations into the development of reflective function revealed that people who are narcissistically organized have great difficulty gaining insight into their minds and feelings and that those who remain committed to substance use may appear to achieve insight, but it has no depth and does not sustain (Neal et al., 2023). My work with Roy, however, showed that there are likely different underlying reasons for these difficulties recognizing and representing emotional states that have important treatment ramifications (Lane et al., 2020). For those who are interested in learning more about themselves and others at a deeply embodied level, the provision of an attuned relational space affords experiences that invite greater knowledge of self and other and also allow greater interpersonal trust to be built.

Those who somatize tend to be caught developmentally in ways that leave other people as either resources to be relied on (but not learned from) or problems to be solved, difficulties to be managed. Pain that cannot be reflected on emerges in somatic symptoms that invite attention and care—or, more perversely, reject attention and care—without having to navigate the complexities of the relational field. The suffering itself becomes the mark of one's humanity in a world in which one has become lost (Aulagnier, 2015). In working with such entrenched difficulties, suggested Aulagnier, we must be able to recognize the importance of "the ensemble of signs and bodily inscriptions which can lend themselves to this function of temporal and relational reference points" (Aulagnier, 2001, p. 96), signs that are inevitably particular to the person in relation to their life story and embodied experience. Such a stance is fundamental to psychoanalysis, whatever theories we follow, from Freud, to Klein, to Winnicott or Lacan.

From the perspective I have been describing in which the body is at the core of human *being* (Ferrari, 2004), the analyst must be open to messages that occur at the level of the body in both themselves and their analysands, tracking the feelings that arise in the moment-by-moment interactions in the sessions (Lombardi, 2018). For those who do not have an integrated experience of body and mind, "orientation toward attention on the body allows an initial contact with reality" (Lombardi, 2018, p. 632). Our insistent intention on the body can invite further distress and resistance, but, as Lombardi (2018) noted, "sensations arising in the body can powerfully illuminate emotions and thought" (p. 633), even when the experience remains, for the moment, at the sensory level.

For those functioning at this level, the lack of grounding in one's own body and being results in a precariousness of mind and meaning. The person becomes easily overwhelmed by sensations that take the form of Bion's (1962) beta-elements, those undigested bits of experience that can feel persecutory because they cannot be metabolized and integrated. Required, then, is a mindful other who can begin to digest the experience. Sitting in a place of empathic resonance helps us integrate the bits into meaningful chunks toward the elucidation of a coherent narrative within which the person can find themselves as a *being* rather than merely a body. This work requires our ability to tolerate, in Leikert's (2021) terms, both "disturbed and toxic emotional contact on one side or a severe *lack* of emotional contact on the other" (p. 683).

For the clinician, it is important to recognize when the person is so saturated by experience that there is no room for reflective thought. Otherwise, the attempt to impose order on the thinking becomes one more assault that further impedes the development of a containing space for reflection. Instead, the focus needs to be on reconstituting a relationship between the analyst and analysand that meets the person in the place where they are. With those who somatize, this often requires a preliminary focus on the person's relationship with their own body and the sensations and feelings that arise as symptoms awaiting recognition, reflection, and consideration. With Tina, much of our work consisted of my attempts to break through the litany of complaints toward an actual encounter, to invite her to meet me—and herself—in any moment of true speech. With others who are similarly ungrounded, who are looking for a way to be with people without being so ashamed that they feel immobilized, I invite them to think about their feelings in the moment and imagine something they might say that is authentic to that feeling. Speaking true can invite others to engage at that level as well, and when the effort fails, we learn something about the other person's limits. In this way, I try to introduce at least the idea of reflective space.

In contrast, we can see in Tina's attempts to symbiotically join with me her determination to obliterate the possibility of reflection. This is the type of joining Marty (1958) referred to in which the otherness of a separate person is experienced as annihilating. For Marty (1968), psychosomatic illness can mark a profound disorganization that leaves the person lost within themselves. My experience of Tina was that facing her utter emptiness was so terrifying and humiliating that she would do anything to avoid it, which left her incapable of any real relationship with her own mind or body, much less with others.

We find Tina at a terrible extreme but, according to McDougall (1989), "we all tend to somatize when inner or outer circumstances overwhelm our habitual psychological ways of coping" (p. 3). This fact can help alert us to moments of too-much when they occur, particularly in work with those who cannot make meaning from their sensory experience. Lombardi (2009) suggested that the "lack of integration of symbolic experience with symbolic elaboration" that we encounter in such individuals "puts us in need of *theoretical and operational tools with which to help them feel and discriminate within their own sensations*, as an indispensable precondition to personal growth and to the capacity to form relationships" (p. 125).

Tina was so devoted to "medicating" away uncomfortable feelings with cannabis that she had little contact with her body aside from moving away from distress wherever she encountered it. She had also become adept at using words to stop speech that distressed her. Unlinking from thoughts and feelings seemed to be her primary mode of defense, leaving all the undigested bits alienated such that she felt persecuted by them and longed only for relief. In our work together, she used words as a wall through which to lodge her grievances and blame others for all of her problems, making it virtually impossible to actually engage with one another in any meaningful way.

I hope that you can see in these cases how critical it is whether the person wants to make sense of their experience or whether they do not. Tina was effectively able to preclude the development of her reflective capacities through her avoidant defenses, whereas Roy and Emily were accessible to attempts to meet them in the places where they were. Tracking Roy carefully, sharing my thoughts and feelings, and listening attentively to his own, helped him feel recognized, affording a sufficient sense of safety in our relationship to develop a meaningful relationship with his own embodied self. From that more secure foundation, his growing reflective capacities helped him build more satisfying relationships with people, with his career and, most importantly, with himself. In my work with Emily, inviting her to be more respectful of her own language registers, as they are enacted through her body, has been useful in helping her build a containing space for herself in the treatment, from which place she has been better able to build satisfying connections with others in the larger world as well.

CONCLUSION

Listening to the language of the body is pivotal in our work with those who have lost touch with their own embodied experience. At times, our minds cannot register meanings, but rather we need to orient toward our bodily perceptions and trust in the value of this level of processing (Leikert, 2021) as we receive messages that mark the unsymbolized experience through the transference/countertransference matrix (Hartung & Steinbrecher, 2018). As the work proceeds, focusing on the mind–body link helps us to recognize inhibited or incoherent material that may only be evident in recurrent somatic symptoms so that the story being told through the symptoms can begin to unfold (Lombardi, 2017). As we work to integrate these embodied experiences into the story that has not yet been told in words, we gradually increase the person's capacities for symbolization (Hartung & Steinbrecher, 2018).

In recognizing the hazard—and the promise—of our own desire, we are in a better position to meet the person who is working in relation to truths told by the body and not yet symbolized by the mind. In that way, the analyst's willingness to engage deeply with their own primary and secondary processes—and to allow them to communicate with one another—provides the space in which the reflective capacities of the other person can also evolve. In the next chapter, I look at eating disorders as a particular case of ways in which distress may be lodged in, and symptoms expressed though, the body.

8 EATING DISORDERS

In this chapter, I focus on eating disorders, which arise in the context of early difficulties around feeding and being fed with parents who are not sufficiently able to meet the child where they are. Eating disorders may be seen as part of the larger group of addictive problems that persist because the behavior eases the distress without resolving the underlying problem.

We ground our thinking in the psychoanalytic perspective that presumes that symptoms are communications not yet elaborated into words, in contrast to the medicalized perspective that views symptoms as problems to be managed or eradicated. The focus on wellness and symptom reduction has not been particularly helpful with addictive behaviors, and yet, psychoanalytic clinicians are left working against the tide, trying to find the sense in maladaptive behaviors in ways that illuminate the developmental and relational difficulties needing attention. Although a focus on the eating disorder itself can be useful in moderating symptoms, failing to address the underlying issues tends to make these efforts short lived. Notably, there is

---

Portions of this chapter have been adapted from "Meaning, Metaphor, and Metabolization: The Case of Eating Disorders," by M. Charles, 2021, *American Journal of Psychoanalysis*, *81*, pp. 444–466 (https://doi.org/10.1057/s11231-021-09324-9). Copyright 2021 by Springer Nature. Adapted with permission.

https://doi.org/10.1037/0000455-009
Echoes of Trauma: Meaning and Identity in Psychoanalysis, by M. Charles

evidence that psychoanalytic therapy is more effective than cognitive behavior therapy in enhancing mentalization in individuals with eating disorders (Katznelson et al., 2020).

From a psychoanalytic perspective, eating disorders mark developmental difficulties that impede the ability to take in nourishment and to symbolize embodied experience. Mentalization deficits are found in persons with anorexia and with bulimia, but anorexic individuals show greater deficits (Simonsen et al., 2020). Whereas both groups show decrements in emotional awareness and emotion regulation, Gilboa-Schechtman and colleagues (2006) found somewhat different patterns of deficits, with bulimic persons lower in impulse control and anorexic persons lower in emotional awareness. At the core, however, we find difficulties recognizing feelings (interoception; Jenkinson et al., 2018) and tolerating uncomfortable feeling states (M. S. Davis & Marsh, 1986). Across categories, individuals with eating disorders tend to make use of maladaptive rather than adaptive strategies in their attempts to regulate their emotions (Prefit et al., 2019).

The greatest deficits in reflective function are linked to anorexia (Tasca & Balfour, 2014), with particular impairments in the areas of cognitive appraisal and mental flexibility, consistent with the tendency toward rigid control in that population (Puttevils et al., 2021). Both groups show difficulties identifying feelings: Emotion recognition is more problematic for anorexic subjects, and affect regulation is more problematic for individuals with bulimia (Gilboa-Schechtman et al., 2006). These findings are consistent with research showing greater identity disturbance in people with anorexia and greater impulsivity in people with bulimia (A. E. Miller et al., 2021).

The intellectualizing defenses found in anorexic individuals are linked with a hypervigilant orientation that underlies their greater capacity to mentalize about others than self (Adenzato et al., 2012). Consistent with this external, intellectualizing stance, they perform well on tasks that evaluate the capacity to represent others' cognitions and beliefs (theory of mind) but poorly on those that require evaluation of emotional functioning. This type of intellectualized, third-person conjecture (Gallese, 2014) is encountered again in Chapter 9 as we consider obsessive defenses. The difficulty anorexic individuals have in identifying feelings has been linked with deficits in interoceptive awareness more generally, suggesting a dissociation from feelings as a way of managing distress (Oldershaw et al., 2019) that results in some of the difficulties we explored in the previous chapter. Although cognitive behavioral strategies may not impact the interoceptive awareness, the ability to identify and more adaptively regulate emotions has been shown to improve with treatment (Amianto et al., 2016).

THE RELATIONAL CONTEXT

The deficits found in eating disorders can be traced to the early relationships we have been discussing that inhibit the development of self-regulatory functions and the progressive differentiation of self from other through which identity is formed. The improvement found in reflective capacities in the context of psychoanalytic therapy may result from the extensive interpersonal engagement that helps to promote affect regulation, differentiation, symbolization, and interpersonal awareness.

With eating disorders, we often find parents not yet sufficiently developed themselves to provide the type of secure containment that recognizes the needs of the child in real time (Charles, 2006, 2021b), leaving maternal—and paternal—efforts intrusive, lacking, or both. The lack of the parental mindfulness through which the child's attempts at making meaning might be anchored leaves the child at risk of profound disorganization. Without intervention, these deviant family patterns and deficits tend to be passed along from generation to generation (Strober & Humphrey, 1987).

In the histories of those who develop eating disorders, we find difficulties developing a sturdy identity in relation to parents who have not yet consolidated their own and who rely on surface presentations to buffer deficits in their metacognitive capacities. In cultures with a heavy reliance on thinness and surface presentations as markers of value in women, eating disorders afford a useful sleight of hand, a means for hiding internal deficits and avoiding distressing emotions. Eating disorders are also prevalent in men at rates that are increasing (Gorrell & Murray, 2019). As with all addictions, the repetitive turn toward destructive behaviors masks the underlying difficulties that are being insufficiently managed. Momentary relief from distress without resolution of the underlying problem itself becomes addictive.

The intense focus on control and restraint found in anorexia has been linked to parental misattunement to the child's emotional needs (Strober et al., 1990). But this defensive strategy leaves the person even further out of touch with the relational context so crucial to building interpersonal meanings. Anorexia is linked to deficits in symbolization such that meanings cannot be reflected on, but rather are concretized and enacted through the body (Skårderud, 2007), which is in line with Kleinian descriptions of the symbolic equations that denude meanings of their possibilities (Segal, 1957). Not eating solves the problem of desire in the moment, but at the price of exacerbating the hunger and the longing, tightening the addictive cycle. The focus on overriding internal signals obstructs the development of reflective capacities and interpersonal relationships, which leads to the deficits we find in the ability to accurately read or anticipate others' emotional states, leaving needs and feelings enigmatic (Brockmeyer et al., 2016).

Bulimia, in contrast, is linked to deficits in self-regulatory capacities that are not tied to such severe deficits in mentalization (Pedersen et al., 2015). There are, of course, overlaps between these positions: My clinical experience suggests that, to some extent, people with bulimia are often "failed anorexic individuals" who have achieved higher levels of self-development or are less profoundly alienated from their bodies. Case illustrations later in the chapter explore these dynamics and demonstrate how theory might more usefully inform our technique. In this chapter, we also consider how metaphors can be a valuable tool for bridging gaps between mind and body and between one being and another in our work with those for whom embodied experience remains largely unsymbolized and unintegrated. The desire and distress that cannot be recognized by the mind remains spoken through the body, awaiting translation and transformation.

MEANING AND SELF-EXPERIENCE IN EATING DISORDERS

Psychoanalysis offers rich metaphors that can help bridge gaps between embodied experience and verbal language. When experience has become concretized, however, the metaphors offered by the clinician can be useless or even feel persecutory, taunting the person with their limits rather than extending them. Our failed attempts to steer the conversation toward exploration are important markers of the need to be respectful of the resistance and turn our attention to the point of difficulty rather than try to override it. Such a stance enables us to be open to the counternarratives that evolve and meet the person where they are, so we might pick up and work with the meanings offered back to us.

As we have seen, deficits linked to early relational failures mark problems in symbolization. Meanings become concretized, and the symptom imposes itself as the problem, a salient feature of eating disorders. Offering metaphorical language rather than concrete solutions or symptom management invites entry into the realm of primary process, the condensed, image-driven meanings that speak the language of feelings and possibilities. Although this language may not be easily accessible (or even wanted!), the gentle but consistent offering keeps open a space in which reflection can develop.

Development is key. Reflective deficits result in insufficient differentiation between self and other, leaving parents unable to adequately nurture their children. The neglected child, then, is in the position of either soothing the parent by accepting the role of self-object or frustrating them, inviting further neglect and rejection. In families with eating disorders, we find mothers either filling themselves through the child—conceptualized by Vlahaki (2012) as a symbiotic enmeshment in which survival is at stake—or teaching them to survive in a world with insufficient supplies—a pathological form of caring for another who must be like oneself.

Whereas the bulimic individual tries to metabolize what has not been metabolized by the mother, the anorexic individual closes off the possibility of being eaten from the outside. As Fairbairn (1952) recognized early on, in the face of inadequate parenting, the child's survival depends on feeding the parent. For people with anorexia, such feeding is accomplished by allowing the mother to feed in effigy while the child remains sequestered. This may be seen as an obsessive defense in which the person sacrifices themselves in their effort to avoid loss, whereas bulimia is linked to hysterical defenses in which there is the illusion of having everything (Lacan, 1960/1977f).

The anorexic person's fear of taking anything in has been termed by Williams (1997) a *no-entry system of defenses* against unmetabolized parental projections that threaten to intrude and overwhelm the developing child. In contrast, those who are more psychically open to parental projections tend toward a disorganized attachment pattern and are more likely to develop bulimia. Taking in but also ejecting marks ambivalent efforts toward object relating and provides a vehicle for self-soothing.

Each trajectory marks parental failures often linked to unresolved mourning and the intergenerational transmission of trauma prevalent in families in which eating disorders emerge. The preoccupied parent cannot reliably offer the empathic attention and marked mirroring essential to healthy self-regard (Mayes et al., 2007) and identity development (Fivush et al., 2011). Complicating the dilemma, eating disorders thrive in secrecy, leaving the developing life story foreclosed by fantasy as though life challenges could be worked through in an internal negotiation between hunger, tension, and relief. That impossible challenge is at the core of the addictive cycle, exacerbated by the shame attendant to the secrecy.

Eating disorders often manifest at the beginnings of puberty, when developmental demands impose themselves through bodily changes that are inherently destabilizing. With no secure internal foundation and a lack of containment in external relationships, people with eating disorders find that these changes can provoke panic and fears of annihilation (Ferrari, 2004). The intense demands of the body at this time have been linked to the onset or exacerbation of symptoms of eating disorders, agoraphobic anxieties that lead to anorexia, and claustrophobic anxieties that lead to bulimia (Romano, 2013). Without effective intervention, the repetitive cycling of the symptoms further entrenches the dangerous division between body and mind. Ineffective intervention that does not address the underlying sources can drive the disturbance further underground, entrenching the alienation and, with it, the terrible isolation.

The lack of integration central to eating disorders invites a relentless focus on the body in a way that precludes reflection, thereby furthering the chasm of developmental tasks that cannot be met. If we think of development in terms of recurrent choice points between growth and evasion, then we can see how profoundly early failures in containment leave the adolescent feeling at risk of what Bion (1965, 1970) termed *catastrophic change*. This failure can manifest in either of the two main stances we find in eating disorders: the disavowing and the evacuative (Freedman & Lavender, 2002). In both cases, bodily experience cannot be formulated and reflected on. The challenge, clinically, is to help the person become more grounded in what Winnicott (1971) called *true self* versus *false self* experience. The analytic process affords opportunities to develop one's own internal capacities for the self-regulation and self-knowledge essential to facing challenges that may otherwise feel catastrophic, including relating to others as separate, autonomous beings.

From this perspective, we can think of Bion's (1967a) admonition to the clinician to avoid memory or desire as a warning against taking the position of the intrusive parent, a reminder not to feed our own ego at the other's expense, even by being clever or "helpful." This abstention helps us be present with those seeking assistance as they confront their own anxieties, to take the transference (Mitrani, 2001) and tolerate moments of great intensity, when, as we go deeper, it is difficult to find anchors through which to make meaning.

In contrast to the no-entry defenses of anorexia, the challenge in bulimia is to deal with foreign bodies that have been projected inside and become a tie to the mother that one is reluctant to give up, a secret solace for what is missing. Opposing this dangerous seclusion, Reiser (1990) encouraged a stance of actively investigating the bulimic episode so as to discern clues to the meanings being managed and portrayed. Early feeding cycles have their own prosody that form a basic template underlying the aesthetic, embodied patterns that evolve (Charles, 2002b, 2021a). For those grappling with early or unmetabolized experience, the countertransference becomes an essential tool for meaning-making—as we increasingly inhabit their universe through our interactions—offering a reflective other with whom to more actively symbolize embodied meanings.

These emergent patterns afford an evolving map of an internal landscape (Charles, 2010) that reflects the scenes in which embodied meanings are stored (Lorenzer, 2016). Symptoms can only make sense in relation to the story being told through them, including the bulimic cycle itself (Schwartz, 1986). That cycle is illuminated by Lewin's (1951) depiction of an *oral triad* that includes sleep along with wishes and fears relating to eating and being eaten. Purging affords tension reduction, an altered state of consciousness that perpetuates the bulimic cycle by attenuating the distress without resolving the underlying issues.

THEORETICAL METAPHORS USEFUL IN WORKING WITH EATING DISORDERS

That relief also serves to evacuate the imminence of discomforting potential meanings as they arise. This reactivity to potential meanings is important to track when working with those with eating disorders for whom disavowal and evacuation can be powerful strategies for desymbolization (Freedman & Lavender, 2002). These types of regressive oppositions to meaning-making are formulated in the psychoanalytic literature in terms of Klein's (1946) early ideas on projective identification (see also Charles, 2018), Bion's (1959) attacks on linking, Lacan's (1953/1977b) gaps and empty speech, and Green's (1998) work on the negative. Much as projective identification arises as a means for communicating distress, desymbolization, too, can serve progressive functions, allowing unsymbolized meanings to present themselves in concrete form. The underlying pattern that emerges can be seen as the ground through which the particular Imaginary of that person takes root and takes form—as the unconscious offers us symptoms when symbols cannot yet be discerned.

I use Lacan's (1964/1977e) term, the *Imaginary*, advisedly, because it holds the complexity of the *particularity* of each individual's meaning structures drawn from personal experience. Psychoanalysis presumes that, within the world of consensual realities governed by the Symbolic (the realm of consensual language), each person's unique lens colors and shapes the meanings encountered. For Lacan, coming to grips with the meanings that symptoms mark enables us to live more fully as ourselves rather than to recursively hide. Anorexia and bulimia embody meanings that cannot be further symbolized so that the concretized displays show us "qualitative configurations . . . [that] may well be the signposts of distinct organizing fantasies, which shape and even impel the trajectory of the clinical course" (Freedman & Lavender, 2002, p. 167).

Recognition of the defensive style through which desymbolization is occurring helps us inhibit our own desire to push past the person's defenses and focus on working through the impasse. This desire to push past discomfort meets the anorexic individual's desire to not take in anything offered, a position Bion (1967b) conceptualized as an evacuative model of defensive foreclosure. The refusal of food meets a refusal to make meaning, where the nonmentalizing mode of *psychic equivalence* (Klein, 1946) is "pervasive, the integration of affect and representation is absolute, and the communicative stance is one that signals the absolute irrelevance of the other" (Freedman & Lavender, 2002, p. 184). This defense suggests that the person with anorexia functions at the narcissistic level of personality organization in which other people are problems rather than persons, whereas the person with bulimia often functions at the borderline level at which instability in relationships is the hallmark.

Bulimia can be linked to Green's (1998) model of disavowal through the *work of the negative*: In disavowing any particular desire, the bulimic individual is left desiring everything, making desire itself both insatiable and repugnant. The analyst's ability to enter into these states through the transference/countertransference matrix and to mentalize the experience provides the possibility of a transitional and transformational space, grounded in what is presented—in eating disorders—as the gutted terrain of the other's Imaginary. Recognizing the shared desire to move away from the utterness of despair helps the clinician meet the person *where* they are as a necessary condition of finding our way through. We see this principle in the child development literature: the importance of meeting the child's distress before trying to attenuate it, recognizing that whatever is avoided will derail any developmental efforts.

In this difficult terrain, metaphors help bridge the abstract and the concrete by mapping content onto form (Lakoff & Johnson, 1980). Metaphors provide a bridge from the patterned feelings of the primal and primary process to the secondary elaboration of more abstract thoughts. This is the terrain of psychoanalysis: sitting at the juncture between thought and feeling without splitting off either. As we have seen, in eating disorders, we find various means of partitioning off meaning from metaphoric possibilities. The challenge, then, is to provide a bridge back toward meaningfulness by embedding the nonverbal communications in the metaphors evolving in the treatment.

When the interpersonal world feels dangerous, meanings close down and metaphor becomes metonymy, something fixed that does not invite reflection (see Modell, 2005, 2009). Opposing this rigid constriction, the analyst affords a vicarious experience of meaning-making through their own mentalization (see Gallese, 2009). Embedding these experiences in the other person's metaphors invites an integrated discourse between two minds and two bodies in which meanings might be revitalized, transformed from concrete austerity into more fertile ground for reverie and for play.

Bion's (1959) attacks on linking and Lacan's (1953/1977b) empty speech are useful metaphors in our work with those who have suffered from intrusion or neglect (Charles, 2012). To investigate the challenge of keeping open the conceptual space by making use of metaphor in ways that keep possibilities open by including those offered by the other, let us look at the cases of Alice and of Kim (discussed previously in Charles, 2012).

CASE ILLUSTRATIONS

When parents fail to hold essential boundaries between self and other, it is difficult for the child to orient toward embodied needs, thereby also foreclosing the narrativization through which identity is built. The person with an eating disorder is both telling and untelling their story, unable to link ideas with feelings and with one another or to take seriously the need to confront and come to grips with their life as it has been. The analytic work, then, takes up the challenge of making meaning from the embodied experience that has not yet been symbolized.

In a universe ungrounded in embodied experience, interpersonal contact becomes dangerous rather than providing opportunities for learning, and symptoms mark points of difficulty that may have no words for expression. Meaning-making can seem catastrophic, and the shift past one's own legitimate need can become a passage into action that retraumatizes rather than an enactment through which meaning might be made (Lacan, 1962–1963/2014).

I use the case of Alice and the case of Kim, each in their early twenties, to illustrate these dynamics and point to differences that arise in working with those with anorectic versus bulimic symptoms. Survival needs pushed each of these young women toward fragmentation; they were unable to know or adaptively perceive information vital to making sense of danger as it arose. Each repeatedly came up against the limits of what she could usefully know in ways that made dying seem the only possible recourse. Part of the work, then, entailed my ability to perceive what each could not know but needed to know and to hold this information in mind as I tried to help them discover ways to encounter these impossible meanings without disappearing or falling into bits.

Part of the challenge for the psychoanalytic clinician is to hear the person's story clearly enough that we can note the disjunctions, gaps, and points of impasse as they occur. Recognizing the patterns of a person's stories is the training we need to help them see what they are telling us without quite noticing. If we can recognize the story as story, we can think about the relations between elements and notice what is too present and where the gaps are, and perhaps offer these ideas with sufficient displacement to make them more accessible, respectful of the powerful relationship between shame and secrecy. Creating transitional space can be pivotal in working with persons with eating disorders to try to attenuate the terrible shame at the core of the dilemma.

With eating disorders, the absent vitality is key. Whereas the person with anorexia may be disorganized by the possibility of liveliness, the person with bulimia may actively kill off that possibility. The story is an assertion and a hypothesis as to how the world works, telling us what is known and what is unknown, whatever is missing that might be needed to build a life. Thus, in the transference, we look for the details in which life might be grounded. With those whose feelings are largely unknown to themselves, we must find the story through the feelings, as inchoate as they may seem.

When the confrontation with lack and limit occurs too early, attempts at survival are brittle and wear thin, and accomplishments become empty and meaningless. For Alice and for Kim, attempts to transcend the pain did not afford sufficient opportunity to confront or resolve the underlying problems. Starving themselves provided physiological relief from their distress, but the very austerity that helped them survive pulled them relentlessly toward death. As we have seen, partial relief becomes addictive and is difficult to give up.

Although many of their symptoms were similar, the underlying issues and defensive structures were not. Alice had learned to defend herself from intrusive, disorganized parents whose unmetabolized projections threatened to inhabit her. Her desperate attempts to avoid being inhabited by her mother left her precariously tethered to life. Kim, in contrast, was trying to survive while being inhabited by her mother's projections. She moved relentlessly toward death in empathic resonance to her lovely, but suicidal, mother without sufficient paternal presence to impose a limit.

With each of these young women, the challenge in the treatment was to hold open a space in which they might find a way to claim a life without making demands that left no room for them to find their own desire. Care easily became intrusion, and space neglect, as I struggled to avoid becoming entangled in a perverse engagement on one side or the other of their ambivalent desire to live and to die. Although each disappeared as a subject, the mode of disappearance was not the same, requiring attentiveness and attunement in our engagements.

With Alice, there was a critical absence of the mother in the moment of flooding, so that the fundamental issue was to ward off meanings that might imperil self-regulation. As is often the case with people with anorexia, neither parent could face the idea that the child had needs that were not being filled, leaving Alice caught between pretending she had no needs and desperately needing someone to have in mind what she could and could not manage. Further, the lack in the parental couple left the father seeking sustenance from the daughter, which made becoming a woman dangerous.

In the transference, I was confronted with the challenges of how to know anything without imposing my awareness on Alice and how to build a structure in which meaning might be held without shaming or annihilating her. Even positive recognition threatened her with the specter of the engulfing mother. That dilemma left any moments of empathic engagement perilous as we teetered between desire, denial, guilt, shame, and self-retribution. In a world in which connection was dangerous and reality was unstable, needing nothing and remaining safely disembodied seemed to be the safest refuge. Conjecturing the critical absence of the mother in the moment of affective flooding, my task was to remain present and available without needing anything from Alice as we worked to tolerate the moments in which all hope and meaning collapse through the embodied memory of the passage into action—the point at which she disappears.

For Kim, the prohibition against knowing anything about her mother's absence left us trying to catch ghosts of meanings that were always at risk, not of ebbing away but of having already ebbed away as she was confronted with the ways her own life force seemed to threaten her mother's survival. For Kim, too, neither parent had been a reliable presence. Although the father could recognize the mother's failures, he was insufficiently available during moments of need. The unknowable trauma had been her mother's suicidal depression that left her utterly unavailable to the family. This terrible truth was exacerbated by Kim's recollection of the father blaming her for the mother's distress. Preserving the fantasy of the mother's availability left no room for Kim's own needs and feelings, leaving Kim in the space of fantasy. Unable to make use of her mind more actively, her fantasizing was a deadly indulgence that foreclosed living her life. This is the territory of the developmental challenge of Winnicott's (1971) use of the object in which sufficient transitional space is needed for the child to learn to inhabit a world where two separate and individual beings can survive an encounter.

Alice and Kim each described being lost in relation to a father who attacked her and a mother who could not save her. The intrusiveness of Alice's mother was so toxic that fending her off was paramount, but the father's desperate neediness and lack of boundaries was equally threatening. Kim's mother's intrusiveness and the father's absence were less apparent, pushing her into resonance with the loving but depressed mother who was unable to fight for her own life sufficiently for Kim to claim her own. For each young woman, there was no reflective space through which to find herself as a separate agent. Alice's efforts to construct a real other fragmented and came apart, whereas Kim was paralyzed by the loving but elusive representation of mother. Alice was left defending against a descent into the psychotic disintegration she associated with her mother, whereas Kim's unconscious identification was with the mother who chooses death.

In these stories, we see a passage into action that is difficult to forestall because of what remains unknown. Unlike the enactment that invites meaning-making, the passage into action forecloses it. For Kim, marking this passage would mean facing her mother's willingness to abandon her. Failing that, Kim is left with the surface appearance of her mother as present, lovely, and loving but needs to reckon with what was absent: her mother's will, her determination to hold on to her own life so that she could help her daughter build one. In the transference, the challenge is to look beyond the allure of the fantasied but deadly union with the mother and to face the underlying tragedy. In that effort, we can begin to discover the missing details in which Kim's life might be grounded. With Alice, in contrast, the challenge is to recognize the missing voice of the mother as a marker of maternal deficit. Facing the need underlying the deficit affords the possibility of finding some sustenance that does not fragment and come apart in the very act of seeking it.

MAKING USE OF METAPHOR

As we have seen with somatic disturbance more generally, part of the challenge in eating disorders is to recognize the internalized drama that leaves the person at an impasse, paralyzed by an inability to condemn or accept parts of the parent they find within themselves. Food becomes the currency through which the ambivalent desire to live or to die is played out, complicated by a libidinized relationship with their own pain. Positioned as the person who must give and never take, the anorexic individual moves relentlessly toward death by denying themselves sustenance. Alice spoke most evocatively—and desperately—through the "silent screams" she needed someone to hear and orient toward (Charles, 2006, p. 261). The bulimic individual, in contrast, takes in too much without being able to derive sustenance.

Kim's solution was to become captivated by the internal fictions that took the place of living. Symbiotically tied to her suicidal mother, she could only enjoy beauty in secret—in alignment with the mother's desire for death—but never in the service of building the life that would leave her mother behind.

So then, how do we work with such individuals? How do we offer opportunities they might be able to make use of? Psychoanalysis provides rich metaphors that can help us survive our encounters with the formless and deadly universes inhabited by such patients. It also helps us appreciate the importance of metaphor as a transitional space that can reduce the shame through the displacement.

When early relationships have been so dire and deadening, the linking of two thoughts or objects can feel treacherous, leading to what Bion (1959) termed attacks on linking. Having what is known in one moment and then utterly inconceivable in the next is unnerving for the clinician. In my work with Alice, I felt at times as though we were in the movie *Groundhog Day* (Ramis, 1993), in which the main character lives through each day only to find himself back at the beginning again. Most perplexing for me, it was after a particularly good session that I was most likely to find us back at square one the following day.

In retrospect, I think I insufficiently appreciated the danger she felt at the possibility of relying on someone. Anything good would be erased, leaving us to begin again, a process that seemed to be repeating Alice's experience of circling around a story that cannot be told, that no-entry position described by Williams (1997). Paradoxically, this type of *fort-da* ("gone"-"there"; Freud, 1920/1955b, pp. 14–15) with meanings that might or might not be linked together seemed to allow Alice to work at building a relationship in which she is in control, the very assurance of erasure enabling us to begin building some scaffolding, conveniently underground.

When working with an individual with anorexia, it is easy to fall into the fantasy of saving themselves from themselves, the clinician's concordant desire to escape from the messiness of living. The challenge, rather, is to try to stand steady in our encounters with the relentlessness that destroys anything that might hold hope or promise. In playing out this dire and deadly encounter with moments when object constancy has failed and there is no way to link ourselves with one another, we are challenged to manage being killed off while still remaining present. Alice's reliance on me felt so desperate and dangerous that she would titrate it by starving herself or otherwise putting herself—and the treatment—in jeopardy. Killing me off as a potential resource seemed to help her not kill herself as we played at acquiring sufficient reflective space to achieve object usage.

The inevitable ruptures made possible moments of repair as she worked to tolerate her distress and hold me in mind beyond her experience in the transference. In turn, I worked at building possibilities from the bits she offered me, such as dreams of a kitten who needs to be fed but is terrified by any approach and fights viciously. Alice's dreams afforded us symbols through which to build a conceptual map of her treacherous internal world in which nothing could be trusted to be as it seems: Vulnerability was dangerous, and care could not be counted on.

Recognizing Alice's psychic reality as it was represented in her dreams helped me speak more directly and empathically to the dilemmas she played out rather than merely be reactive to them. This attunement to her metaphors, culled from her lived reality, helped me find my own reflectivity during times of strain and avoid trying to save her from herself in ways that denied her value and her agency. As Alice began to be in greater contact with her own embodied experience, the metaphors that emerged afforded us some solid ground. Locating myself in her metaphors helped me attend to shifts in her self-experience rather than override her feelings with my own. Working together to build her reflective capacities opposed the darkness that occurred when her mind shut down and nothing was left but chaos and despair.

When working with people with bulimia, the challenge is different. There is an apparent taking-in that masks the interpersonal chasm, a facade of engagement that obscures the underlying sea of chaos and fragmentation. In such cases, we see the type of empty speech Lacan (1953/1977b) referred to: speech that skims over the surface and threatens to lull us into mindlessness. Failing to recognize the meaninglessness introduces a note of perversity into what becomes a pseudorelationship until we can recognize that we have been drawn into complicit acceptance of something that has no meaning. I often find it difficult to recover in such moments because I believe I have failed to do something I should have been doing. Shifting focus to recognize that feeling of failure as a signal rather than a concrete reality becomes the challenge.

In working with those whose development has been foreclosed and whose symptoms—and the meanings they mark—are lodged in the body, repetitions within the work can signal a traumatic moment that has become frozen in time. Much as is played out in the bulimic cycle, repetition ritualizes the traumatic event, taking it out of the realm of terrible realities to be suffered by transforming the suffering into an ecstatic state. In the repetition, there is both a living through of the event and its denial, replacing real loss with a mythic absence whose reality is denied (LaCapra, 1999). Breaking through a moment of empty speech creates an opportunity to look deeper into experiences that have eluded language, including what it means to be in relation to another being.

Much as we found with Alice, for Kim, too, keys to the meanings of her actions came through in her dreams. In various guises, we find representations of the traumatic moment of loss of the mother. There is a jarring disjunction between the absence of discourse regarding the mother's suicide attempt when Kim was 8 and the representations in her dreams of a struggle to hold on to a mother who was always in danger of slipping away. In Kim's early dreams, neither parent could be relied on as an enduring presence, but rather became monstrous or evanescent.

Jarring as well is the disjunction between Kim's well-put-together appearance and her massive collapse in late adolescence. It is difficult to build a story through which to make sense of her collapse or of the discrepancies in the picture she both presents and covers over. In my efforts to resonate to Kim's meanings and learn her language, I recurrently found myself trying to overcome the gap by assiduous attention to my work, as though if I just listened harder or had more wisdom, if only I could be other than I am, then everything would be all right. Finding myself in the position of the insufficient object, I was left to wonder to what extent I was identifying with her or being cast as the reciprocal in her story: caught between the absence and abusiveness of each parent and Kim's belief that she should be able to "do better," even though she cannot.

In this story, we see the bulimic cycle in which the taking-in never satisfied a hunger that could not even be acknowledged. We see how Kim became lost in the belief that she could not afford to have needs or feelings because her feelings did not matter in relation to her mother when she was a child. Unlike Alice, however, Kim fabricated a symbiotic bond in a relentless move toward an empty fullness that attempted to find the mother where she never was but should have been. The metaphors that emerged from Kim's dreams and poetry showed her desperately trying to soften the reality of a mother who was too preoccupied with her own distress to attend to the daughter. Her identification with what Green (1986, Chapter 7) termed the *dead mother* was extremely resistant to treatment because of the terror of losing/killing the mother if one were to leave her behind by facing the need for real, embodied others rather than empty fantasies.

We can see in these young women's relentless movements toward death both an accusation and an attempt to point to the missing maternal and paternal functions (see Charles, 2000a). For the person with anorexia, there is the struggle between relying on the therapist as the person who can envision that living might be possible and the fear and resentment of intrusion in relation to their own efforts to make room for themselves in life. Through engagement with an empathic other who can support these struggles without overriding the person's autonomy, they can begin to mentalize what formerly existed only in the realm of inchoate meanings or actions and to recognize links between feelings and meanings.

For the person with bulimia, in contrast, there is often a pretense of engagement. The emptiness must be exposed for the person to find themselves as they learn to regulate themselves sufficiently to embody the empty spaces with meaning. Finding the hole they have fallen through—and inviting it to be filled with some intention that can be sustained—is an arduous, and in some ways heartbreaking, achievement, but through this process, there is the possibility that life can impose itself as something the person might choose for themselves.

The dangers are real as the person struggles with fears of abandonment and even psychotic disorganization as they grapple with the interdependence that would be required if they were to imagine more actively living their life. With Alice, the challenge was to avoid imposing meanings, allowing her to come upon them and form her own links so that she could find her own tether. With Kim, the challenge was to offer meanings, to refuse the emptiness that had left her untethered to her life, by inserting the absent affective, embodied details as they emerged from her stories and dreams.

NOTE OF CAUTION

As we try to conceptualize differences that might lead a person toward anorexia or bulimia, it is important to keep in mind that we are dealing with psychic reality. To illustrate, we can consider another case involving two sisters who each sought psychoanalytic treatment in young adulthood. Each had been born into a home in which the intergenerational trauma of failed mourning played out in successive generations of mothers and daughters. One sister had anorexia; the other, bulimia. The maternal grandmother's mother had been dying when she was a child, and her daughter had internalized her own mother's feelings of loss and abandonment as well as her negative self-identity as a woman. The girls' mother's feelings of emptiness and devaluation left her, at times, profoundly depressed and inaccessible as a source of support or object for positive identification, the type of unreliable parenting that can lead to disorganized attachment.

These sisters had been positioned in opposition to one another: As the older sister was the favored child, positioned as the savior/confidante, the younger daughter felt barred from a family system in which there seemed to be no room for her. The older sister was left with the task of keeping the mother alive—at times literally—and learning to live austerely, feeding herself on knowledge and the accomplishments that marked the value she could not find in herself or her family. Achievements also provided a vehicle for escape from the mother and what she represented. The younger sister, in contrast, was left to feed herself in effigy of the maternal care of which she had been deprived, turning to secret feeding rituals for sustenance. In adolescence, these rituals began to take the form of the bulimic oral triad through which tension reduction is achieved in the absence of more direct paths toward self-soothing.

Their different positions in the family left these young women with different trajectories in their difficulties obtaining nourishment. The older daughter retained a cognitive awareness of the parental conflict and maternal deficits but at the price of being cut off from her emotions. The younger daughter, in contrast, was caught up in the world of emotions, unable to sufficiently metabolize and integrate her experience to find a stable place in the world. Each remained split off from herself and from one another until psychoanalysis provided them each a space through which to recover aspects of being human that had been delegated to the other. As each integrated feelings into meanings, they began to recognize how they had been divided and their growth had been impeded by the mother's failure to recognize each as a legitimate individual and by the father's inability to move beyond his own limits and take a stand on their behalf. These insights enabled them to free themselves from their destructive habits and to more fully live.

CONCLUSION

Individuals with anorexia and bulimia are each caught in the dilemma of trying to live without having been able to count on others sufficiently to develop the self-soothing mechanisms essential for identity development and effective self-reliance. Self-denial at this primary level means denial of feelings, leaving no ground in which to build a self. Working with such individuals without imposing oneself on them provides the interpersonal scaffolding through which development can proceed.

With people with anorexia, the focus is on the development of a relationship with one's body and mind, whereas with individuals with bulimia, the challenge is to develop a relationship with one's embodied desire. With each, the clinician must be willing to reckon with the ravaged internal landscape left in the wake of the failed developmental efforts. Through the prosodies and working through of the analytic relationship, the interplay between the metaphors embedded in our theories in relation to those drawn from the patient's internal world provides the nourishment needed for psychic survival.

In this chapter, we encountered two different types of defensive structures that are subsumed under the rubric of eating disorders. In the following chapter, I continue to explore distinctions between those who depend more on feelings to make sense of their experience and those who depend more on thinking. Psychoanalysis has long recognized the importance of integrating these two aspects of meaning-making. Chapter 9 continues this exploration by taking a look at the obsessive defenses that find difficulty obtaining traction to the extent that they are not anchored in feelings that can be reflected on.

9 BORDERLINE VERSUS NARCISSISTIC POSITIONS

Before looking at narcissism in Chapter 10, it seems important to try to tease out some of the issues at play in those whose development has been impeded such that they find themselves in the territory termed *narcissistic* or *borderline*. One factor crucial to these distinctions that has been undertheorized is obsessiveness. Freud's original case histories looked first at hysteria (in which the predominant symptoms were embedded in an oversaturation of feelings) and then at obsession (in which there was an overreliance on thinking that was not grounded in feelings).

Perhaps in part because *hysteria* became a problematic term, this division has receded from view. If we think, though, about the distinctions between the anorexic and the bulimic stances discussed in Chapter 8, we see the move toward either the more intellectualized defense, embedded in thinking, or the one more embedded in showing feelings. This disjunction can also be found in distinctions between the narcissistic position and borderline position: The narcissistic position relies more on thinking, and the borderline position is more embedded in feelings. We have considered ways in which unexpressed feelings become symbolized. In many ways, those we term borderline are more accessible to psychoanalytic treatment because

https://doi.org/10.1037/0000455-010
Echoes of Trauma: Meaning and Identity in Psychoanalysis, by M. Charles

they are object related, albeit without stability. In contrast, those we would term narcissistic pose particular challenges because they are not. Much as hysteria became a problematic term, so, too, did borderline. At the extreme, the term became a marker for the pathologization of feelings and of women (Charles, 2020). Currently, narcissism has become the catchall term that threatens to become meaninglessly derogatory. And yet, as we will see in Chapter 10, it also marks some of the developmental difficulties associated with complex trauma. Before turning to narcissism, in this chapter I investigate more directly some of the differences in the metacognitive capacities of those more mired in intellect or in feelings, unable to adaptively integrate both functions.

CONCEPTUALIZING BORDERLINE AND NARCISSISTIC DEFENSES

Attempts to understand the etiology and treatment of narcissistic versus borderline conditions have been beset by a confusion of tongues both within and across diagnostic categories. In research conducted through the Erikson Institute of the Austen Riggs Center that looked at the development of metacognitive capacities over time, we found that borderline defenses are linked with greater affective lability but also greater metacognitive abilities, particularly in relation to the person's own thoughts and feelings, capacities that further develop in the course of intensive psychoanalytic psychotherapy (Neal et al., 2023; see also Semerari et al., 2005). In contrast, narcissistic defenses are linked with an intellectualized capacity to solve problems that tends not to be well grounded in feelings and that has particular deficits in the ability to recognize, reflect on, and differentiate one's own or others' thoughts and feelings (Dimaggio et al., 2002). In narcissism, we most often find entrenched intellectualized, obsessive defenses, but there are also those with narcissistic difficulties who are more histrionic. The affective lability in such cases can make diagnosis difficult, impeding treatment efforts.

Although both of these diagnostic categories point to the type of massive parental failures resulting in overwhelming experiences of helplessness that become precursors for later feelings of shame, humiliation, and alienation (A. Schore, 2012), their differences have important ramifications for treatment because they are linked to different developmental trajectories, defenses, and functional impairments. Notably, narcissistic personality disorder has been linked with alexithymia, whereas borderline personality disorder has been linked with heightened fear responses that inhibit reflectivity

(Decety & Moriguchi, 2007). The greater reflective capacities of individuals with borderline symptomatology make insight-oriented therapies user friendly, providing a scaffolding that helps stabilize the dysregulation at the core of their difficulties (Charles, 2020). At the core of the borderline dilemma seems to be a hyperresponsiveness to others' affect, and to threat in particular, that leads to difficulties making sense of self or others during moments of emotional arousal (Fonagy & Bateman, 2008).

In contrast, narcissistic individuals seem to be impeded in their capacity to discriminate emotions in self and other, leading to theory-driven accounts of mental states, as described by Gallese and Goldman (1998), in contrast to ideas driven by the simulation of embodied experience we find in more normative development. Our research findings have shown that their reflective capacities do not tend to develop substantially—even with intensive psychotherapy (Neal et al., 2023)—with notable exceptions, as I will illustrate later. What does seem to develop for those caught in a narcissistic position is the ability to make use of what is learned toward more adaptive behavior. Ideas can be taken in and applied without necessarily finding referents in self-experience. Development occurs in what Gallese (2014) termed the *third-person realm of intellectual reasoning*. In this way, we see profound deficits in making meaning from embodied self-experience that require sufficient respect from the clinician to enable us to help the person manage despite their deficits, even as we work to try to ameliorate them.

One important factor that may help account for the different trajectories we find in treating those caught in the narcissistic position may be the extent to which the lack of self-knowledge is linked with alexithymia or difficulties with interoceptive processing (Palser et al., 2018). These two separate but interrelated issues suggest there may be different underlying reasons for the impediments in recognizing and representing emotional states in terms of deficits in apperceptive versus associative capacities (see Lane et al., 2020). *Alexithymia* is a construct that relates to impairments in emotional awareness and regulation, pointing to

> difficulties in identifying and describing feelings, difficulties in discriminating between feelings and bodily sensations of emotional arousal, markedly constricted imaginative processes . . . a cognitive style that is concrete . . . and a high degree of social conformity with little contact with their own psychic reality. (Bankier et al., 2001, p. 235)

Bankier and colleagues (2001) found that an obsessive thinking style is prevalent in men who have trouble distinguishing emotions from bodily sensations. Such difficulties lead to an increased focus on external events over internal experiences or feelings (Zackheim, 2007).

In contrast, *interoceptive awareness* is associated more directly with conscious awareness of emotions and the processing of emotional stimuli (Herbert et al., 2011) and helps to organize meanings in relation to subjective experience (Craig, 2009). Heightened interoceptive awareness in the absence of being able to make meaning from the signals results in anxiety precisely because of the diffuseness of the signals (Palser et al., 2018). We consider these difficulties as we focus once again on Bob, whom we first encountered in Chapter 7. Learning more about the internal deficits underlying subjective emotional experience helps us better understand the difficulties of those who have trouble making meaning from the basic rhythms of experience that underlie the unconscious underpinnings of symbolization. Recognizing the tendency to intellectualize as a sign of possible deficits in the ability to make meaning from primary embodied experience helps us conceptualize and work with the profound difficulties we encounter with those who are obsessive and overly intellectualized. Given the huge obstacles to be overcome by such individuals, one essential factor seems to be the extent to which the person wants to change or whether they are so entrenched in the perverse satisfactions of their egocentric position that they are loathe to give them up.

METACOGNITION AND REFLECTIVE FUNCTIONS

The disruptions in early attachment we have been discussing lead to deficits in metacognition, notably the "comprehension of action intentionality, comprehension of pretending, and comprehension of the beliefs on which behavior is based" (Semerari et al., 2007, p. 108). Being able to think about our thinking provides the type of "third" perspective that enables us to contextualize an understanding of self and other beyond the immediate moment (Charles, 2012; Muller, 2007). However, when that perspective is not sufficiently grounded in self-experience, thinking can become ruminative, obsessive, and maladaptive.

Because this instability impedes the development of the internal monitoring so essential to making sense of others' minds, there are far-reaching effects (Gallese, 2013). Semerari and his colleagues (2007) highlighted the important distinction between having a theory of mind that enables one to recognize mental states in the third person—through an intellectual lens—and having a *monitoring mechanism* that is oriented to oneself in the first person. Deficits in monitoring can be seen as social and emotional processing deficits linked to the attachment difficulties associated with abuse and neglect, impairments found at the neural level in individuals diagnosed with personality disorders

(Flasbeck et al., 2021). These findings are in line with the recognition in psychoanalytic theory that conditions of trauma and neglect teach children to be vigilant to others' affect to the neglect of learning to monitor or manage their own feelings (Fairbairn, 1952).

Between the embodied self-experience and the intellectualized third-person conjecture, suggested Gallese (2014), lies another realm of experience that he termed *the second-person perspective*. "When exposed to others' expressive behaviours, reactions and inclination, we simultaneously experience their goal-directedness and intentional character, as we experience ourselves as the agents of *our* affects, feelings, and emotions, the owners of *our* thoughts, fantasies, imaginations and dreams" (p. 5). When all goes well, we are able to orient to our internal experience and recognize similarities and differences between our own and that of others.

According to Gallese (2014), the second-person perspective requires the basic constituents of metacognition described by Lysaker and his colleagues: *self-reflectivity*, awareness that mental states exist; basic *awareness of others' minds*, the capacity to distinguish self from other; and *decentration*, the ability to recognize the existence of different, legitimate perspectives (Lysaker, Erickson, et al., 2010, Lysaker et al., 2011; Semerari et al., 2003). Gallese (2014) proposed the term *mindreading* as "a non-meta-representational way of understanding others, basically sharing a common feature: the mapping of the other onto the self, reciprocated by the mapping of the self on the other" (p. 7). From that perspective, we can see that patterns of metacognition in different character typologies mark different trajectories in managing interpersonal engagements in the face of early environmental failures.

Gallese (2009, 2014) helped us distinguish some of the functional aspects of the internal and external monitoring that support and sustain the implicit relational knowing so crucial to normal development. When there is a history of neglect, traumatic memories stored in implicit memory may impede the development of symbolic processes and reflective functions (Bucci, 2002), making defenses brittle and insufficiently adaptive (Stern, Bruschweiler-Stern, et al., 1998; Stern, Sander, et al.,1998). Further, Mancia (2008) suggested that

> continuous or repeated frustrations and disappointments can also contribute to organizing a young child's fantasies and defenses, which will be deposited in the preverbal and presymbolic implicit memory, where they will mould the structure of an *unrepressed unconscious nucleus of self*. (p. 203)

As we have seen, these internalizations come to structure memory, meaning, and the self in ways that become further entrenched in direct relationship to their tendency to preclude growth.

THE INTERPERSONAL CONTEXT

As we learned in Chapter 2, failures to mourn interfere with the parent's ability to be sufficiently present with the child to assist them in making meaning from their experience. This gap interferes with the recognition and integration of nonverbal communications so that the child may be receiving affective messages that cannot be overtly recognized or discussed. The parent who has worked through past difficulties is more available to recognize their own distraction in ways that help the child transition back to a state of equilibrium. Notably, intergenerational transmission of trauma often results in mixed messages that impede the child's ability to make sense of their own experience. Deficits in the ability to recognize embodied feelings, meanings, and intentions and link them with categories of experience impede the development of abstract reasoning so crucial to later learning (Knox, 2009). In this way, intergenerational trauma can interfere with the development of the capacities for abstraction and generalization that facilitate learning, leading to the borderline dilemma in which affect becomes overwhelming because it cannot be sufficiently reflected on. Making the picture even more complex are the enigmatic messages (Laplanche, 1997) parents give to children through the affective loadings that speak from the parent's unconscious to the child's unconscious. These messages speak from unintegrated trauma as well as from the cultural injunctions and shame- or fear-bound aversions that have shaped the parent's mind and being (Apprey, 2024).

When affective signals cannot be differentiated, the diffuse arousal tends to be experienced as an anxious discomfort to be managed or moderated, resulting in avoidant or obsessive, intellectualized defenses. Taking seriously what we know from studies of mirror neurons, we would do well to have in mind the links between emotion regulation and identity so that our offerings support development rather than oppose it, paying close attention to ways in which learning can itself be regulating. An analytic stance can invite containment and reflection by putting the difficulties into context. An attitude of being curious together affirms that meaning can be made without imposing any particular meaning on the person, inviting the person to make meaning from their own experiences. Paying attention to the balance between thinking and feeling is particularly important with our more obsessive patients, whose defenses work toward intellectualized learning as a way of not having to feel emotions they have difficulty making sense of and may need help distinguishing and naming.

Findings about mirror neurons also remind us that, in attending to our own arousal, and working toward downshifting when tensions get too high, we are supporting the affect regulation that is an essential underpinning of cognitive flexibility (Gallese et al., 2007). Recognition of the direct effects of relationships on behavior is crucial to any understanding of insight-oriented treatments given what we now recognize about factors that enhance and impede the development of the mentalization capacities so crucial to adaptive living (Fonagy & Luyten, 2009).

Self and identity are most adaptively built through relationships that are sufficiently attuned and attentive to symbolize experience in discursive terms. Severe character pathology marks deficits in development that require the clinician's attentive interest so that we can help build the symbolizing capacities essential for well-being and adaptive living, thereby also attenuating the depressive turns that accompany chronic failure. Psychoanalysis suffers from a confusion of tongues, but at the core it is about building shared meanings within a relational context, providing a space for the development of metacognition.

CLINICAL ILLUSTRATIONS

If we think about the narcissistic and borderline positions developmentally, those we term borderline have unstable relations but are nevertheless object related. The deficits are associated with unreliable representations that become further impaired under conditions of high emotional intensity, a phenomenon familiar to all those who work clinically with such individuals. These difficulties can be traced to the pattern of hypervigilance to threat and rejection linked to attachment anxiety, childhood trauma, and stress (Flasbeck et al., 2021). Although such individuals' apperceptive abilities may be intact, enabling them to identify internal states, there is an associative impairment that impedes their ability to integrate disparate data into a coherent narrative or to differentiate a subjective experience from a concrete reality, to know that their thoughts or feelings are not necessarily an accurate representation of reality (Semerari et al., 2005).

As an example, think of Elizabeth, an elegant woman in her late fifties who describes herself as "a child of neglect." She is aware of deficiencies in herself that she has passed along to her daughters despite her best efforts and her profound love for them. She has sought treatment now, hoping to stabilize herself sufficiently to be of greater use to them in their own struggles without further undermining her internal stability. We can locate Elizabeth's struggles precisely in the borderline realm. She is remarkably attuned to and able to discriminate subtleties in her own internal experience but easily becomes dysregulated and derailed in the presence of others, leaving her unable to reflectively make use of her self-knowledge. We can conjecture that her early history of adaptation to a violent father and a mother who could be warmly wonderful but turn monstrous without warning left Elizabeth attentive to external danger without being able to effectively read the signals that might help her orient more adaptively to safety or danger.

Interpersonally, although we see Elizabeth resonating to the plight of young women her children's age, she seems so attuned to her own sense of being a child and being a mother that she has trouble reading signals from those who are present with her at the time. Seeing how out of touch she becomes in the presence of others, we can understand her urge to return to the safety and solace of engagements with nature and other forms of self-soothing. In the safety of her own mind, she can reflect on her experience, but it is difficult to translate those reflections into adaptive action.

In contrast, individuals diagnosed with narcissistic personality disorder show severe deficits in self-reflectivity that impede the establishment of interpersonal relationships. Those we would characterize as narcissistic appear to have relationships, but these relationships are largely illusory, based on self-esteem management rather than actual interpersonal engagement (Dimaggio et al., 2002). People tend to be viewed merely as characters in a self-referential drama rather than actual persons in their own right. There is an egocentric failure to differentiate others as having autonomous, separate, and legitimate perspectives. There is also a tendency toward alexithymia, that profound deficit in the capacity to accurately read one's own internal workings that invites "an excessive use of values in making life choices and programming actions, to the detriment of the emotions" (Dimaggio et al., 2002, p. 422). The overreliance on intellect over feelings often results in obsessive defenses that keep others at bay.

The more libidinally organized narcissist seems to be struggling in a world in which obsessive defenses arise because internal experience cannot be sufficiently monitored or moderated. As an example, we can look once again at Bob, the man who, in his mid-fifties, had come to a standstill in life and career, so overwrought by anxious obsessions that he was unable to work or to engage with others. Having tried every other type of therapy, Bob sought psychoanalytic treatment, hoping, perhaps, to get to the root of his troubles. His obsessive defenses had been fed by the cognitive behavioral treatments meant to relieve them so that, when I met him, he spent several hours trying to relate to me the exact type of obsessive-compulsive disorder from which he was suffering. My attempts to make sense of what he was saying were not sufficiently near to his own discourse to be parsable, and he became increasingly frustrated, warding off any effort I made at engagement. I suggested that maybe we should turn to the task at hand: Rather than trying to identify his symptoms or syndrome precisely, perhaps we could try to better understand the contexts in which they occurred.

This invitation seemed to ease the impasse, although our engagements were still impeded by his obsessive style. I noticed that my attempts to join the conversation still tended to ratchet up his own discourse. It was as though leaving room for another mind was potentially catastrophic. Rather, Bob would try to keep me (and others) at bay by anticipating what they might add from their own perspective and factoring it in himself. This would seem to be the type of competitive avoidance of shame that tends to be linked to a poor prognosis in psychotherapy (Kealy et al., 2023; Richter et al., 2023) and seemed to be obstructing the very learning Bob was hoping to accomplish. Eventually, we came to a catastrophic moment in which I insisted on saying something at the end of the hour that he had been fending off. The gist was that other people might have a different perspective that might be worth listening to. He came back the next day, having been overwhelmed with shame and anger and outraged, hurt, frightened, and angry at my attack on him. I listened attentively to all he had to say and then acknowledged the hurt while also recognizing the need to leave room for the something-more he had come to learn about. Linking that dilemma to the shame and self-esteem issues he himself had marked helped us reach a moment of equilibrium together.

Here, we find the thin-skinned narcissist whose libidinal needs leave a bit of room for rupture and repair. These libidinal needs keep Bob engaged, despite how difficult our encounters can be. As we struggle to make translations between his universe of ideas and mine of feelings, I try to build conceptual links through which he might more easily find his way into this foreign realm of embodied meanings. He tells me that he is working at making room for others by shortening his own speech and making space for others. I suggest that he is attending to the form of the conversation but not the relational elements. He is confused. I tell him that structuring a conversation so that each person has space is not the same as being interested in what the person is saying. I say that it likely matters to him when he feels that a person is listening in a way that shows that they care about his thoughts and feelings. This finally registers because it marks precisely what he feels is lacking in his relationship with his wife. Recognizing the real deficits in being able to recognize embodied experience and translate it into words is crucial in this work, lest we leave the person lost in relation to our own empty speech.

Another example is John, a man in his early thirties who seemed unable to discriminate between different feelings or to make sense of relationships (see Chapter 13 for an explication of this case). John's lack of contact with his internal world was so stunning that he almost seemed autistic. His obsessive defenses were so compelling that he could lose hours in selecting the "right spoon" and had lost his home because of the accumulation of debris he had been unable to manage. In his dreams, he was looking for the secret key that would unlock the meanings he felt were withheld from him, meanings he could intuit but seemed inevitably out of reach. We find allusions to this type of secret key in Freud's (1909/1955a) early work on obsessional characters in relation to the elusive meanings little Hans felt were being withheld from him to which his father seemed to hold the key.

Lysaker's ideas about metacognition helped me to organize a useful understanding of John's difficulties and the work needing to be done (Lysaker, Dimaggio, et al., 2010; Lysaker, Erickson, et al., 2010). Taking seriously that reflective functions begin with the capacity to orient toward and name one's own internal experience, John and I start working toward differentiating the possible feelings that might be lost within the dark, looming black cloud of negative affect. Also essential is my insistence that his dilemma must, somehow, make sense, if we can sufficiently understand the contexts in which the difficulties arose. From that vantage point, his story begins to emerge, first in my mind and then, reciprocally, in his. Our work consists of being interested in the feelings he cannot find, particularly as they begin to surface in the displacement of his dreams. The dream space seems to afford sufficient safety to work at his difficulties and develop a consensual language through which he can use me in the service of his development.

At times, the internal dysregulation is so profound that no thinking is possible. This was the case in my work with Chris, a man in his early fifties whose life had come to a standstill in middle age. Unable to build a career or relationships despite his strong intelligence, he had returned to his parents' home, angry, assaultive, and ashamed. His entry into my office seemed to take the form of his dilemma with his parents. At times, he seemed to be so tortured by my presence that the moments were barely endurable. His hypersensitivity to sound exacerbated his sense of overwhelm. It was only when I tried to help him find another therapist who might better suit his needs that he was able to settle down sufficiently to encounter me as a person who might have something of value to offer. This case reminds us that when affect regulation difficulties are at the core of the dilemma, they must be taken seriously before any real work can be done. Meeting a person in such a state respectfully and empathically takes a great deal of effort because of their presumption that being seen means being devalued. With Chris, being able to recognize, together, that his own negative self-evaluation was at the core of his difficulties helped provide a moment of meeting from which to proceed, in part because it marked my position of not agreeing that his position was hopeless. This point of differentiation between two persons is crucial to one being able to effectively make use of the other.

In the cases of Bob, John, and Chris, the developmental failures were profound, but there was a desire to break through the impasse and develop a language through which to describe feelings and ways to build more meaningful relationships. In contrast, we have those individuals I term *perverse narcissists*, who are so devoted to managing their esteem needs that their grandiosity makes it difficult for them to engage with, much less learn anything from, anyone. Rather, they seem to hope perhaps to steal some needed knowledge so they might spare themselves the injury inherent in someone knowing more than they. Encounters with such individuals seem to exist within predictable patterns of tension-building, rupture, and a repair in which nothing is learned that cannot be erased as we begin the cycle once again. I think, for example, of a young man who suffered from his love for a young woman whose needs often conflicted with his own. Wanting someone's love and attention, I told him, is not the same as loving someone.

Another man's major symptom was his intense suicidality, which he wielded as a weapon. Most essential was his need to be the most extreme sufferer, leading him to be vigilant toward and envious of the suffering of others. This became evident when he learned that someone in his circle was dying of cancer. He began to obsess over the possibility that this might be his fate as well. I spoke with him about his envy that made him adopt the difficulties of others as though they were his own. These markers of meaning seemed to have little impact on him in the moment but did make his habitual defenses a bit less easy to shift into. Although he still relied on his grandiose investment in his own suffering, over time, he began to also take small steps to build a life.

CONCLUSION

When we encounter those with obsessive defenses, helping them find ways to access their inner experience more fully becomes the foundation on which a more satisfying life might be built. When third-person formulations become the predominant means for managing the feelings and relationships that otherwise seem overwhelming, offering a formulation of the contexts that led to the impasse can provide a conceptual framework that helps them better tolerate their uneasy forays into the realm of feelings. Respecting the profound deficits in making sense of embodied experience that seem to underlie such difficulties is an important precondition for building a relational space—and meaning structures—through which these capacities might develop.

Having highlighted some of the important differences between those who are caught at the borderline level—with an overreliance on feelings—and those caught at the narcissistic level—with an overreliance on thinking—we are in a better position to look more intensively at narcissism. Although narcissism has become an overused term, its predominance also marks the prevalence of developmental difficulties in current times. If we think of metacognition as a developmental progression through which internal and external data can be increasingly recognized, reflected on, and integrated, being able to recognize where a person is caught can be crucial for the clinician. In Chapter 10, we look at narcissism and its treatment.

10 NARCISSISM

In Chapter 9, we focused on two different trajectories in the development of metacognitive capacities. What we term *borderline dilemmas* are linked to severe deficits in affect regulation that make relationships unstable. In contrast, *narcissistic difficulties* are linked to deficits in recognizing and making use of affective signals such that there is a reliance on thinking without being anchored in embodied meanings. In this chapter, I focus on narcissism, looking first at the etiology of the term and then applying current theorizing to a clinical illustration.

ETIOLOGY

Early on, Freud (1914/1957b) recognized that, along with the libidinal urges toward pleasure in living, there were darker forces within us, destructive forces he subsumed under the heading the *death drive*. In this classic paper, he noted that narcissism in parents is crippling to the child. This insight presages recent work by attachment theorists and infant/parent researchers, who noted that perhaps the most destructive force waylaying development

https://doi.org/10.1037/0000455-011
Echoes of Trauma: Meaning and Identity in Psychoanalysis, by M. Charles

in children comes from failures in mourning that leave parents unreliably available to attend to the needs of the child (Liotti, 2004; Main & Hesse, 1990), the type of small-t, complex trauma that impedes growth. Parental failures can invite overwhelming experiences of helplessness that become precursors for later feelings of shame, humiliation, and alienation (A. Schore, 2012). As Symington (1993) noted, "Narcissism is nearly always the product of trauma" (p. 73).

In this early paper, however, Freud (1914/1957b) was not thinking about trauma, but rather theorizing about how we move from what he termed a *primary narcissism*, a preliminary self-focus, toward a greater appreciation of our inherent need for others. He introduced the idea of the *ego ideal* as an adaptive resolution to the problem of narcissism in which the perfection that has not been achieved is held as a self-potential that might offset the present failure. In theorizing the shift from the illusion of omnipotence to the recognition of lack and limits, Freud discussed sublimation as a means for managing the space between the wish and the actuality.

More recent explorations have shifted away from ideas of primary narcissism to focus on Freud's later ideas regarding life and death drives. In his paper on this subject, Rosenfeld (1971) distinguished between libidinal and destructive aspects, much as we discussed in the previous chapter. Rosenfeld tied the libidinal pull to omnipotent control and an overidealization of self, and he linked the destructive end to omnipotent aggression. Whereas the libidinal focus is on humiliation at dependence, the destructive focus is on envy. Destructive envy can be highly organized and difficult to discern, presenting particular clinical challenges because any potential change is seen as weakness and is resisted. Maintaining the self-idealization requires vigilance and deception.

Rosenfeld (1987) later refined his ideas to focus on what he termed *thin-skinned* narcissists, characterized by their vulnerable fragility, versus *thick-skinned* narcissists, characterized by envy and a profound inaccessibility to feelings. These distinctions have also been termed *vulnerable* versus *grandiose* (Bernardi & Eidlin, 2018) and can be conceptualized in relation to the oversensitivity to feelings one cannot easily make sense of versus difficulties processing feelings, as discussed in Chapter 9. Akhtar (1989) suggested that these presentations are two sides of the same coin depending on which aspect is overt and which is covert—the grandiosity or the vulnerability—but there may be differences in apperceptive versus associative abilities that have profound ramifications for treatment (see Lane et al., 2020). Whereas some individuals present with the types of apperceptive deficits associated with alexithymia, for others, it is the linking of troubling meanings that is resisted.

Whatever the presentation, narcissistically organized individuals pose particular problems interpersonally because the threat to their own subjectivity impedes their ability to tolerate or even imagine an actual relationship with the analyst as a separate person (Bernardi & Eidlin, 2018).

CLINICAL ILLUSTRATION

As an example, let us take the case of a young man in his late twenties who has come to a standstill in his relationships and career. Very bright and intellectually competent at times, Luca can appear quite dull. His speech comes slowly, and it is not clear until he speaks whether he is planning to respond or if he is even tracking what is happening around him. He appears timid and withdrawn, his eyes wide and dark. He grounds his story in an angry father and nonprotecting mother, describing having soothed his father's rages through apologies that left him feeling as though he had, as his father had insisted, been responsible for those rages. I can see a part of Luca that recognizes this falsehood and is angry, but it remains hidden behind the part of him that has adapted compliantly to the needs of the family.

Despite this timid, even frightened presentation, as I read Rosenfeld (1971), I can recognize Luca in the descriptions of destructive narcissism and its impact on treatment. Like Rosenfeld's patient, as Luca becomes more engaged in the therapy, he withdraws and becomes more symptomatic. He complains of sleepiness and misses sessions and, in his suggestions of possible resolutions to this dilemma, shows that he would like to make the analyst responsible: The sessions are too early; he can't respond to his alarm even though he tries. Might the analyst call to awaken him when he doesn't arrive on time? But changing the sessions to later in the day only makes him feel cared for; it does not increase his attendance, and he does not answer his phone when I try to call. He also keeps his voicemail full so that a message cannot be left. I imagine that the phone ringing provides a felt sense of someone being there without Luca's needing to actively engage. As tends to be true in narcissism, through this enactment, I find I am merely offering myself as a character in his drama. He stages events so that he can feel my presence without having to interact. Even though my efforts have failed, however, they seem to have made a mark, and he returns to more active engagement in his treatment with a deliberation and a sense of pride that comes forward when I meet his attendance with a smile rather than an attack.

Luca saves grievances and only brings them up after the fact, often with a vague hint of a smile that I find hard to parse. Is it pleasure, shame, discomfort?

He says he was frightened to mention the grievance, a stance that leaves him always the silently suffering victim of others' aggression or inattention, a replay of the parent–child dynamics. There is an already-done-to aspect to relationships that ensures hopelessness and leaves others little room to play anything other than their assigned parts. When he does let others in, however, their anger and aggression come forward along with his, leaving him pulling back into the victim stance once again, decrying others' unwillingness to allow him to have his feelings without attacking him.

In our sessions, Luca refers to abuse he cannot talk about. But then, when the events begin to come forward in his dreams, it is unclear to what extent he positions himself as the victim. Rather, in the first incident he mentions, he insists that he was the instigator but then felt used by the person he was using, leaving him feeling defiled, dirty, and ashamed. His self-disgust seems to be at the core of what makes memory problematic, including the recognition that he, too, was used, a fact that shakes his need to imagine himself in control.

Luca reports that he never felt good about himself. In the context of an angry, aggressive father and a subservient, self-effacing mother, he reports feeling at fault for his father's rages. There does seem to be a part of him that enjoys having the power to provoke, the part of him that seems to watch me from behind the presentation he puts forward to gauge what I do and do not register and to what extent he is safe with me. There are hazards on either side: If I see his competence, I am dangerous; if I fail to see it, I am a fool.

Luca does have friends, but they complain that he disappears and that they are afraid to confront him when they have a grievance. They sense his anger, but he refuses to acknowledge it. Rosenfeld (1971) noted the importance of interpreting the envy and its destructiveness when it gets isolated and all-powerful. Failing to interpret leaves the analyst in precisely the quandary I find myself in with Luca. However, the part of him that is beginning to trust me allows him to bring in a dream that is remarkably similar to the one described by Rosenfeld in which his patient dreams about the destructive part of himself. Luca dreams: "A person has a knife to my throat. I wake up and feel he is still there, hiding. I am scared. It is very real." He then brings in another dream:

> Someone is trying to attack me. This keeps happening and it seems very real. Then, there is a friend there, and I decide to fight back, and I manage to overpower them. In that part of the dream, I am aware that it is a dream. It is very strange.

In reporting each dream, Luca is careful to note the parts of the dreams that seem real and the parts in which he is aware of dreaming. I am aware that there are meanings he is trying to communicate that I cannot quite grasp, but I can recognize the value of this intention. I find these dreams remarkably consistent with Rosenfeld's patient, who began to dream of a powerful man who stood for the destructive part of himself. The patient noticed that the destructive impulses at night increased after any progress in the analysis. I could recognize this pattern with Luca, which I marked internally for future reference, waiting for a moment when an interpretation might be more experience-near. Finding a moment when the person is close to the insight helps them to make it their own rather than reactively resisting uncomfortable impositions.

At times, the critical, arrogant part of Luca would come through and be visible in the sessions. Recognizing his agency helped to invite the more actively competent part of himself into the work rather than leave it outside, where it remained inaccessible, destructive, and unintegrated. Encouraging him to bring his anger forward and to speak with people rather than remain isolated and wounded helped him establish more authenticity in his relationships. This path, however, was fraught with the need to recognize others' anger at him for how destructive his refusal to engage with others—or even in self-care—has been. There is a poignancy to seeing how intimately tied these destructive defenses were to his felt sense of danger should his potency be revealed, leaving his actual capacities unable to develop and flower in his daily life. This is one tragedy of narcissism: that everything becomes pretend in relation to the need to deny the shameful sense of utter deficiency at the core of the disturbance, a difficulty we also encountered with Chris in Chapter 9.

DIFFERENTIAL DIAGNOSES

Conceptualizations of narcissistic disorders have been plagued by confusions between various levels and types. In considering this issue, Kernberg (2014) distinguished between the borderline level of identity diffusion when aggression—and fear—predominate versus a more primitive resolution typified by a defensive, grandiose self. Aggression tends to be tied to more severe psychopathology, whereas libidinal dominance is linked with more effective defenses and higher levels of functioning. In malignant aggression, suggested Kernberg (2014), "aggression is still mostly directed against internalized object relations reflected in conflicts with the external world" (p. 867). At the extreme, offered Kernberg (2014), "aggression is directed not only against all internal relations with significant others, but against the very self" (p. 867). The result is what Kernberg (2014) described as "severely self-mutilating narcissistic personalities" (p. 867) likely in relation to the type of profound deficits in early relationships that Green (1986, Chapter 7) pointed to in his descriptions of the *dead mother syndrome*. There is a poignancy in recognizing the damage and deformation that occurs as the child tries to survive within the constraints of such fundamentally lacking and destructive early relationships.

To guide our work with such persons, Kernberg (1970) suggested three variables to consider beyond the diagnostic category per se: the relative *cohesion or diffusion* of the self, the relative *maturity* of the defense mechanisms, and the degree of *contact with reality*. These distinctions also help us better understand confusions we encounter in trying to differentiate the person with borderline difficulties from the person with narcissistic difficulties, suggesting that we may find elements of each disorder in the same individual that run not in a continuum, but rather orthogonally. The *Diagnostic and Statistical Manual of Mental Disorders* (5th edition [*DSM-5*]; American Psychiatric Association, 2013) has included in its definition of narcissistic personality disorder recognition of both the instability of self-esteem linked to identity disturbance and the difficulties with empathy and intimacy linked to interpersonal deficits.

Notably, these deficits can all be viewed through the lens of the mentalization capacities that depend on both affective and cognitive engagement with empathic others to develop (Fonagy et al., 2002). Those we would term narcissistic have greater impairments than those we would term borderline in their abilities to navigate the emotional and interpersonal worlds, to link thoughts with feelings, and to put these into context. Whereas the narcissistic individual tends to talk about others as though they were characters in a self-relating drama, the borderline individual does have relationships with others, but they are unstable.

Dimaggio and his colleagues (2007) differentiated four variables implicated in these intra- and interpersonal impairments: *identification*, the capacity to distinguish and define with increased nuance and complexity one's thoughts and feelings; *relating variables*, the capacity to recognize relationships between these internal events and put them into context; *integration*, the capacity to reflect on and organize mental states of relevance or importance; and *differentiation*, the capacity to recognize that one's mental states, including both ideas and feelings, are subjective and fallible. The major deficits in narcissism are in the areas of *self-reflectivity*, awareness of one's internal states, and *decentration*, the ability to recognize and respect another, different perspective (Dimaggio et al., 2002). Without these capacities, other minds tend to be difficult to read, and difference easily signals danger.

Notable deficits found in narcissistic individuals include a lack of empathy in the context of excessive entitlement, envy, and arrogance (Bilotta et al., 2018). These defenses further impede the ability to establish satisfying relations with others. In our own research using interviews from the Follow-Along Study at the Austen Riggs Center, we found that narcissistic individuals tend to make up for deficits in self- and other-awareness by figuring out how to manage events despite those deficits, whereas borderline individuals tend to be able to reflect on their own feelings and ideas as well as those of others without necessarily being able to integrate this knowledge or make adaptive choices based on it (Neal et al., 2023).

TRANSFERENCE/COUNTERTRANSFERENCE DYNAMICS

Transference/countertransference dynamics can be highly charged with narcissistic individuals. The underlying terror that robs the person of real engagement (Meltzer, 1968) demands that the analyst learn to bear the transference so that they can offer the possibility of relationship. Kernberg (2014) noted salient transference/countertransference dynamics with narcissists, including

> the activation of a dominant transference relationship between a grandiose, entitled, superior self and a depreciated object, reflecting the patient's pathological grandiose self, and a complementary, devalued, inferior, paralyzed counterpart, usually projected onto the therapist but sometimes enacted by the patient himself. (p. 867)

We can consider Luca's difficulties in relation to the notion of the thin-skinned narcissist. He is so afraid of his anger that he is often not even aware of it. To the contrary, he becomes hurt and confused when others accuse him of being angry.

Breaking down this dilemma, we can see that several things are happening. First, accusations of anger—and even Luca's own internal recognition of it—activate the relationship in which his father accused him of being responsible for his rages. If Luca is indeed angry, he must be the rageful, terrible person who was responsible for his father's attacks. Second, whatever anger he is aware of also seems dangerous because it might explode and attack and alienate others. That would confirm his inherent badness and prove that his father was right. His inability to make sense of his heightened internal emotional experience makes it threatening in the absence of strategies for the affect regulation that might afford internal relief and interpersonal repair. These difficulties are further complicated by the notion we encountered in his dream, which marks the greater safety in being the perpetrator rather than the victim.

Because of his history of freezing during his father's rages as a way of trying to stop them or at least diminish his own pain, Luca finds himself at an impasse in moments of danger. That impasse is furthered by his confusion regarding his anger, which has become not a signal that something is wrong that needs attending to, but rather that he is wrong and needs to disappear. His disappearance during moments of assault has left him helpless but also feeling responsible for the attacks he did not fight off. In his dreams, we see him working at trying to mobilize the part of himself that might fight off such an attack, trying to find a way to be assertive without being destructively combative.

In the consulting room, we see the effects of this confusion regarding the possibility of being powerful without being destructive. Because of the precariousness of "truth" on these occasions, reassurance becomes a lie, verification that the other is duped and useless. This defense has mixed results: relief at a grandiose victory and despair at another possibility lost. Actively recognizing the complexities of the experience as they are linked to past and present dilemmas helps invite the possibility of thinking further together rather than merely inviting retreat. In moments of impasse, my intent focus on my internal self-regulation helps to set in motion his own so that we can move back to thinking together about the difficulties he is facing.

A DEVELOPMENTAL PERSPECTIVE

Kohut (1966) took a developmental view on narcissism, noting the idealization of the parent that potentially paves the way for the healthy development of object ties and object love. From this perspective, we can consider how Luca's father's rages and his mother's inability to protect him subverted the process of internalizing standards of behavior grounded in loving relationships. To the contrary, his drives were blocked by the dictates of a corrupt superego that imposed impossible standards, impeding the path from narcissistic investment to object love. Crucial to that path, for Kohut, is the development of healthy narcissism in the child, the sense that one is valuable and loveable. Failing that, "traumatic onslaughts on the child's self-esteem [can drive] the grandiose fantasies into repression" so that, rather than being modified, "they tend to vacillate between an irrational overestimation of the self and feelings of inferiority" (Kohut, 1966, p. 252).

In pointing toward how developmental failures invite shame, which further inhibits the achievement of mastery and resilience, we can see how Kohut meets the Kleinians. Kohutian Andrew Morrison (1983) marked shame as *the pivotal affect* underlying narcissistic disturbance, reflecting "feelings about a defect of the self, a lowering of self-esteem, falling short of the values of the ego ideal, a flaw in one's identity representation" (p. 299). Shame severs us from others, resulting in a sense of being endangered by the imminence of abandonment or rejection. We can see in Luca's case ways in which he was thwarted by failures in what Kohut (1977) terms the early mirroring parental functions and the later empathic idealized-identificatory aspects. Neither parent was able to prioritize his needs and feelings when they conflicted with their own, leaving him, as Fairbairn (1952) described, vigilant to the needs and feelings of others at the price of developing agency in relation to his own internal experience. The failure to make meaning from internal experience leaves feelings in the realm of noise rather than useful signals.

For Kohut, when the primary needs for mirroring, merger, and idealization have not been met, the goal in psychotherapy is either to repair the damaged self through repeated engagements with an empathic other or to modify "the compensatory structures, by establishing more flexible and realistic ambitions, goals, and ideals" (Morrison, 1983, p. 307). We can see both these processes at play in my work with Luca as he takes in another way of experiencing and imagining himself through his interactions with me and is exposed to alternative conceptualizations of himself in relation to his history, his present, and his future possibilities. His primary experience and imaginings take place at a nonverbal level, whereas his consideration of alternative ideas occurs at the conscious level. I would contend that both are essential in our work with such fragile persons, helping to build the capacities for self-reflection in relation to others who may be similar and different in important ways while we also support the development of their capacities for affective self-regulation.

Notably, metacognitive failures underlie the deficits in empathic capacity that Kohut (1966) traced to parental narcissism. In today's world, we see deficits in parenting accruing across the generations, resulting in increasing narcissistic deficits in the population. This situation seems to lead to the type of lack of grounding Lifton (1995) referred to in his descriptions of the *protean self*. As societal demands continue to morph without sufficient grounding in custom and culture, we lose our moorings, inviting shame in relation to an empty self. Shame is a difficult emotion to experience, calling on the analyst to face their own shame and learn to first tolerate it and then be interested in it. This positioning enables us to be more empathic toward and interested in the other person's experience as well, helping them to move beyond the aversion to introspection that often accompanies shame.

In contrast to Kleinians and Kohutians, Rothstein (1979) viewed narcissism in relation to an unsuccessful effort to emerge as a separate self, resulting in feelings of separation anxiety, dependence, and loss. This leaves the person attached to an internal fantasy of oneness that is unsustainable in reality, but without the wherewithal to tolerate separateness, there is no path for development. Rothstein, too, highlighted the parental failures that result in narcissistic self-preoccupations and the urge to control the object. The lack of responsive engagement results in an unsatisfied need that can feel to the other person like a demand or a need for control, making it important, clinically, to respond to this demand empathically and also to recontextualize it by linking it to the unfulfilled need so we might legitimize the feeling in ways that attenuate the shame.

Rothstein (1979) highlighted the inevitable rage that accompanies this level of profound unfulfilled need and the fear, as we see with Luca, that the rage will utterly destroy any possibility of relationship. This fear becomes isolating in ways that magnify the feelings, at times—as with Luca—resulting in a desire for death as the only possible release. In this context, the child's defiance can be seen as a wish to vanquish the unloving frustrater. As Luca recalls fighting back with his father, we can recognize the anger and elation described by Rothstein as implicit in the narcissistic victory.

Luca links the end of this phase to a staggering moment when his father landed a blow to his head that literally stunned him. For Rothstein (1979), when a loving representation of the father is not internalized, "a tenuously internalized representation of an angry, jealous, potentially retaliatory castrator exists within the 'self-as-place'" (p. 46). This leaves the child with the sense that their autonomous strivings will result in annihilation. That cycle of anger at frustration and desire to overcome obstacles and achieve mastery has become so fraught with danger for Luca that it results in terror and feelings of fragmentation, resulting in symptoms of dissociation and the sense that he is losing his memory and even his mind. This type of cycle can keep vulnerable individuals caught in the narcissistic position unless they can encounter another person who can tolerate the interpersonal tensions sufficiently to help the person learn to reflect on them.

DISTINGUISHING BETWEEN NARCISSISTIC AND BORDERLINE CONDITIONS

In an attempt to distinguish between the narcissistic and borderline conditions, Meissner (1979) suggested that the narcissistic character tends to have greater ego deficits but greater cohesion than the borderline character, which tends toward fragmentation. Because of this greater cohesion, Meissner posited the narcissistic position as more highly developed. I think his theorizing goes in the wrong direction. In my experience, narcissism suggests a greater degree of psychopathology and an earlier developmental quandary.

My thinking on this is based on clinical observations. As noted in the previous chapter, those who might be classed as borderline have unstable object relations but are related, whereas narcissists appear related but tend to experience others as merely characters in a drama rather than persons in their own right. My view would seem to be in line with Meissner's (1979) depiction of the more exploitative narcissism. For him, it is only at the antisocial or psychopathic end of the spectrum that narcissistic individuals fall within the borderline spectrum. His depiction of more needy and demanding presentations seems in line with Rosenfeld's (1987) and Kernberg's (2014) depictions of thick-skinned narcissists.

Looking further into Meissner's (1979) theorizing, we can recognize the greater instability in the borderline position but can also consider that the personality that is unstable not only lends itself to greater fragmentation but also, potentially, to growth. The narcissistic personality may be more cohesive, but the relationship is to the self and not to others. In this way, there is an inherent resistance to any growth or change, particularly to ideas offered by another. In interpreting, therefore, we need to be mindful of the tendency to oppose any thoughts that might intrude from another's mind. This recognition helps us orient our interpretations within the frame of the person's needs and interests given that anything that pushes from the outside will likely be experienced as either irrelevant or dangerous.

Luca, for example, often experiences my words as noise. As he rouses himself to greater awareness, he realizes he has no idea what I just said. In those moments, I recognize, out loud, that likely I have gone too far and that we are learning what is too much and what is not enough. I do this to counter the more familiar position he takes of being the one who always fails and is always at the hands of the uncaring other.

In his attempts to explore commonalities and differences between these positions, Meissner (1979) separated out a narcissistic dimension characterized by "superiority and grandiosity in one direction . . . [and] inferiority and shame-filled insignificance and worthlessness in the other" (p. 194). He also posited an aggressive dimension that "expresses itself in terms of polar attributes of hateful, evil, and powerful destructiveness on the one hand, and impotent, helpless, weak vulnerability on the other" (Meissner, 1979, p. 194). Notably, he suggested, these polarities are always linked. If the insignificance is coming forward, the grandiosity is never far behind.

Although these polarities are present in less extreme form in those with less severe psychopathology, what characterizes the narcissistic personality is that self-maintenance depends on preserving the narcissistic introjects. For Meissner, the borderline carries the additional burden of an aggressor–victim introject, something we see in Luca. I am not convinced, however, that the borderline disorders are, as has traditionally been seen, more severe than the narcissistic ones. This remains an area to be further considered.

To aid our efforts, André Green (2002) introduced the ideas of positive and negative narcissism, reminding us that "the convincing evidence of the value of this concept depends on the coherence of the descriptions and their match to clinical issues" (p. 632). From Green's perspective, there is a narcissism that aims toward unity and oneness versus one that aims toward nothingness and moves toward psychic death. He suggested that positive narcissism "impoverishes relationships with objects [but] it is less destructive than negative narcissism . . . which aims at the subject's self impoverishment nearly to the point of annihilation" (Green, 2002, p. 637). Luca's efforts toward engagement helped him learn to tolerate failures sufficiently to continue to work at building relationships. As he learned more about his internal experience, he was able to also apply his insights toward better understanding others, which began to add quality and dimension to his encounters.

THE ANALYTIC CHALLENGE

Beyond questions of definition, there is the issue of how we work with such people clinically. Bromberg (1983) suggested that as field theory perspectives have come to the fore, we can see how deficits in early experience "can lead to structural pathology of the representational world itself . . . [leading to] character disorders traditionally considered untreatable by psychoanalysis" (p. 360). Viewing narcissism as a function of waylaid development in relation to a personality that has prematurely and inflexibly coalesced in ways that make it hard to use others in the service of growth invites an explicit focus on the development of a therapeutic relationship.

For Bromberg, the first challenge for the analyst is to become a person in their own right with individuals whose stability depends on the illusion of self-sufficiency. Treatment, he said, requires a view of the "analytic situation as an open, empathic, interpersonal matrix within which the patient's representational world has maximal opportunity to become systematically repatterned and restructured at increasingly higher developmental levels"

(Bromberg, 1983, p. 369). The relative lack of an observing ego in such persons makes it difficult to consider possibilities.

In accordance with the principle offered by Levenson (1978)—that "it may not be the truth arrived at as much as the manner of arriving at the truth which is the essence of therapy" (p. 16)—and also with Lacan's (1964/1977e) ideas regarding the stumblings through which meanings are revealed, Bromberg (1983) suggested that it is the analyst's flexibility within the analytic setting that affords the possibility of change: "The analyst is committed to an approach rather than being bound to a technique" (p. 371). In line with Kohut, Bromberg recognized that progress requires the development of a sufficient internal structure on which subsequent growth can rest and the belief that such structure can be built. In being freed from the grip of "the narcissistic transference as the primary source of ego-sustenance," there is the possibility for "personality growth to be self-perpetuating; that is, for the patient to internalize the analyst's analytic function as an aspect of his ego autonomy" (Bromberg, 1983, p. 372).

Much like optimal parenting, Bromberg (1983) noted the need for the analyst's interactions to be moderated by sufficient empathy to allow engagement and by sufficient anxiety to allow growth, suggesting that severe narcissism does not

> require a different form of treatment; it requires a greater sophistication and personal maturity on the part of the analyst in adapting to the patient's shifting need for affirmation in a way which enriches rather than contaminates the analytic field. (p. 377)

Unlike Kohut's focus on mirroring, Bromberg (1983) suggested that the early stages of the work should include interpretations that are grounded in an empathic recognition of the person's story as they have experienced it. In this way, there is an invitation to the observing ego without a direct challenge to the resistances. This stance is particularly important because of the intense vulnerability to shame (Bateman, 1998), which tends to further inhibit the development of relational ties.

Bromberg's view is in line with my own: that what we term *narcissistic psychopathology* points to an impasse in social and emotional development that leaves the person managing self-esteem needs in ways that preclude further growth. Our challenge, then, is to provide an environment in which the person's self-perceptions can be challenged in ways that allow the possibility of an alternative perspective so that we might "facilitate the acceptance and integration of unpleasant but accurate experience of oneself that would otherwise be discarded because it is too discordant with one's interpersonal self representation" (Bromberg, 1983, p. 383). Crucial to these efforts is our ability to recognize, through our countertransference reactions to the alternations between grandiosity and vulnerability, that we are dealing with narcissistic vulnerability (Bernardi & Eidlin, 2018).

Aiding us in our empathic engagement with such individuals is our recognition that narcissistic difficulties are linked to the type of complex trauma and neglect we have been discussing. Gerzi (2005) highlighted two types of repetition compulsion in those who have experienced trauma: One is the recurrence of the traumatic experience; the other is the recurrence of what he describes as the *hole* left by it. This notion of the hole helps me in my conceptualization of Luca's difficulties by considering how he constitutes this hole. It suggests that his not-remembering and avoidance of precisely the experiences that might repair his damaged interpersonal relationships are a function of what has become a primary defense against narcissistic injury. Not-knowing smooths the edges of the traumatic reexperiencing but does so at the price of growth.

When working with trauma, clinicians need to be able recurrently to come back to life. Concepts such as Bion's (1992) notions of dreaming the session can help free up our unconscious mind and attenuate the affective intensity that can obscure meanings. Affirming our faith in the primary process underbelly of experienced meaning helps afford sufficient play within ourselves to consider how our unconscious may relate to the unconscious of the other. Profoundly being-with without becoming lost can be a challenge, although at times we need to become lost for meanings to begin to take hold.

Allowing ourselves to become lost within the transference/countertransference matrix helps us to be present with whatever might evolve, which is in line with Parsons's (2007) recognition that our openness may "evoke capacities, and functions, in the analyst's psyche, of which he was not previously aware" (p. 1453). There is a compelling truth to nonverbal meanings (Coltart, 1992; Shapira-Berman, 2022), making it important to allow ourselves to experience them with the other person and allow meanings to evolve, working at the level of Winnicott's (1971) playing as doing. At that level, our statements become interpretations that *touch*, in Sirois's (2012) terms, rather than those that might intend to teach. The crucial issue here is to try to stay at the level of experience so that the person's thoughts can evolve in relation to that experience, which is in line with Winnicott's (1971) suggestion that the play "*be spontaneous and not compliant or acquiescent*, if psychotherapy is to be done" (p. 51).

As we saw in Chapter 6, playful being-with helps to develop the person's metacognitive capacities as verbal language is attached to nonverbal experience. When the person's early environment has not provided sufficient foundation, the potential space afforded by the analytic environment can help the person to encounter their own truths and learn from their own experience. Our trust in the growing relationship helps to build that sense of trust and safety in the other person as well, providing containment that can help sustain us through the bumps that lie ahead. As Winnicott (1963/1965) said,

> I have tried to state the need . . . to recognize . . . the non-communicating central self, for ever immune from the reality principle, and for ever silent. Here communication is not non-verbal; it is, like the music of the spheres, absolutely personal. It belongs to being alive. And in health, it is out of this that communication naturally arises. (p. 191)

LOOKING FORWARD

At just the point when Luca began to get traction in his treatment and decided to postpone going back to school so he might consolidate his learning, his parents pulled the plug on his treatment. Luca literally fell down the drain, reverting to sleepless nights and days hidden under the covers. He would make it to our last session of the week but was missing everything else, including working on discharge planning with his social worker.

This dilemma marks the lack of reflective capacity in the family that has been part of the developmental context in which narcissistic impasses occur. Our considerations thus far show the narcissistic dilemma in relation to a future that cannot be imagined because the tools through which to realize it have not been constructed. The treatment, therefore, is most useful when it helps to build the reflective capacities of the person so that problems can be recognized within the contexts in which they occur. Such considerations enable a looking forward in which a different future might be imagined because there are ideas regarding what might be needed to build a path toward that future.

Luca had learned to rely on his treatment team to provide a containing structure when affect intensified and meanings broke down. Before a week's break for vacation, we were able to get to the point at which he could recognize that his collapse was a message that he was not ready to leave. Notably, he directed this message to his treaters, who had no power in the matter, rather than to his parents, who did. When confronted with these data, this recognition seemed to rouse him, and he attended his next psychiatry appointment in full. The psychiatrist told Luca that he was forcing people to give up on him. Luca was ashamed but accepted the all-too-familiar interpretation. His interim therapist tried to help him make meaning of the message. The psychiatrist's interpretation touched a familiar wound in ways that precluded insight in the moment but also marked something important, enabling Luca to hold the moment in mind (see Sirois, 2012). Coming to meet with his treatment team to discuss his failures to show up, Luca spoke with a great deal of shame about the importance of that interpretation and how helpful it had been. In the moment, I felt embarrassed that I had failed to deliver that seminal message.

In our next session, I wondered about the enactment, and whether my shame was a concordant countertransference reaction. I inquired into his experience. "You give me room to think," he said. The following day, I wondered aloud about his actual experience of the team meeting. "The psychiatrist felt like my mother," he said.

"I'm wondering if you actually agreed with her or if it was more in the order of a performance you felt demanded of you," I said.

He thought for a bit and smiled—a genuine smile. "The latter," he said.

This interchange helped me get my bearings in the transference/counter-transference matrix, leaving me freer to engage. We talked about the work ahead—between us and after discharge—so that we might consolidate his learning and factor in his needs, his feelings, his desires to actively use internal and external resources and fight for the kind of life he wants.

"When I go down that hole," he says, "I forget. I can't even see anything."

"If you start forgetting," I say, "contact me, and I will remind you."

To be alone in the world is a terrible thing. In our roles as clinicians, we find ourselves in odd positions with those seeking assistance. There is a limit to what we can do. But we can be there when a light is needed in the darkness, so they can find their thread once again and keep living.

CONCLUSION

The narcissist lives in fear of the truth that will reveal their ultimate smallness and insufficiency. Our job is to recognize this fear empathically, hold it, and speak to it in ways that recognize its legitimacy as one stopping point in a journey that is ongoing. As we have seen, in working with such vulnerable individuals, we need to be able to ride the waves of aggressive contempt and wounded vulnerability to build relational resilience within the person and the relationship. In doing such work, it is important to keep in mind the emptiness at the core of the narcissistic individual's world. We need heroes. And mentors. People who believe in us. When that function was not filled early on, it becomes difficult to believe in the believer. That difficulty results in a terrible isolation toward which we must be empathic if we are to persist in our efforts to cross the divides.

In this chapter, we discussed how we might work with individuals whose metacognitive development has been stunted by insufficiently attuned parental attention. The narcissistic position may be seen as a last bastion in the effort to sustain engagement in an interpersonal world one does not understand. In the next chapter, I turn to what Lacan (1955–1956/1993) termed *the psychotic position*. In this way, he stressed that psychosis marks not an inherent deficit, but rather a position someone has taken when they cannot bridge the gaps between their psychic reality and the interpersonal world.

11 PSYCHOSIS

In Chapter 10, we considered obsessive defenses as a desperate way to hold on to one's place in a world that seems alien and alienating. In this chapter, let us look at the psychotic position as one in which the link has been lost between the person's psychic reality and that of the consensual world. Psychoanalysts recognize that a story is being told through symptoms that seem strange precisely because the person is alienated from the consensual social world, a position in striking contrast to medicalized views. Davoine and Gaudillière (2004), for example, highlighted ways in which psychotic symptoms mark a story that cannot otherwise be told, leaving the person holding on to meanings essential to their own self-knowledge but inexpressible in consensual language. These authors suggested that it is within the transference/countertransference matrix that meanings that have been inscribed in time can register in the clinician in ways that enable the person themselves to further mentalize the meanings they carry. This would seem to be the territory of Abraham and Torok's (1975/1994, Chapter 9) intergenerational haunting, in which *encrypted secrets* carry the shame associated with the trauma in ways that haunt future generations. Apprey (2024) described this haunting as occurring when trauma is carried across the

https://doi.org/10.1037/0000455-012
Echoes of Trauma: Meaning and Identity in Psychoanalysis, by M. Charles

generations but cannot be symbolized, integrated, and worked through in terms of *transgenerational errands,* noting ways in which a person may become the symptom-bearer for the family.

This rich history of theorizing makes a psychoanalytic lens valuable in opening up channels for development for those who may be further marginalized when viewed from a medical diagnostic perspective. From Freud's (Breuer & Freud, 1895/1955) "archeological dig" to Lacan's (1964/1977e) recognition of some of the hazards of that digging, there has been a growing recognition of the possibilities that a psychoanalytic perspective can offer. Stepping back from our attempts to "understand" as a way of controlling or eradicating symptoms invites the person to confront their own impediments to growth and begin to think about their troubles with another person who can meet them where they are. This stance helps provide a space in which the person might learn and grow through encounters with their own unconscious. Bion (1962) warned against the hazard of the *received knowledge* that can preclude learning from our own experience. Taking seriously his admonitions against becoming lost in our own memory or desire (Bion, 1967a), along with Lacan's (1964/1977e) warnings against becoming lost in the desire of the other, we see that we can spoil the space with our own investments, reminding us to lean in with our interest and lean back with our intentions.

PSYCHOSIS AS A MARGINALIZED POSITION

In this work, we do well to learn the lessons from the literature on attachment and parent–child relationships that reminds us to have our eye on the person who is developing so that we recognize and keep in mind their needs, feelings, interests, and desires. In this way, the consulting room becomes a space in which the person might come to know themselves (Bion, 1990). As noted in Chapter 2, self-knowledge is hindered when the person has been so marginalized that they cannot find themselves in relation to others in meaningful ways. Often, the truth-teller in the family is cast out and left to flounder while the rest of the family tries to keep their own blind eyes intact. Although a not-knowing is legitimately at the core of any encounter with another being (Bion, 1967b), there is also an ethical imperative to heed the call from someone's otherness across that gap without trying to elide precisely what is unique and particular to them (Lévinas, 1974/1991a).

In any form of caregiving, there is a risk that whatever we are blind to will undermine the other person's developmental efforts. Psychoanalysis affirms our inevitable blindness, reminding us that the unconscious is alive and well in each of us, guiding our movements in ways we might be able to recognize but can never entirely anticipate or control. This recognition invites the clinician to provide a space in which embodied knowledge might grow; to lean in with our reflective attention and curiosity such that possible meanings might be considered; and to have faith in the process, as Coltart (1992) encouraged. Transference is ubiquitous, and enactments are a form of embodied exploration. We need to be able to tolerate the repeated encounters, bumps, and collisions that reveal our own fantasies but also allow glimpses of the person who is ambivalently trying to find and conceal themselves from view. Recognizing the precarity of this process can help us to lean back with our theories and judgments so that the person might find their own path. Working at tolerating the bumps and bruises and remaining open to what might be revealed help provide the conditions under which learning might occur.

Recognizing ways in which development is impeded when parents are not sufficiently available to their children is crucial to this view of psychoanalysis. Taking seriously Winnicott's (1971) admonition to recognize the particularity of the child and their needs helps us find ourselves in relation to the challenges faced by those who seek treatment. Lacan (1964/1977e) highlighted the tendency to defer to the desire of the other that is both a prerequisite and an obstacle to human development, depending on what is at stake. Early development proceeds in relation to the person who meets our needs, holds our hand, and, optimally, stands at the right distance and believes in us as we take our first independent steps, neither too close in nor too far away. The clinician must be willing to find the right distance through which to support the other person's development while not standing in the way, to recognize the story being told of failed or thwarted development, and to look for places where what has been foreclosed might be reopened and worked through. Both Bion (1990) and Lacan (1964/1977e) warned against the hazards of our presumptions of privileged knowledge, and Laplanche (1995, 1997) reminded us that the shadows of those presumptions fall hard, most insidiously when we are not aware of them.

In this volume, we have traced how psychoanalysis helps us recognize ways in which the unconscious holds the patterns of meanings that inform and undergird an individual's life, mind, and ways of being (Charles, 2002b). Again, we find Lacan and Bion pointing in the same direction: in the particularity of the individual being Lacan (1975–1976/2016) recognized in his exegesis of the sinthome and in the ubiquity of the dream space highlighted by the Bionian field theorists (Civitarese, 2006; Ferro, 2009). Recognizing the potency of these patterned meanings shows how the unconscious offers form as a vehicle through which hidden truths might reveal themselves. This recognition opposes our tendency to simplify, concretize, and diminish the richness and profundity of the embodied meanings through which identity is formed.

From this perspective, psychoanalysis, like all profound change, is fundamentally disruptive, even *catastrophic*, to use Bion's (1965, 1970) term. This disruption provides an alternate lens for investigating the nexus between subjectivity and the contexts in which it is evolving. Rather than positioning ourselves as interpreters of entrenched meanings, we can open up possibilities "by disrupting and disorganizing" congealed meanings so that the "functions become clearer, including its functions for us" (Parker, 2005, p. 177). We must be willing to have our own ideas disrupted as we try to imagine the other person's experience sufficiently to more fully meet them where they are. From that place, we might find a way through together.

As we have seen, perhaps the greatest catastrophe occurs when parents cannot mark the child's experience as worth orienting toward, inviting the child to be not the legitimate subject of the conversation, but rather the object of scrutiny, irritation, devotion, or blame. If we think in terms of Winnicott's (1971) depiction that the baby needs to look into the mother's eyes to discover themselves through their reflection there, we can see the tragedy of the child who encounters empty, preoccupied eyes. But, as we have seen, the eyes of adoration or disdain can also provide a misrecognition that derails development rather than affording the beginnings of a stable foundation.

When the parents are not stable within themselves, the press toward moving on rather than coming to terms with difficult experiences leaves parents less available as resources in the crucial function of identity development that depends on the child's ability to emerge as the focus of the parents' interest in a moment of need. In turn, the clinician needs to be sufficiently stable in their being that they can tolerate their own dysregulation and move toward reflection in difficult moments in ways that invite the other person to do the same. Our ideas about mirror neurons help us hold steady in our negotiations with difficult moments, affirming the importance of modeling truth and integrity as we locate ourselves in relation to our own feelings and in relation to the other (Gallese, 2009, 2014).

The attachment literature has highlighted different ways that children react to insufficient parenting. Some become clingier, whereas others reactively detach in ways that impede their ability to find their way into the social matrix. I continue to be haunted by an image from a presentation by attachment researcher Stephen Suomi (2011) of an ape clinging to a tree, looking lost, alone, and terrified. I see that look in lost young people I encounter who have been unable to find their way into the social world. Without sufficient grounding to be at home within oneself, it can be impossible to find a home in the world. At times, these individuals find respite and rescue in a psychoanalysis that affords them the possibility of self-discovery within a matrix of recognition and respectful care.

THE LOST CHILD: GROTSTEIN'S *ORPHANS OF THE REAL*

Lacan (1955–1956/1993) usefully pulled away from reified ideas regarding diagnostic categories to locate psychosis as a position. For Grotstein (1995), psychosis marks an *orphan of the real* "*whose illness can be described as the result of a premature awakening from the protective blanket of innocence*" (p. 287). To not further disenfranchise those who have become profoundly lost in relation to self and others, it is important to recognize the developmental contexts in which such difficulties arise. In this chapter, I consider the plight of such individuals, who are caught between the characterization that is evolving within family and culture, and their own needs and feelings as they experience them.

In contrast to biomedical views of psychosis, psychoanalytic theory, clinical experience, and personal reports have suggested that people are driven mad by their experience and that respectful engagement is crucial to well-being, particularly for those whose perspective is idiosyncratic or those without the power to advocate for themselves (O'Loughlin & Charles, 2015). We are all born dependent on others for the care and meaning-making that inform identity development. If caregivers are interested in our particularity, they can help us find our way rather than lose ourselves in our accommodations. Idiosyncrasy, however, can leave us off-balance, and even small differences affect our sense of self-in-world.

Born into a family with greater respect for facts than feelings, I had an uneasy entry into the world of diagnoses and medical meanings. I could always see something of myself in textbooks and those seeking treatment, which, I think, made me a better clinician but also increased my wariness of the harm that can be done by misunderstanding. That caution invites me to recognize how profoundly diagnostic utility depends on the clinician's vision and integrity, inviting us to track carefully the details, trajectories, and affective resonances of each person's story and to be very interested in what they are trying to accomplish and where they encounter obstacles, including with us. Someone once told me that our job as parents is to help our children with their problems and that *we* will be one of their problems. I think this is true for the clinician as well.

In those early days, I yearned for external validation for the facts I discovered through my feelings. On that journey, I found in Bion a father who, like my own, came from that far remote other side of the brain in which categories and "reason" prevail. Bion (1962), however, helped to combat my father's indictment of me as a "messy kid whose intelligence was wasted" on her by desperately trying to get to the place where I live: that land of primary, embodied experience that I now think of as the aesthetic realm. Please note the irony in needing a man to validate the woman's perspective, something we continue to struggle with despite all we have learned. I encourage you to take this as a cautionary tale to remind you to try to notice when you are letting someone else's "knowledge" override your own. In this work, we need to be able to bring our own voice and being to the table and encounter the bumps and bruises rather than avoid them. That is how we learn from our experience, and we cannot invite those we work with to take that ride unless we are willing to do so as well. Nowhere are these fundamental truths more at stake than in our work with those who struggle with psychosis.

Bion's (1967b) clinical work was grounded in his early experiences with individuals struggling to find words through which to symbolize their experience. In later writings, we see him working toward a recognition of how catastrophic major change can feel, highlighting the eternal choice point between growth and evasion (Bion, 1977). The realm we term "psychotic" represents one cliff we encounter as we move toward truths that glimmer beyond the knowledge we have received. This cliff becomes a fundamental reckoning point for those drawn by the desire to create meaning, which, in Milner's (1987) words, wells from "an internal necessity for inner organization, pattern, coherence, the basic need to discover identity in difference without which experience becomes chaos" (p. 84). Milner's ideas are grounded in her own work with a woman whose traumatic underpinnings became symbolized through the drawings that eventually enabled the two of them to find words through which to build the narrative that helped to establish for the woman a more solid identity (Milner, 1969).

IDIOSYNCRASY AND MARGINALIZATION

Lacan (1955–1956/1993) spoke of psychosis as a position rather than a disorder, a marginalized position in which speech becomes distorted and it is difficult to hold meanings between people. My clinical experience speaks to the validity of this perspective: that people are driven mad when sense cannot be made from their experience and that psychotic symptoms tell a story that cannot otherwise be told. Context is everything. Cultural values affect how human qualities are perceived, but marginalization tends to be experienced as a mark of personal deficit rather than a social problem. Countering that tendency, psychoanalysis helps to contextualize character by viewing symptoms in relation to the story being told. This stance is crucial with extreme states in which the possibility of holding meaning is critical.

When there are meanings that cannot be parsed within the family system or the cultural context, symptoms mark the forbidden meanings in disguised form. In families in which the sequelae of trauma is carried across the generations, inconsistent parenting leaves children both vulnerable and dependent (Liotti, 2004; Main & Hesse, 1990), inviting a "madness" that is socially constructed, driven by the desire to avoid facing difficult truths. Such socially constructed madness can become the inherited legacy of the symptom-bearer, a gift to a family that cannot tolerate knowing prohibited intergenerational truths (Apprey, 2024, Davoine & Gaudillière, 2004). When meanings cannot be parsed, it is difficult to make sense from embodied experience, alienating us not only from others but also, more terribly, from ourselves.

Disorganized attachment, schizophrenia, and posttraumatic stress disorder are all diagnostic terms lodged within a system of medical meanings. However, qualities deemed problematic through that lens may be prized by cultures that consider them *extra*ordinary (Johnson, 1981). For example, the experience of "oneness" can be found in both mystical and psychotic experience (Heriot-Maitland, 2008), an immersion into a primary unity that also typifies the aesthetic moment (Milner, 1987). The profound openness to experience and the capacity for absorption integral to creative engagement can be capsized by fear and misunderstanding. Cultural definitions held within the social structure can either contain the person or alienate them in ways that may drive them mad (Brown & Charles, 2019a, 2019b). Notably, the limits in understanding of those defining such meanings can alienate us from qualities that have deep and profound social and human value, and therefore from ourselves and from one another. Our fear of the unknown can lead us to founder the developmental efforts and creative capacities of those very seekers who might otherwise open up possibilities for us all.

CLINICAL ILLUSTRATIONS AND SOCIAL CONTEXT

Let us consider a few clinical illustrations to contextualize our exploration. First is a young man in his mid-twenties who considered himself to be a "mad" painter: only able to paint during frenzied periods in the middle of the night. His painting instructor said he was not a mad painter, but rather a gifted artist who had trouble finding his way into painting without the ritual he had developed. Believing that there was a forced choice between sanity and painting, the young man quit treatment. We can hope that, at some point, he revisited these questions sufficiently to have been able to paint and also build a life.

We can also consider the daughter of a disturbed mother and well-intentioned but distant father. The daughter became distressed in early adolescence at encountering erotic feelings considered damnable within the tight constraints of her religious community. Driven mad by forces she could neither control nor tolerate, the institutions she turned to told her she was psychotic and treated her accordingly. Some years later, in her mid-twenties, she found herself at the Austen Riggs Center, where we take a stand regarding trying to make meaning from symptoms rather than merely trying to make them go away. This woman credits this institution that treated her like a person with likely saving her life. Although she came to the limits of what medical treatment could offer, she had recovered her dignity as a human being and was able to build her own resources through diligent devotion to self-care and personal and spiritual growth. We can wonder what her path might have been if she had been nested within a religious community that valued her idiosyncrasy and truth-seeking and preserved a protective space for her efforts at growth.

A third example is a young man in his late twenties who, discovering the term *schizoid* and feeling that this was a lexicon that recognized his particular difficulties, sought psychoanalytic treatment. He, too, worked diligently at personal growth, using many of the strategies used by the young woman mentioned previously, including engagement in various spiritual practices in the service of truth-seeking. Never having been diagnosed within the lexicon of medical science left him freer to make his own meanings from the visionary experiences that ensued from his spiritual practice.

We also have an intellectually gifted young woman in her early thirties who became derailed in adolescence, unable to sustain life at university despite her capacities. Her family valiantly tried to support her in her struggles but were perplexed by the impasse at which she found herself and frustrated at her seeming inability to manage ostensibly simple tasks of daily living. When she finally began to recover memories of early sexual abuse, this idea was so impossible for the family to face that they decided she must be psychotic. At that juncture, their "loving" attempts to "help" her were so contaminated by their insistence on her craziness that her family became utterly lost to her. Her efforts at recovery entailed working at building a story in which the loving parents of her childhood could so utterly and profoundly fail her. It was a long and painful process, which required learning to accept and meet her parents in the places where they were rather than insist that they meet her in her own.

We also have examples of people who pursued the path of truth-seeking and spiritual growth more directly, recognized by their communities as exemplary. We have all likely met such people who seem to emanate a peaceful wisdom in ways that can be soothing and even inspirational to those around them. Some have previously been deemed psychotic. The working through of our personal demons can take many forms, and there is likely a price for any path. At some level, we are all utterly alone, and yet we are social creatures, profoundly dependent on one another. When we encounter such a person in our consulting rooms, what may matter most is to be respectful of the person and their struggles so that we might support them in their journey forward.

In each of these examples, there was some inner drive or truth that led the person on an uneasy path, often including moments of visionary experience. The unknown presents both allure and fear. Current medical views of psychosis represent a particular conceptualization—and pathologization—of experiences formerly linked with healing and religion (Johnson, 1981; Littlewood & Dein, 2013). And yet, extreme events have also been held in high esteem (Johnson, 1981; Koss-Chioino, 2003). Meanings are inevitably contextual, inviting us to consider more carefully links between what is termed *madness* and the contexts within which the symptoms are being read. Social isolation and marginalization can render the person deviant and mark their communication as invalid (Vardy & Kaplan, 2008). And yet, much like Bion's (1970) depiction of the relationship between the establishment and the mystic, the person who speaks from the margins may be offering messages that are relevant to other members of the community, affording vicarious benefits to the extent that they are encountered with interest (Cook, 2004). Pathologizing such experiences distances us from potential learning about our own humanity.

As we sit with those who find themselves situated outside consensual culture, it is important to try to hear the call of truth and enter as empathically as we can into resonance with the experience. From that place, we are in a better position to find links between their words and experience and our own, and to have a sense of where the difficulties arise for them. It is difficult to witness extreme suffering, and yet, in such respectful engagement, the person who has become lost might begin to locate themselves in relation to the life story that could not previously be formulated. Human development depends on those unique individuals who reach out into the darkness and help us all move beyond the places where convention limits our growth

(Bion, 1990). Rather than fearing that we might mistake craziness for creativity, perhaps we would do better to cherish idiosyncrasy where we find it and try to assist those we encounter in getting their bearings and finding their way—and, in the process, also learn that each person has their own gifts and stories to share.

PSYCHOANALYSIS, TRAUMA, AND SOCIAL CONTEXT

Psychosis often marks trauma that needs to be remembered but has not yet been symbolized and so, as Winnicott (1963/1965) suggested, needs to be experienced for the first time within the transference. Psychoanalysis helps provide a frame through which we can be attentive to the various language registers (Ferrari, 2004) through which these stories might be told, particularly when latent meanings lurk beneath the surface presentation. That perspective invites us to consider how our clinical minds might be informed by the embodied resonances we experience in the countertransference and the patterns of the stories we are offered. Bion's Grid (Bion, 1977/1989), discussed in Chapter 1, insists that meaning is found not so much in the content of a story, but rather in the functions being performed (Charles, 2002a). From that framework, we can consider the story within the story.

People often come to us suffering from the impact of their life story but committed to a narrative in which children are expected to flourish in an environment largely empty of sustenance. We encounter the striking difference between the fantasy of parental love and care and what may be needed in real time, perhaps during a moment of crisis. We see how the person struggles in relation to the bonds of a love that does not recognize them sufficiently as an individual to allow them to grow.

The attachment literature has shown that if early engagements build sufficient self-regulatory capacities, then the child is free to learn. If not, then that fundamental instability conditions all later learning and experience (e.g., Fonagy et al., 2002), also impeding the development of the epistemic trust on which human relations depend (Fonagy & Allison, 2023). Disruptions become traumatic because they derail. To survive, the child learns to orient to the parent's needs and feelings rather than their own. Even when they rail against the parent's lack or limits, they have internalized a sense of internal badness or deficit in relation to the accusations they experience from the parent.

Because the antecedents are more difficult to discover, inherited trauma is more likely to haunt us than trauma that is experienced directly. The untold story courses through us in the rhythms of affect-laden meanings. These embodied, enigmatic messages speak directly but cannot be translated because our parents and their ancestors had not been able to work through the trauma sufficiently to pass along the keys to those meanings. Haunted by their own histories of death and deprivation, parents develop narratives that attenuate their own distress. But distress that is displaced and avoided becomes a pitfall, a hazard for future generations that unfolds in the lives of the children (Apprey, 2024). When the ancestral history has been encrypted, development is foreclosed (Charles, 2019; Derrida, 1996). When the keys to the secret meanings are lost in an archive that has become impenetrable, the secrecy itself can be perversely satisfying. The satisfaction depends on an essential not-knowing in the dyad, resulting in an impossible enmeshment between parent and child. Unresolved, these types of secrets further alienate us from ourselves and from one another, as we see unfold so disastrously in the lives of those deemed "psychotic."

Parental failure to be sufficiently separate to recognize the child's legitimate needs undergirds this type of tragedy. Failure is experienced as shameful, and, in people's stories, we see not only failures in the parental roles but also a failure to hold steady against external pressures. Social acceptance often comes at the price of self-denial, thereby tainting identity with the shame inherent in that denial. Shame breaks the interpersonal bond, making it difficult to encounter the type of repair that might be found through human connection. In Lévinas's (1974/1991a) terms, the human "face summons me to my obligation and judges me" (cited in Lawton, 2005, p. 214). But parents' failures to come to grips with their own histories impede their ability to recognize the needs and feelings of their children, leaving the children at odds with themselves, searching for a place in a world into which they never have been truly invited.

In my work at the Austen Riggs Center, I have had the privilege of being able to work with families along with the individual family member seeking treatment. This work affords a vantage point through which to see the collisions of disparate stories in real time and the possibility of helping family members to hear one another's stories more lovingly without the full force of their defenses in play. We all hide and displace aspects of self as a way of not facing our own negative self-identity. From a Kleinian perspective, our life stories provide a means for projecting bad feelings outward, trying to keep them at a safe distance (Klein, 1946). Optimally, this distance affords the possibility of working with difficult truths—taming them, perhaps. However, when this maneuver fails, the parent's failures impede the child's ability to integrate bits of their own life experience into a coherent narrative. As we know all too well from clinical experience, these disowned bits inevitably persecute us from without, constant reminders of precisely what we are denying. When parents turn a blind eye to children's needs that conflict with their own desires, these acts of betrayal obstruct the redemptive potential inherent in the human encounter (Lévinas, 1969/1991b).

There is a universality to trauma in that we all commit little acts of murder that deny aspects of reality to those around us. This very truth, however, makes a demand on us to try to fight against the desire to turn a blind eye, to look even harder in difficult moments. Caruth (1991) suggested that "history, like the trauma, is never simply one's own, that history is precisely the way we are implicated in each other's traumas" (p. 192). A loving acceptance of our own limits helps us in our invitation to others to accept their own.

CASE ILLUSTRATION

When individuals who are lodged in the psychotic position by family and culture enter our consulting rooms, we have the opportunity to invite a different ending, one in which parent and child (of whatever age) can each survive and perhaps find themselves and one another in the process. We know that change has an impact within the family structure, so augmenting individual intensive psychotherapy with family work affords opportunities to help family members adapt positively to the changes taking place. These encounters can help family members face their troubles together rather than become further mired in defensive maneuvers against their ongoing suffering (Charles, 2023). It is difficult for well-intentioned parents to face ways in which their child's needs have not been met. And yet, it is precisely in orienting to the family member's experienced reality that healing might happen. Recognition of the legitimacy of each person's feelings and perspective invites each into a more textured understanding of the other as we try to orient to each individual's experience and empathically engage with them in their struggles. Crucial in this regard is recognition of the concreteness of metaphor in psychosis, requiring the clinician to be respectful of the gap between the other person's relationship to the metaphor and our own.

Identity forms within the context of consensual meanings built in respectful, intimate engagement with one another. When the family has been unable to integrate an individual into the family story, a psychoanalytic perspective can provide an arena in which what has been forced into the realm of concrete metaphor can be reflected on and integrated into a story in which each person's perspective can be recognized as legitimate and meaningful.

I think, for example, of a young man in his late thirties who described himself as Atlas, holding up the world. This was the position in which he found himself in his family of origin, standing accused of being the source of whatever suffering prevailed. Paul had been wounded by what felt like a forced exclusion from the world of human beings, driving him ever further from the dangerous realm of feelings and embodied meanings. When I first met him, he had been so distanced by his suffering that he could only speak from the realm of ideation. Our work entailed traversing the gap between his precise meanings and my embodied sensibilities, often bumping quite jarringly against disjunctions between the two. Our growing ability to meet in the middle helped Paul to recognize the hazards of the relatively rigid code of ethics he had adopted, facilitating forays into the discomfortingly messy world of human feelings.

As Paul learned to accept his own humanity as well as others' needs and limits as legitimate, he slowly began to find his own place within the social surround and within his family. His family members, in turn, slowly learned to hear Paul's sincere and poignant attempts to engage rather than become defensively polarized by his idiosyncratic phrasings. My own challenge was to recognize the good intentions of family members and ways in which each could become hurt and hurting while I tried to invite greater reflectivity through my speech rather than merely inciting greater reactivity. This work required recurrently taking a stand for the importance of each person being able to get their bearings and find their way, in the process learning more about self and other and recognizing that each has their own perspective. Opening up to the other's perspective not only affords greater insight but also enlivens the whole. Crucial in this regard was my own willingness to be bumped into and found lacking or offensive and to take these accusations seriously, reflect on them, and try to respond empathically to the injured party. Modeling mentalization is pivotal in this work.

When the family cannot tolerate the demands made by the child whose needs go unmet, the child must either capitulate to the family's limits or go rogue, attempting to safeguard their core identity by remaining outside the bounds of consensual reality. This situation results in an impasse in which the price of "care" seems to be annihilation. One such moment occurred when Paul's mother became increasingly distressed as she became more empathic to her son's distress. She seemed to catch herself, announcing defiantly that she would not be taken in by the forces of darkness. At that point, she seemed to position herself even more firmly in her own story of a family history of joy and gladness, leaving her son alone in his private hell.

Left positioned, once again, as the source of all badness, Paul and his mother were left caught in what Lacan (1964/1977e) termed the realm of the Imaginary, the personal universe each of us inhabits—apperceptive rather than perceptive—even when it seems to match with the experience of others. The clinician hopes to support the ambivalent urge to break through the confines of the Imaginary—the transference relationship—into something more authentic. Such engagement both demands and makes possible a different level of truth-telling but can require facing what feels like catastrophic change when we break through the limits of the story as it has been told.

So, opposing his mother's preference for a romantic fantasy that covers over her son's distress, Paul insists on a bare truth that takes no account of people's feelings. Rather, he is motivated by a fierce desire to divest of the "upholstery" with which most people cover over truths that feel too raw. His family's efforts to reach out to him fail as their words become further barriers to the closeness each both longs for and occludes. Much like Bion's (1970) description of the relationship between the *establishment* and the *new idea*, Paul became the mystic who spoke truth in his own particular haiku form, unupholstered and seemingly obscure, yet cutting to the core as best he could. His desperate efforts to find something real in relationship were obstructed by his failure to take feelings into account. Countering this stance, family therapy helped to affirm the legitimacy of each person's speech, inviting the parents to shift from their efforts to "help their crazy son" to a more respectful engagement with his truths alongside their own.

This repositioning meets the challenge posed by Lacan (1964/1977e): for the parents to see themselves being seen rather than positioning their son as the alien being. In this type of movement, the seeking of "one's own in the alien, to become at home in it, is the basic movement of spirit, whose being is only a return to itself from what is other" (Gadamer, 1975, p. 15). That vantage point invites respect for the truth-seeker's bumps and bruises as we help them build a navigational map in relation to their own experience. Paul had found himself positioned as the excluded voice who speaks back to the family about the blindness that keeps them alienated from one another. Relegated to the position of holding the meanings that have been excluded from the family consciousness—Atlas holding up the world—Paul was left to find his place as *a* knower rather than *the* knower—a subject in his own right—leaving family members to face their own truths and lies. Over time, his efforts, and those of his family, succeeded, and he was able to recognize increasingly the relationships between context and meaning. His ability to have his own mind in relation to others that were different than his own—but might be legitimate in their own right—enabled him to begin to build a home in the world and a valued place in his family.

BUILDING TRUST AND THE CAPACITY TO PLAY

Those who do not fit within the family discourse are often left—or thrust—outside the gates. Their suffering makes a demand on the clinician as a witness to the tragedy, marking the ethical imperative that Lévinas (1974/1991a) said is lodged in the human face. For me, that call links directly to my memory of Stephen Suomi's (2011) avoidantly attached young apes, whose alienated attachment style has left them unable to learn the skills or relational knowledge that might have facilitated the transition to a new home. I see that suffering in those, like Paul, who have been pushed outside the gates by family and social structure, left to suffer in a wilderness that seems endless and unendurable. Structurally, I see this dilemma in the terms that Lacan (1955–1956/1993) referred to as the psychotic position, marking that the experience of being left outside shapes the individual in a process of abjection in relation to the social surround from which they are excluded (Kristeva, 1980/1982; Vanheule, 2011).

Recognizing the force of abjection and marginalization in the etiology of what we term psychotic disorders, individuals in northern Finland have developed what they term the *open-dialogue method* (Seikkula et al., 2006). Based on a humanistic, person-centered approach to human struggles, teams of health providers go into the homes of families where an individual is suffering from a psychotic break and talk with the sufferer and family members about the problems they are encountering. In the process of listening, talking, formulating, and respectfully engaging with one another, the affective intensity within the family is attenuated, and family members are invited to more adaptively think about their dilemmas. If you think about what we know about mirror neurons (Gallese, 2009), it makes sense that such engagement helps to set a process in place whereby the alienated individual and other family members are provided models of reflective thinking and effective problem-solving, which also helps provide the type of epistemic trust so crucial to relationship building (Fonagy & Allison, 2014, 2023).

This is the type of process I was able to work at with Paul and his family, but, as clinicians, we can bring these insights into our work with individuals too. That frame of reference helps us to take seriously—and try to think and feel our way into—speech that can otherwise sound odd, metaphoric, or even inconceivable. Psychoanalysis helps us recognize ways in which what seems inconceivable can be a function of our defenses against the suffering that is marked by such speech. In describing himself as Atlas, holding up the world, Paul was marking his experience of alienation and the privilege afforded by this marginalized position. This phrasing aptly describes the position in which he found himself in his family of origin: accused of being the source of whatever suffering prevails. Although his speech was unconventional, it also was quite precise and cogent but lodged at that odd juncture of concrete metaphor that is often called psychotic.

In the transference, we inevitably find ourselves in the various positions inhabited by family members. Entering deeply, one can imagine the good intentions, presumptions of care, and personal limits that may underlie a person's defensive moves. Taking seriously the story as we know it, we work to recognize empathically how the impasses have been built. Looking for the story to provide meanings rather than blame helps us find our way out of the mire.

This work requires *our* resilience. At times, I would think Paul and I were on steady ground, and then, suddenly, a shift would occur, and I would become suspect: one of *them*, those well-intentioned caregivers whose utter blindness makes them dangerous. I struggled with the me-them, insisting that there was a *me* guiding my speech and behaviors but that I also was willing to think about how the *them* in me might color or inform my speech. My willingness to struggle provided some assurance, but at times, the stumbling was so jarring that I was thrust off-balance.

In one such moment, when Paul's fear erased whatever meaning had been intended, I was taken aback, as though the wind had been knocked out of me. In trying to describe my experience of the moment, Paul named the Gravitron, the carnival ride in which one is thrust backward, spinning. We could both recognize that I was, for those moments, in the place where Paul spends much of his time, and how difficult it is to get one's bearings, much less think or engage with another person, from that place.

Paul's depiction of himself as Atlas seems apt if one is willing to allow the possible meanings to accrue and resonate. Such recognition, however, requires a willingness to take one's own place on the Gravitron and recognize how bits of refused meanings pile up and take their toll. In these efforts, it is useful to consider how these myths and metaphors might mark a place where the person is stuck and how reflective consideration might open up the possibility of a different ending or path. Paul's family may, in some sense, need him to stand in the position of Atlas, holding up the world, but perhaps the world will still exist even if he lets go of his burden? I made this suggestion to him as one possibility as I also reflected on the question of how we might use this myth in more creative, generative ways, to move from the ostensible burden of universality toward finding new possibilities and transforming the fixed meanings together.

This turn brought me back into the realm of the reflective space through which meanings can be considered, played with, and amended. That ability to play within one's own mind, and also with others, affords us the flexibility needed to make our way in the world. Paul came to an impasse when his trauma was marked, but there was insufficient parental attention to provide a lifeline for him to hold on to. The consulting room, however, afforded him an attentive other on whom to rely while he tried to find his way into the social matrixes of past, present, and possible futures. At times, psychoanalysis provides the play space within which intrapersonal needs and feelings can be encountered, marked, and put into context. With these basic building blocks of metacognition in place, there is room to encounter and make sense of the others with whom we might engage in the interpersonal learning that is essential to socioemotional development.

CONCLUSION

With Paul, what seemed to invite the designation of psychosis was the forcefulness and one-sidedness of his truth claims. The strength of the claims, however, could be seen in relation to his desperation as he tried to cling to something he could reliably know. Learning to meet his assertions with interest and respect, while also having another point of view, afforded us an arena through which he could learn to test his own ideas without anyone needing to be destroyed, affording him entrance into the realm of embodied meanings and engaged and rewarding interpersonal relationships. Once again, the use of the object provides a helpful metaphor in thinking about the passage into autonomous identity, perhaps most crucial in working with those whose struggles bring us into such dangerous territory.

In this chapter, we considered how we support the development of those so alienated from consensual culture that their symptoms tend to further marginalize them. We ended with our discussion of applying theory to particular types of clinical difficulties. Next, in the chapters in Part IV, I consider more broadly how to make use of what we have learned in this volume and from our own experience in our clinical encounters with those whose development has been waylaid by trauma and neglect.

PART IV INTEGRATING THEORY AND EXPERIENCE

12 THE OBLIQUE ANGLE

Psychoanalysis and the View From the Side

In Part IV, I weave together theory and personal and clinical experience as a way of trying to model how I integrate these disparate aspects into my actual work. I hope that you can travel alongside me in this journey so that you might make use of these offerings as interactive models rather than prescriptions. We need to have theoretical models in mind, but be able to carry these loosely so that we can find ourselves—and those we work with—within them. In this chapter, I begin with a theoretical construct—a metaphor—that caught my attention in ways that played on me and that I was able to play with. As I hope you have noticed, being able to play is a particular strength we bring to and develop in this work so that we can move beyond places we get stuck, meet the challenges we encounter, and invite playfulness in those we work with.

LACAN'S PARADOX

In *The Four Fundamental Concepts of Psychoanalysis*, Lacan talked about the paradox that "you never look at me from the place I see you" (Lacan, 1964/1977e, p. 91). Beyond the problem of transference, there is also this

https://doi.org/10.1037/0000455-013
Echoes of Trauma: Meaning and Identity in Psychoanalysis, by M. Charles

question of "the relation between appearance and being" (p. 94) that Lacan (1964/1977e) contended does not lie "in the straight line, but in the point of light—the point of irradiation, the play of light, fire, the source from which reflections pour forth" (p. 94). "If you wish to see a star," he said, "you will be able to see it only if you fix your eye to one side" (Lacan, 1964/1977e, p. 102).

I have been intrigued by Lacan's (1964/1977e) notion of the *oblique angle*, the view from the side, in part because of the inherent mystery entailed in seeing beyond our limits but also because of ways in which women and other marginalized groups have been placed as the object of a gaze that is not their own. From that perspective, the marginalized person is in a "sinister position," speaking indirectly: the Greek chorus, commenting from the side regarding whatever has been omitted from the scene as it is represented. Although this can be a difficult position to speak from, we need that type of countercommentary to break into ideas that seem to make sense because of the conventions of culture but also hide other potential meanings. Bion (1970) noted the essential tension between the establishment and the new idea that is essential to vitality and to growth. The clinician who can recognize the conversation that is difficult to break into because it makes sense is in a good position to disrupt the sense, from which point the nonsense might be explored. This tension—between whatever is established and the need to break into it so that development can occur—keeps us always off-balance, precisely the place where a new perspective might be taken and creativity might emerge.

As a left-handed person in a right-handed world, I fared better than my uncle, who was severely punished when he tried to write with his left hand. In contrast, I can recall my grandmother's trying to figure out how to crochet backward so she might teach me that skill. Even earlier, I began my academic career by writing in such a way that my older sister (playing teacher) had to read my productions in the mirror. But it was not only my left-handedness that was problematic in my family. My inherent emotionality, my *passion* as it were, was read in my family as a sign of a somewhat despicable vulnerability—at best, a concerning lack of the manners that, for me, marked a constraining and inhibiting conventionality. There was always a "too much" to me that made my mother elusive: I was always more (and other) than she had bargained for. In turn, my father, an engineer, contended that my intelligence had been wasted on me, leading me, I imagine, directly to a similarly left-brained psychoanalytic father figure who valued passion as an indicator of important meanings yet to be discovered.

I found in Bion (1977) an authorization I had been seeking: to value and learn from my own experience, wherever that might take me. My feelings seemed to be the truest ground on which I could stand, a ground Bion affirmed through his ideas of the "truth instinct," thereby opposing the anxious thread in psychoanalysis with an optimistic and idealistic vision that invites faith in one's ability to track one's own becoming. That faith is certainly grounded in the self-analysis of Freud, the very capacity, I would contend, that we hope to set into motion in our work with persons seeking assistance so we can set them free—not only from their inner demons but from our authority.

This issue of authority has been compelling for me, having grown up in a culture that devalues much of what is sacred to me. As in childhood, when I spoke to an authority that did not recognize me as valuable in my own right, as a woman, I have felt that I stand "outside the gates," speaking toward an authority that is not my own, somehow hoping to be authorized by someone who fails to understand me. Although I found in Bion that authorization, I had yet to fully encounter and validate my own. Therefore, this issue of what stands between the subject and their object remains a compelling question for me. It is a clinical dilemma captured in the diagram Lacan (1964/1977e) offered in which the analyst is looking from the side to have a view of what stands between the person and whatever projection of self they are trying to impose on us precisely because of the beliefs that keep them from being able to merely and more truly be. We are inevitably caught in the act of trying to misdirect the other person's attention because we have lodged in them our own self-contempt. In the realm of the Imaginary, our ideas color what we see. If I am lost in my own self-loathing, I find it everywhere, much like Klein's (1946) ideas regarding projective identification. What I cannot tolerate finding in myself attacks me, seemingly from the outside. Sleight of hand is everywhere.

SEEING FROM THE SIDE

To compound the difficulty, humans, being the technological animals we are becoming, build contraptions to try to get around our essential dilemmas in being human. So then, medications and medical interventions are supposed to solve "depression," but losing sight of the reasons we are depressed keeps us from solving the underlying problems, leaving us needing more and better "solutions." We try to capture ourselves from various angles, looking for some key to a mystery we hope to cover over and that we are terrified to reveal. It is kind of like the mystery story in which we are offered so many red herrings that we miss the obvious hiding in plain sight. Our ambivalence leaves us saying we want to hear or see something, and then we close our eyes and ears and hum loudly all the while!

The gaze from the oblique angle, in my fantasy, exposes us rapt in this enterprise, catches us in our games, busy pretending that if we close our eyes tightly enough, no one can see us. In part, the appeal of the oblique angle is an aesthetic one, capturing a movement in the dance, a moment in the mystery. My hope is that in pondering this notion, we will come closer to an appreciation of what this angle both hides and reveals: perhaps a means for finding our way back into the dance.

We present the world with our best face or, at times, our worst face, but there is always a face being presented that, in some sense, stands between us and the world, imposing a barrier that keeps us safe from the shock of too much contact. Our first relationships with others are embedded in this direct contact, whether of gaze, touch, or sounds reverberating between us. I recall with poignancy my 1-year-old granddaughter intoning repeatedly, intently, like a mantra, almost under her breath, something that sounded suspiciously like "ice cream," words my ears did not want to register at that point in time, her intention being inconvenient to my needs. Months later, there was no mistaking that word. It was said with utter clarity, with hopefulness, exuberance, or determination, depending on the context, and she would glower or look amazed when the word did not produce the intended aim. Such is the magic of the spoken word.

She works at other words now, words that are not easily perceived despite my earnest attempts to understand. For this child, although our busy lives often take our attention away, there is still the attempt to understand. That intention guides her securely into a universe in which meanings may be made and received, in which eyes are made to be looked into, a smile brings one in return, and a cry brings comfort often enough.

In contrast, the young adults I work with could not be sufficiently received, for whatever reasons, despite their parents' good intentions, and they are left with an empty space where self-grounding should stand. Into that void, I offer my interest and my curiosity so that we might, together, help them inhabit their own life story. The older adults, such as Chris (see the case explication in Chapter 9), have an even greater challenge as they confront the lost decades in which they were largely absent from their life. Orienting from the lament to the possibility becomes the challenge.

Increasingly, we think of mentalization and reflective function in relation to the process of becoming a self. Many of the people we work with have the appearance of proper selves, but underneath there is no *there* there, no real ground on which to stand. In working with people who present the appearance of a self to avoid falling into the chasm that always awaits—the empty space where the self would be—we cannot encounter them directly. Rather, they stave us off at any cost in desperate attempts to not be located in the place they fear to be found, the place that marks, for them, their essential vulnerability that would invite contempt, disdain, and disparagement.

Klein (1957/1975) marked the essential humiliation built into seeking assistance, reminding us of the price people pay in entering the consulting room and attempting to reveal themselves. That juncture—in which the intent to reveal is countered by the need to obscure—is precisely where Lacan's (1964/1977e) metaphor of the oblique angle can be useful, reminding us to look from the side so we might, perhaps, catch a glimpse of the person in action. If we can catch them at their game, we might find a way to engage empathically with the subject behind the presentation, whoever is hiding behind the curtain trying to orchestrate the scene.

It is *that* person with whom we are trying to engage, the very person who closes their eyes and hopes that if they do not see us, we will not see them. Let us try to take in how young this dilemma is, this place where we can believe that if we close our eyes, we will not be seen. There is a poignancy to that hope that demands our respect for the very real challenge it poses in our work with adults so profoundly waylaid in their early development.

CASE ILLUSTRATION

Consider my work with Nikolai (introduced in Chapter 6), a man in his early fifties who is staking everything on our work together because of his sense that I know something about him that he cannot quite grasp but seems of great importance. He also, however, fears being seen as the pathetic person he believes he is, so he goes to great lengths to impress me and keep me at bay. Seeing me seeing him poses impossible challenges for this man, whose narcissistic vulnerability is as fragile and brittle as the finest, most transparent bone.

A familiar pattern emerges: He spends the better part of the session complaining or philosophizing. I remark on his tendency to already have the answers such that he seems to have little interest in anything I might add to the conversation. He appears to be interested in what I am saying but is often merely waiting for me to finish speaking so he can bury my words under a rash of his own and thereby dispose of them. "You don't really understand," he says, as he begins, once again, to explain himself to me. If that does not work, if I persist in trying to say something to him about what I see, he may tolerate the intrusion. But in the next session, he will be ready for me with a renewed onslaught detailing what was wrong, what I was missing, and how I continue to fail to offer him any relief. At times, I seem to become so threatening that he turns me into a caricature who can then be dismissed because, of course, such a person could never understand.

I tell Nikolai that I am sure that I am wrong about many things, but if that is all I am, then likely he should not waste his time or his money coming to see me. I suggest that if he *is* going to work with me, it may be important to find something useful in whatever it is I am offering.

From the point of direct engagement, we are often at an impasse in which I am the impossible mother overriding all his sensibilities. From the side, however, there is a poignancy as I watch him fending off the very information that might be useful because my gaze itself is so humiliating. We talk about this difficulty: that he is so certain of his own deficiency that being seen is inherently shameful. So, then, he talks about wanting intimacy but fends off real engagement instinctively, vehemently, and virulently. At the point of contact, his defenses go into gear, and he is gone, safe within the armor he created so long ago.

In our conversations, I try to unpack the meanings behind the words so that I might better understand what he is saying, what he is moving toward and what he is moving against. I can tell when we are facing one another directly because of my countertransference feelings in relation to his grandiosity and heavily shielded hostility. In such moments, I become the powerful, overbearing, intrusive mother who tries to break through his defenses rather than recognize their meanings, and so must be fended off at any cost.

In such heated moments, I am immobilized but, as I catch myself, I try to see him from the side, from which place I can recognize, once again, the little boy who climbed inside his armor so long ago to protect himself from repeated rejections by peers and ridicule from family. Turning away from the shame and humiliation, he became preoccupied by solving puzzles, always keeping his toys to himself so that he would be the holder of the prize rather than the person left behind.

From that place, I can see the dilemma we are caught in, such that he must hide from me the very troubles with which he is faced. He comes to me seeking not the understanding he claims, but rather to have a misperception affirmed, the search for misrecognition described by Lacan (1949/1977c). We find ourselves in the territory alluded to by Bion (1963, 1965), in which statements can be used for very different purposes. For Nikolai, there are truths that must become lies and lies that must become truths, making it quite difficult at times to have any ground on which to stand.

I tell him that I think he has the idea that if he could just "say it right," then I would understand, and things would change. So, he keeps trying to tell me what he has already told me, hoping that this time it will stick. But,

I tell him, I do not think that his problems will be fixed by a more accurate description. I think that I am hearing what he is saying but have a different perspective, that it is likely what he cannot see and cannot describe to me that he needs to learn something about.

We are caught in a terrible dilemma in which he is desperately trying to maintain the grandiose façade he has erected, and I am hoping to invite the person behind the mask into being. Paradoxically, it is when he is most present and vulnerable that he is most likeable, whereas his grandiosity can be extremely off-putting. He wards off the opportunity to learn something more because he fears what he might find. In this way, he also wards off the very intimacy he longs for.

CONTEXTUALIZING THE CASE

Often, suggested Lacan (1960/1977f), it is only in our stumbling that some greater truth might be revealed "by which we would arrive at the paradox of conceiving that the discourse in an analytic session is valuable only in so far as it stumbles or is interrupted . . . when there is a cut in false discourse" (p. 299). In Bion's (1977) terms, we need to be able to recognize the lie—but recognize it in a way that invites the person to encounter it and work with it rather than just try to make it disappear.

My psychoanalytic "home" has been in object relations, grounded in Winnicott, Klein, and Bion, who helped me recognize people's symptoms in terms of the developmental journey that had been waylaid. In my own journey, I have been heartened by the embodied offerings of women such as Milner, Coltart, and Kristeva. Their ideas have been useful in helping me construct a story in which the person's problems make sense and also in being more profoundly present, enhancing my ability to make use of my feelings, odd associations, and bits of reverie in enlarging the field of our imaginings.

I did find, though, that these theories and the metaphors they offered were not sufficient to help me find my way with many people I worked with, particularly in encounters with those who were profoundly lost in relation to themselves. It was with great interest, then, that I encountered the clinicians from GIFRIC, the Freudian Interdisciplinary Group for Research and Clinical and Cultural Intervention in Québec, who were using metaphors from Lacan in ways that were directly clinically useful (see Apollon et al., 2002).

Most notable was the centrality of the Subject in Lacan's (1964/1977e) thinking. We all read Lacan differently, so I can only give you my version of the ways in which this question of the Subject, opened up by his theories and metaphors, has informed my work. If, at the core of our work as clinicians, there is the question of the Subject and their desires, then it must be the Subject we seek that is the presence, the directive, the agent I am looking for when I cast my eyes to the side, so I can see that direction, that *directive* in motion.

I find it crucial to have a sense of the developmental flow of the person with whom I am faced, to try to discern where they are caught in a developmental impasse that could not be broken through, but rather had been foreclosed and avoided. Like a pearl in an oyster that forms around a grain of sand, some of our complexities may be lovely presentations and yet cohere around a point of distress that can be painful. When the pain began before we had the tools to make sense of it, it hides in plain sight beneath the surface, and we encounter it in the ways in which the pain is avoided.

Recognizing the elusiveness of the symptom that marks the spot but also represents the way the person's character is revealed through the marking, Lacan (1975–1976/2016) coined the term *sinthome* to offer us a more complex and respectful way of thinking about idiosyncrasies of character, the ways in which the Real, Imaginary, and Symbolic—experience, mind, and culture—formulate themselves within a given person's mind and experience. I like this way of conceptualizing what is essentially transference, because it holds the multiplicity of the dimensions in which our relationships to self and other are constructed, recognizing that our ideas of self and other inevitably exist within the terrain of the Imaginary. Essential, then, is the extent to which that Imaginary can be informed by reality and consensual meanings as we encounter them.

The term sinthome holds the paradox of our own mystery, our own essential being, that truth to which, Bion (1990) reminded us, the person themselves uniquely holds the keys. In turn, we know that there are keys and, in looking for their traces, we invite the other person to turn inward to find them, to take seriously the signs, signals, and symbols as they present themselves.

For those children who encounter interest in their own particularity, self-development can proceed, but, most notable for our purposes here, there is a collision that occurs when the child cannot break through the idiosyncrasies of parental apperception, when the child cannot be recognized because they are not the child the parent hoped to see. If we are caught by the gaze that directs and misdirects us—the parent who is looking in a different direction for the person who is not-us, the person they had hoped to find—then, as Winnicott (1971) put it, the baby looks in the mirror but cannot find themselves there.

ANOTHER CASE ILLUSTRATION

If we think of what we know about the ways unresolved mourning impedes the development of a coherent identity in the child because the parent's attentive face cannot regularly be found, then we can imagine the plight of those who use their intelligence and resilience in trying to put together a package that can be received. I worked with one young woman, for example, who was bright, creative, and highly accomplished. She was, in particular, the apple of her father's eye, delighted as he was by her ability to push past any obstacle and accomplish any goal she set her mind to.

When I first met Val, a young woman in her very early twenties, she had sought treatment because of her inability to move beyond a traumatic experience that she could only register as traumatic because of the utter impasse in which she found herself. Val had the idea that she should be able to surmount all of life's challenges and that to not do so would be to fail. Initially, she attempted to seek treatment without ever really coming in for a landing, merely pausing to obtain sufficient information to enable her to go on with her life.

Val was highly reactive to bumps and bruises and could easily become so dysregulated that all she could do was draw herself up to her full height and cement a pleasantly disdainful smile on her face. She could, however, think about these collisions once she had settled down, and she could then talk with me within whatever parameters she could tolerate. We learned to respect her limits, and her limits grew, although it took some time for me to recognize that my tendency to offer her ideas when she was dysregulated was maddening to her. We can know something in principle and utterly fail to apply it!

Helpful to Val in breaking through the wall she had created—a wall through which it was difficult for her to receive an idea that conflicted fundamentally with her own—was a family meeting in which she was able to recognize that her parents' defenses were so like her own. Seeing, for example, her father's condescending unwillingness to even consider a story in which his daughter might not be the exception to every rule helped Val recognize how she becomes trapped by the need to be that exception, which keeps her from coming to grips with the very real trouble she is in.

Rather than merely coasting on the grandiose edge she had been riding, Val could recognize that she was imprisoned by the need to do so. She came up against her longing to be accepted for her whole self, her longing to feel real. We could begin to recognize the paradox of how she could place so much value in her ability to immerse herself in the wonders of the universe and yet be so constrained that she could not truly play.

Play can only be free and creative to the extent that one can rely on an environment sufficiently safe in which to land. In psychoanalytic therapy, we hope to provide such an environment, but to accomplish this is often a challenge because we encounter the gaps, the no-man's lands that are also safety zones, the chasms that need to be encountered, the minefields that need to be traversed and survived. I find that being able to offer the missing pieces conceptually—and tentatively, without imposing—helps the person build a story in which the fragments that could not be assimilated can come together into a coherent narrative.

For example, Val's extreme reactivity to nuances in word or tone could make an offering absolutely indigestible. Back in the safety of her own mind, however, she could calm down and begin to think about what had distressed her. As our work proceeded, I often felt anxiously reactive as well and found myself wondering how to talk to her about her diagnosis and its implications, fearing that she would feel discarded and diminished.

I talked to her about my ideas regarding ways in which her development had been foreclosed. Despite her deep investment in her idealization of her parents, she was able to recognize herself in the difficulties I described: a sensitive, bright, and highly emotional child who might have needed more containment from her parents. She stumbled over my words, however, particularly words like *containment* that she found impossibly constraining. Working hard together, we were able to come to the idea of being "held," an idea that was more experience-near to her sense of feeling empty and alone and wanting close physical contact as a way of reconstituting herself.

I found myself thinking repeatedly about the film *Girl Interrupted* (Mangold, 1999), wondering if this might be a way to offer her the diagnosis I thought was correct but feared would be disorganizing. At one point, she told me her mother was reading a book about mental illness and wondered if it was a good one. I had not heard of it, I replied. "Can you recommend one?" she asked. "Actually," I said, "I would suggest your parents see the film *Girl Interrupted.*" Val was sitting curled in her chair, her head to the side. She was silent, and I wondered what she was thinking. Then she smiled and said, "I love that film." After another silence, she said something about her good fortune in being matched up with me. As she left the room, she said she felt like crying. That, I thought, was the containment of the right interpretation at the right time, Sirois's (2012) interpretations that *touch*.

DISCUSSION

When working with young people whose intellects far outpace their ability to engage empathically with their own primary experience, I often suggest that they wander over to the shop and play with the mud (clay) or muck around with the paint. I hope that they can find a way into the playfulness that has eluded them, that seems to be an important antidote to their overly intellectualized and remote stance in the world, one that might help them rediscover—or perhaps discover for the first time—an ability to become absorbed into their experience in ways that have eluded them.

It is not just those seeking our assistance who must struggle with tensions between reason and the primary process so crucial to psychoanalytic exploration. Just as people come to us caught behind an image of the self that they believe they need to be, one that leaves them unable to access many of their basic capacities, so, too, the clinician can believe they should be other than they are. I can remember a moment after completing psychoanalytic training when, sitting behind someone lying on the couch, I searched for the voice of the psychoanalyst, but it came out just sounding like me. At the time, I was glad there was no one standing over my shoulder who might overhear me.

Although I thought I made my peace with being myself, that moment had reverberations, even years later, when a member of my Kleinian clinical seminar group said of my work, with disgust and frustration, "That is not psychoanalysis!" Deeply wounded and feeling confused, angry, hurt, and misunderstood, I was grateful for the gentle voice of the consultant, a psychoanalyst who was also an anthropologist, who seemed able to see my work in context and recognize its value. This moment marks the importance of being able to lean in and orient toward the person before us and the trouble they bring rather than resort to theory or technical concerns during difficult moments. As you can see from this example, this is true in our interactions with colleagues as well.

It is only many years later that I truly feel comfortable—if anyone can ever be comfortable in this work—but at least I feel at peace with the way I practice, believing that I stand in a place of integrity—or at least have a sense of how to strive for it, some faith that I can survive difficult moments—and knowing that it has value for those I work with. When I lose my way, I can always invoke Winnicott (1971), Bion (1990), Coltart (1992), and Lacan (1964/1977e, 1975–1976/2016) to remind myself that I need to meet the moment as wholly and fully as I can, which means leaving to the side, as best I might, the voice of the psychoanalytic superego that threatens to overturn my efforts to be real, to be true to what the moment demands.

I think it is particularly important for those entering this field—for our future—that we stand in our utmost humility as we support other clinicians in their journeys. This is not a field in which there are answers. This is a field in which, if we are lucky, we can find the questions that will open up the answers that have formed like hardened brittle crusts—to break through the answers that cover over whatever remains unexplored—and encounter ourselves companionably, from the side, on a journey that is ours to discover.

In making that journey, metaphors often become guideposts that point to some of the complexities worth unpacking along our way. One such complexity can be found in Lacan's later work (1975–1976/2016), when he moved beyond the *Name of the Father*—the authorization that comes from the consensual—to point toward the idiosyncrasies of meaning that reveal the individual in their own particular essence. Although many people find Lacan challenging, we can locate him in parallel to Winnicott (1971), perhaps the most accessible psychoanalytic theorist. It may be that all roads lead to Winnicott, or else that each psychoanalytic language is infinitely translatable into any other because we are dealing with the same clinical facts: the fundamental challenges of being human. Personally, I think that the greatest value of having all of these theories—beyond the fact that one will likely be particularly user friendly to each of us, which is likely the Achilles' heel as well—is that their multiplicity allows the view from the side through which precisely what becomes dogmatic, closed off, and therefore counterproductive can be opened into and explored, something further revealed. We can think about Winnicott's ideas about the space of creativity, which is the space of the self, as commensurate to Lacan's (1964/1977e) Subject. For Winnicott, the space is a potential space, an optimistic, idealistic view, very lovely in its essence, and my grandchildren may get there, but what about those who come to me already lost?

Although, in my heart, I would love to open up for them a play space through which they might be divested of their burdens and trip the light fantastic, the reality is seldom so simple. Rather, to open up that potential space with those for whom hope has been an unrelenting trap, and home a place of dangerously empty eyes, I find it useful to bring in the greater complexity of Lacan's (1975–1976/2016) *Borromean knot*, the ways in which experience, mind, and culture—the Real, the Imaginary, and the Symbolic—have conditioned meanings for that individual. To begin to unpack these layers, I try to hear the story as it courses through, as I also try to watch, from the side, the story as it is being told through the *intention* of the storyteller. Through the vantage point of the oblique angle, I try to catch glimpses of the person in motion as they direct and misdirect my attention toward and away from whatever it is we are ambivalently seeking.

Bion (1962) located the oedipal dilemma in the desire to turn a blind eye, in this way highlighting the essential choice between growth and evasion that is always in play. Whereas Nikolai instinctively moves toward evasion, there is a part of him that struggles to find something that might break him free from the terrible nightmare in which he is caught. I think he hopes to steal the answer from me so as not to have to acknowledge his need and, with it, his lack. And yet, that very determination is precisely what keeps him isolated and alone, the little boy who cannot find his way into the world of his peers, a world in which sharing and receiving might be good things rather than utterly humiliating.

Val, in contrast, is delighted to find someone who can see her, even though she might wince at times or even become overwhelmed by dysphoric emotion at what has been revealed. The desires for connection and meaning-making are so strong that she works to tolerate the dysregulation that accompanies greater self-knowledge. Some of these differences can be traced to the developmental differences we explored in Chapters 9 and 10 regarding the narcissistic versus borderline dilemmas.

In his own obscure way, Lacan (1975–1976/2016) pointed to the difficulty, also noted by Matte-Blanco (1975), regarding the limits of human perception in a world with multiple dimensions of experience, far beyond what we can grasp in a given moment. At best, we can intuit these larger truths, but as we refine down the complexities of experience into manageable bits, much is lost in the process. In our struggles to make sense of self and other, we make use of past experience, which is inevitably colored by the idiosyncratic lenses afforded by our own imagination and culture.

In the face of this multiplicity, we work to cohere a usable sense of agency and identity, offering the world a view of ourselves that is in line with how we would like to be seen. We then stumble over the gaps between what we offer and the other perspective that is inevitably not our own. In the cases of Nikolai and Val, you can see how Nikolai stumbles over my perspective because it threatens to erase and override his. He stumbles over it because he privileges it and therefore must destroy it. Val, in contrast, suspects that my perspective can open her own, if only she can tolerate it. She reaches for it, to hold it side by side with whatever is already known. In putting the fragments together, there is the possibility of growth.

As T. S. Eliot (1943/1971) noted so profoundly: Home is the place we start from, but we also begin from the end, the place we have come to. In psychoanalysis, where we begin is always the endpoint we have come to thus far, and our explorations inevitably take us home, back to our origins. Much of the life journey entails affirming basic truths we knew at one time that have become buried over by sense and by nonsense. Both Bion and Lacan could see that many of our most important truths are hiding in plain sight, waiting for us to dim the stark light of our reason sufficiently to discern what lies beyond. Whereas Bion (1990) talked of deepening the darkness, Lacan (1964/1977e) referred to "the screen that re-establishes things in their status as real" (p. 107). The "screen cuts into that which is illuminated without being seen" and "makes the milky light retreat into the shadow and allows the object it concealed to emerge" (Lacan, 1964/1977e, p. 108). In psychoanalysis, what we are seeking is always present. The challenge is to enable it to be revealed.

In families that have carried the burden of too much trauma to integrate and absorb it into the family narrative, the child is left with the impossible task of carrying that knowledge as a stain, a point of darkness that cannot be encountered sufficiently to make sense of it. Such knowledge tends to emerge in the form of a symptom, a symptom that marks the impossible meanings. For most of us, these points of denial become the little murders through which we come to deny aspects of our perceptual realities. At the extreme, however, we drive our children crazy denying the subtleties of emotional meanings that they experience directly and deeply.

In psychoanalysis, we hope to provide opportunities for people to stumble over the truths that foreclose learning, and, in turn, we hope to be up to the challenge of stumbling ourselves. We all have our stories, and for the clinician it is particularly important to plumb deeply into the crevasses of one's mind and being, to give room for those seeking our assistance to do the same, to obtain greater access to their own potential.

I began my life as a left-handed person in a right-handed world, as the second daughter to parents not yet ready for her, as the daughter to a mother who wanted to present her husband with a son, and as a person who had not yet figured out how to value herself with equal weight to the men in her life. Standing outside, at the margins, the excluded middle daughter, I was left always coming in from the side, at an angle. That outsider position became a way of life, countered only by my children, who thrust me precipitously into engagements with others that have reaped rewards I could never have imagined. I am grateful to them and to all those I have worked with and struggled with in various roles who, similarly, have forced me to move beyond places where I have become comfortably stuck by mirroring back to me the fault lines in my own integrity.

But perhaps most of all, I am grateful to my grandchildren, who are teaching me about love that knows no bounds, no limits. What I am learning forces me to work even harder to push the world toward being a kinder, gentler, more loving and accepting place for all of our children, everywhere, most particularly those we encounter in our professional lives: those fragile and precious beings who could not find sufficient light in their parents' eyes and come to us in dire need of repair.

CONCLUSION

In this chapter, I offered you a personal account of how I make use of many of the ideas you have encountered in this volume. As I hope you have seen, we need theory as a way of organizing the multiplicity of data assailing us in our clinical encounters, but these ideas must ultimately be oriented in relation to our own experience of being a human being in the world. From that place, we are least likely to do violence to the person who is ambivalently trying to move beyond their own strictures in our presence. Next, we turn to the very rich territory of dreams and Bionian field theory, which encourages the development of the dreaming functions in those we work with.

13 DREAMS AND FIELD THEORY

In Part IV, we are working at integrating the ideas we have learned into our clinical practice. In this chapter, we turn to dreams and the Bionian field theory that positions dreaming at the core of the clinical work. From early times, people have been intrigued by dreams, using them to discover truths about themselves and the universe. Freud (1900/1953b) proclaimed that dreams are the royal road to the unconscious, showing how complicated and enlightening our dreams can be. People have tried to create lexicons of dreams, but psychoanalysts recognize that it is not the equivalence of image to meaning that is most important, but rather, as Matte-Blanco (1975) noted, the fact that the unconscious has its own logic in which meanings, rather than falling into discrete categories, are amorphous and can blend, merge, and develop. In this logic of dreams, an image can stand for meanings in many ways, and the relationships between images can be more important than the images themselves (Charles, 2003). Each person creates their own lexicon of dream

Portions of this chapter have been adapted from "The Dream and the Image: Creative Transformations in Psychoanalytic Space," by M. Charles, 2019, *American Journal of Psychoanalysis*, *79*, pp. 174–195 (https://doi.org/10.1057/s11231-019-09194-2). Copyright 2019 by Springer Nature. Adapted with permission.

https://doi.org/10.1037/0000455-014
Echoes of Trauma: Meaning and Identity in Psychoanalysis, by M. Charles

imagery, making it important for the psychoanalyst to stand respectfully in relation to both the dream and the dreamer, inviting the dreamer to discover their own truths.

Much as Winnicott (1971) warned not to steal the patient's creativity by knowing too much, but rather to wait, listen, and trust the person to make their own meanings over time, so, too, the analyst must stand respectfully in relation to the dreamer. In puzzling over the dream, we hold open a space for potential meanings to emerge and encourage the dreamer's faith in their own relationship to the dream world, so they might go deeper and range more broadly as they ask their own questions and discover their own answers. Lacan (1964/1977e), Bion (1990), and Winnicott, each in their own ways, warned of the hazards of saturating that potential space rather than recognizing our position as the person who might hold it sacred if we can keep our egos and superegos out of the way.

Notable to our purposes here, dreams can provide a lens into early or traumatic experiences not encoded into language more easily integrated into the life story. Such *inscribed meanings* (McDougall, 1989), Klein's (1957/1975) *memories in feeling*, become a language of the body (Charles, 2002b) that speaks quite directly—if we can heed the signals. We turn away at our peril, haunted by meanings from early experience and unassimilated debris from our ancestors that push toward recognition (Apprey, 2024), Laplanche's (1997) enigmatic meanings transmitted from one unconscious to another. In psychoanalysis, we are always listening with two minds: the conscious mind of rational, secondary logic, and the less conscious registers of primary process; the realm of dream, fantasy, and the primary understandings we often term intuitions.

Learning the language of dreams helps us explore those less conscious meanings to orient ourselves and play with the complexities (Charles, 2010; Lippmann, 2000). It is the process of exploration that is crucial; the journey is always more important than the destination. Psychoanalysis takes a stand for the possibility of knowing more than we think we can know. In that context, the dream, indeed, provides a royal road, a path into the unknown, including a way of translating meanings inscribed by a history that might be unspeakable within the family or invisible because this is just "the way things are" (Davoine & Gaudillière, 2004). As we discussed in Chapter 11, the inability to speak important truths can literally drive us crazy, offering no external reference point for understanding. The dream affords a potential joining place, an opportunity to find meaning together. In this work, the analyst invites respectful curiosity toward whatever has remained unknown and seemingly unknowable as it pushes forward for recognition. Notably, psychoanalysis stands at a respectful distance from the defenses, recognizing the importance of providing a path without insisting it be traveled beyond the person's capacity in that moment.

CLINICAL ILLUSTRATION

Let us begin our explorations with a repeating dream from John, a man in his early thirties (reported more fully in Charles, 2019):

> I am in a fictitious apartment that was bequeathed to me. There are three rooms. Red played a large role, and stairs played a large role. Possibility. One room is like the library in other dreams, lots of diaries with personal knowledge and wisdom bequeathed to me. I'm walking around, not knowing how to make use of the knowledge. A lot of my dreams have to do with wisdom and secret knowledge.

In John's dream, we see the bare but essential bones of his life story, the scaffolding on which our work will rest. John is clearly bright and well educated, but his discourse remains at the surface. His inner life seems utterly enigmatic to him, leaving me to translate the story through my experience. What emerges is a young adult whose potential was waylaid by developmental impasses, leaving him lost and ashamed, caught by the type of small-t, complex trauma we have been discussing. His early life had left him easily dysregulated, inviting frustration and anger rather than soothing. The family value of "good behavior" likely masked family members' affect in ways that made them as unreadable as his own internal experience. John's own anger was seen as so abhorrent that, at a certain point, it simply disappeared, becoming the internal blackness he desperately feared. Despite his high intelligence, his difficulties with attention and organization were seen as a sign of internal deficit, masking the external deficits that left him trying to find his way in a world in which his father's interest was turned elsewhere and his mother's "care" became crippling.

The mother's attempts to moderate the troubles as they were perceived inevitably failed in the absence of the data that would have enabled John and those around him to recognize the contexts in which they occurred. The "attention deficits" in those around him left him further alienated from himself as the primary interpreter of internal and interpersonal meanings. We can recognize in this story the developmental context in which narcissism develops. The lack of effective soothing and the inscrutability of one's own or other's emotions sorely impedes the development of reflective capacities. Despite the mother's best intentions, without recognizing the problems at the core of his difficulties, her attempts to push past the problems increased his dependence, which became a crutch that further crippled him. Eventually, her efforts were so far removed from his needs that he came to a crashing halt, a cataclysm of betrayal so profound that it led him to seek, first, the vacuity of alcohol, and then, to his credit, psychoanalytic treatment.

John's dreams insistently remind us that we are in the realm of metaphor. His dreams reside in the realm of negation; he is always in a place where he is not with people who are not who they are. Opposing his massive concreteness in our sessions, John's dreams are profoundly playful, affording a transitional space in which to recognize and play with the signs and symbols that are markers of meaning in his universe. In these efforts, we are building consensual meanings through which his experience can be organized—and details be noted—opposing his fear of transgressing into the territory that seemed to be forbidden in his family.

John is also learning through that work that people in dreams can be important *markers of relational patterns*, that the very fact that no one is exactly who they are points to the meaning rather than a person. Given the inscrutability of persons in his life—and the lack of permission for intruding into private spaces—being able to play with meanings was essential to his development. If we think about Winnicott's (1971) object usage as the transitional moment in which one becomes a subject in relation to other persons, the parents' offer of treatment, their willingness to give John room to discover himself without their interference, was an extraordinary gift that helped to repair their earlier failures. That gift ultimately paid off for them all, because John developed his own internal resources sufficiently to be able to establish relationships with his family without such intense fears of annihilation.

In our work together, part of what John was learning was the difference between what can be *marked* versus what might be *built*. Marking territory and stepping back to consider what might emerge or, alternatively, leaning in to see what he might feel not only helped John locate patterns of meaning in his dreams but also locate himself in relation to other people as he encountered them in his daily life. As we noted in Chapter 10, profound developmental difficulties associated with the narcissistic position result not just in failures in self- and other reflectivity but also in having sufficient interpersonal space to make meaning of self in relation to others. Developing self-knowledge through the exploration of his dreams afforded John sufficient grounding and interpersonal distance to engage in more satisfying ways with others and to build deeper, more meaningful relationships. Learning to discover, exchange, and refine meanings rather than merely imposing them on one another, John was able to achieve a more autonomous selfhood than had been possible in his earlier years.

As we have discussed, identity develops in relation to the stories we are told and tell ourselves, built on the early interchanges between parent and child that are nested within the familial and cultural contexts from the stories and myths that organize complex sociocultural and historical meanings. Stories require the ability to fix meanings in relation to one another in reliable ways that depend on expected relationships between symbols. At the core of symbol formation are the images that function as proto-meanings, relating back to the primary rhythms that organize all experience (Kristeva, 1986). Within the context of reliable relationships, these affect-laden images can develop over time into rich and more fully elaborated symbols and stories.

Without grounding in embodied meanings between persons, images can remain largely unmentalized signs that point to personalized meanings rather than being useful in communicating with others. At the extreme, images can be ruminative and obsessive, the types of *symbolic equations* (Klein, 1930/1981a) that are so fixed that they destroy possibilities rather than allowing us to play with them. Winnicott (1971) described this difference in terms of a type of empty, repetitive fantasying that goes nowhere versus a dream that can be used in creative ways because it is layered with meanings that can be located within the contexts of historical time and self versus other.

When I met John, he was lost in a universe in which signs could not reliably be read. The danger of becoming even further lost in an interpersonal world that had betrayed him left him adrift in a world governed by obsessive ruminations over meaningless differences and compulsive, repetitive checking and rechecking that titrated his anxiety but could not relieve it. Choosing the right spoon could become so impregnated with meaning that his destiny seemed to depend on it, and the inability to accurately assess value left him saving everything, submerged within the mounting debris. In our work together, intent interest in his experience as he related it helped him describe to me in increasing detail the events that had led him to this impasse. As we integrated the depictions of his life experiences with the patterns we discovered in his dreams, we were better able to appreciate factors that impeded his ability to engage more directly with self and with others in ways that might enable him to more effectively organize his mind and life.

DREAMS FROM THE PERSPECTIVE OF BIONIAN FIELD THEORY

This interest in patterns is also at the core of the work of Bionian field theorists, who encourage us to think of each analytic session as a potential dream space in which a transformation can occur from whatever meanings have failed to come into being through the possibility of meaning-making as an active process (Civitarese & Ferro, 2013). Bion (1977) had the idea that there are proto-thoughts—what he termed alpha elements—that are present but cannot yet be thought about. It is the analyst's job to register these unformulated meanings and begin to metabolize them and bring them into words. This is the process Winnicott (1971) referred to as *containment*; Bion (1977) described in terms of *reverie*; and Kleinians think of in terms of making use of countertransference thoughts, feelings, and images in the service of registering unformulated meanings (Schafer, 1997). From a field theory perspective, however, what each of these stances misses is the *reality* of the transference and the *subjectivity* of the countertransference, something Lacan (1964/1977e) pointed to in his focus on self-knowledge. No one has the corner on truth: The possibility of greater self-knowledge develops in the deepening relational field between us as we begin to recognize our own mistruths and try to come to grips with the ramifications.

The field theorists make use of their recognition of the precariousness of our relationship to "truth" as we might experience it by encouraging us to listen from the perspective of the analytic field (rather than listen defensively or solely in terms of the transference or countertransference). In parallel to the cautions of Lacan (1964/1977e) against presuming privileged knowledge of the other person, Civitarese (2005) suggested that it is only when we listen from the field perspective that meanings can be made that are potentially transformative. For the field theorists, the real work of psychoanalysis happens in the moment as the analyst and analysand work at dreaming together—allowing themselves to be present in both psychic and physical reality—and play with whatever comes forward, thereby inviting meanings to evolve.

For Ferro (2002), the crucial issue is not the depth or "truth" of the interpretation, which would originate in only one mind, but rather trying to be on the same wavelength with the other person so that the analyst's words can elaborate, in the moment, the truth being created in the emotional field between them. This orientation is grounded in the very basic rhythmic resonance of Kristeva's (1986) chora, which likely underlies the passion Bion (1977) referred to that has its own truth value, an indicator that something important is happening that is worth exploring further. The goal in treatment, from this perspective, is to help develop the person's reflective capacities, to enhance their "capacity for symbolizing, and to increase therefore *indirectly also the appropriateness of his reality test[ing] and the consistency of his life story*" (Civitarese, 2005, p. 1313).

Ferro (2009) conceived of the psychoanalytic session as a type of virtual reality in which the central operation is Bion's (1965) *transformations in dreaming*. That transformative process entails not the traditional reconstruction, but rather a *de*construction, *de*concretization, and *re*dreaming of the person's material. This task is accomplished through the analyst's willingness to enter deeply into the material and encourage engagement at the primary process level, in this way enabling the analyst to dream the session. By taking this attitude, the analyst encourages the analysand to develop greater capacities for dreaming, feeling, and thinking, moving beyond what we think we know—or can know—to consider potential meanings that have not yet taken sufficient form to be realizable.

For Ferro (2009), this process is an antidote to *the transformations in hallucinosis* through which we develop stories based on the failures of the reflective capacities of previous generations. From this perspective, we are forced to hallucinate whatever meanings are omitted from the family narrative. The Bionian field theory approach recognizes the intergenerational transmission of trauma as a failure in reflective functions that is passed from generation to generation until the failure can be recognized and addressed by reinstituting the capacity to encounter the split-off meanings and begin to integrate them into the narrative. What seems hallucinated can then be located in relation to whatever truths afford foundation to the perception. The phantoms haunting us are transformed into ideas that can be reflected on.

In this way, Bionian field theory works toward the goals described by Winnicott (1971) in terms of the creative potential in each of us that can be inhibited or facilitated depending on the quality of our relationships. Opposing this type of creative work is the regressive pull of the unconscious that can invoke our reactive defenses against being pulled into the realms of primary process.

Dreams enable us to use images to explore elusive meanings, affording a displacement through which to titrate the anxiety. There is always a sleight of hand at play, as we noted in John's dreams, in which the meaning of the image gets pushed by a distortion that grabs our attention. Lacan (1964/1977e) reminded us that we go to psychoanalysis in search of, not recognition, but misrecognition. There is always our ambivalence to contend with. We would like to reveal something but not too much, in line with our own best and worst images of ourselves.

Another hazard is our tendency to falsely presume universality, and yet the image can only be read in relation to the gaze that positions it (Lacan, 1964/1977e). Awareness of the multiplicity of an image requires sufficient maturation that we can appreciate the separateness of individual subjects and the impact of perspective on what is seen. At some level, we know that the image is open to interpretation, and so, unless we have some assurance that there can be different legitimate points of reference, we can fear being undermined by the gaze of the other that might eclipse our own.

This fear/desire that the other might know us better than we know ourselves is important to recognize so that we can appreciate the dilemma of the person who presents themselves to us, hoping that we might see them more positively than they see themselves but, in that process, conditioning "truth" in relation to their hopes and fears. The failure to proceed through the fundamental transition toward autonomous selfhood marked by Winnicott (1971) in his depiction of the use of the object, or by Lacan (1953/1977b) in relation to the inevitable cut that separates us from one another, leaves us caught in a no-man's-land in which meaning is fraught and dangerous. In such a universe, the signal is mistaken for a sign that cannot be read because it becomes a symbol for a secret meaning that is withheld. Recognizing that fundamental impasse invites us to work at establishing sufficient safety within the consulting room that meanings might, perhaps, be made together.

CONTINUING THE CLINICAL ILLUSTRATION

The case of John illustrates the disaster that can occur when development is foreclosed. His early life left symbols that were not markers of consensual meanings, but rather of meanings that were withheld and foreclosed. His search, then, was for the secret meanings that became subversive precisely because they were off-limits, sequestered away from the consensual. Unable to assert himself as a subject in his own right, his relationships became perverse because they were utterly dependent, leaving him ensconced in perverse meaning structures. Meaning remained hidden, in the hands of the other, keeping him isolated in a paranoid position because of what could not be seen but seemingly safe from the glare of the terrible truths he feared to encounter. The utter incomprehension in his face at times reminded me of Stephen Suomi's (2011) film, which I described in Chapter 11, of the avoidantly attached adolescent monkey clinging to a tree, lost between the home of origin and his inability to find his way into the adult world.

Lacan (1953/1977b) highlighted the importance of speech as a meaningful act that can cut into the false presumptions he termed *empty speech*. Notably, this type of cut can also break into the shame that closes the person's eyes at precisely the moment they need to be open. My work with John required repositioning what seemed to mark his insufficiency to mark, instead, the possibility of his autonomy and independence. This was a process that could only be achieved through my willingness to accompany him on a journey of self-discovery and my unwillingness to stand in the place of the One Who Knows (Lacan, 1960/1977f). For John, the relational world had been so incomprehensible—and so dangerous—that he was caught behind the mask that both protected and denied him. When I met him, he was only able to say no indirectly: through his refusal to engage with others in any real ways. His surface affability obscured the malignant fear and rage surging within.

In the early dreams John brought into the treatment, it was difficult to locate him as a subject with his own desires or intentions. He was, effectively, masked, but the very effectiveness of the camouflage enabled him to lodge questions for us to consider. For example, he reported having been at a wedding in a clearing but then awakening naked and not knowing whether he had raped, murdered, or merely had intercourse. These dreams seemed to ask questions regarding how people use and are used by one another as well as the impact of strong feelings of need, desire, and hostility on ourselves and those we encounter. In the dreams, over time, we could see him moving from the external *no* that denies him as a subject to the self-defining *no* that refuses symbiosis and affirms subjectivity. From that perspective, we could better recognize the complexities of the images and see, for example, how John's alignment with the killer acknowledges the deadly potency of his rage in ways that might also set him free. As we recognized his frightened ambivalence in the saying and not-saying, the problem of having meaning made and the problem of the interpenetration of language, he entered the realm of metaphor in which having a feeling and acting on it occur in two separate realms.

Although these dreams provided a useful way for John to bring his internal experience into the consulting room, until these two realms of meaning and being were more firmly established, the dreams also frightened him. His previous experience had left him so outside the bounds of consensual reality that the normal agreements between people could not hold. Having been so terribly betrayed by the person he relied on most, what could possibly be made of any promise of care or good intentions? His inability to rely on anyone to work toward the establishment of consensual meanings left him in what Lacan (1955–1956/1977d) termed the psychotic position. From that place, agreed-upon boundaries do not hold, leaving the possibility of other minds making alternative meanings a major problem. At the extreme, meanings can seem so concrete that there may be no distinction between the dream and the "reality" (Apollon et al., 2002; Charles, 2012).

It remains for the analyst to orient to the meanings as they might be known if the person could only orient toward themselves sufficiently respectfully to discern that meaning. In the absence of that capacity, suggested Lacan, the analyst must assume that the problem is not a deficiency in the person, but rather in their ability to make meaning from their experience. In his words, "We must listen to the speaker, when it is a question of a message that does not come from a subject beyond language, but from speech beyond the subject. For only then will one hear that speech" (Lacan, 1955–1956/1977d,

p. 214). Images and relationships within a dream can become one of the language registers that carries meanings that are not yet known by the dreamer (Ferrari, 2004).

Terribly betrayed by his reliance on his mother's word, John found himself catapulted out from under her protective wing. Uncertain of his ability to trust anyone, including himself, he now refused entry into the symbolic realm, the realm of consensual meanings that can be agreed on between persons. That refusal left him in the realm of the paranoid-schizoid position, equally afraid of what might come from the outside or from within (Klein, 1946). Feeling barred from the social structure that had taken from him his only home, John was left in a subversive position in relation to the father to whom he had no value and the mother who obstructed development but could not be killed off without threatening his survival. We encounter, once again, the specter of Suomi's (2011) young ape, lost in a wilderness with no safe haven.

Lacking a secure foundation, John was unable to build a cohesive, resilient identity. Even more fundamental, he was unable to validate his perceptions sufficiently to integrate them into a cohesive worldview. This dilemma left John seeking, in his dreams, an enlightenment that continued to elude him as he looked outside himself for a received knowledge that could not be challenged by personal experience in ways that might lead to integration. Countering this desire, his dreams showed the importance of being able to move—not toward the light, but rather toward the darkness of our deepest desires and conflicts to more truly make sense of where we stand in relation to self and other.

Bionian field theory invites us to allow the darkness to deepen, to tolerate our ignorance rather than reflexively trying to overcome it (Bion, 1990). As we accustom ourselves to the darkness so that truths might be revealed, the dream helps us locate our hidden desire as we become accustomed to our own dream language (Ricoeur, 1970). The symbols in our dreams help make visible whatever is most difficult for us to know as we learn to apprehend our own language registers (Ferrari, 2004), undergirded by the primary rhythms of our own experience (Kristeva, 1986; Milner, 1987), and recognize the expressive and relational meanings that have a directly felt truth value (Cassirer, 1957).

John entered treatment wearing the mask that had kept him safe but also imprisoned, unable to read the affective signals that organize both memory and cognition. His dreams afforded sufficient distance to explore important elements from his experience and begin to put together a narrative through which to move from a false-self position to one in which the foreclosed learning might become possible. To move beyond this impasse, we needed first to be able to mark the duality between what is presented and what may be revealed, between the mask we present to the world and the truths that may be hidden even from ourselves. For John, a face was something that could be looked *at* but could not be looked *into*, the impossible dilemma highlighted by Winnicott (1971) and Main and Hesse (1990) in their descriptions of child development gone awry.

John presented an affable face to the world that was initially engaging to those around him but soon wore thin because of the lack of depth they encountered. He seemed to be lost in the developmental failure marked by Winnicott (1971) in his descriptions of the use of the object, unable to find himself in relation to others. Early on, I had the uncanny feeling of coming up against not a person with whom to engage, but rather a cipher, a pseudoself with no clear definition or intention. In counterpoint, John described a terrifying, inchoate, formless, and endless internal blackness that threatened to emerge. In his mind, it took the form of an overpowering rage that would be annihilating. It was only over slow, painful time that he could begin to envision an anger that might not utterly subsume him.

WORKING WITH THE DREAMS

Perhaps more than with anyone else I have worked with before or since, dreams became the definitive playing ground on which the work took place, providing a creative platform through which John and I could play together (Lippmann, 2000). Bland and colorless in his presentation, John's dreams were quite the opposite, striking in their energy and imagery. His early dreams were like adventure stories, invoking the sense that something has or might go terribly awry: "I go off with someone into the woods," he says. "I wake up the next morning, alone, naked, in the room. I go back to the field. My clothes are hanging—filthy." He goes on, "I'm needing to avoid people to keep them finding out." The danger is imminent, but John is uncertain as to what might be discovered. "I'm assuming when I went off with someone in the woods, I either murdered someone or had sex with them. The clothes were hanging like someone saying, 'I know what you did.'"

In the next dream he reports, he is "on the run from a crime. I was like a predator who was stalking a train station, but I wasn't actually a predator." In this dream, we meet a character who will become very familiar: someone who is trying to be his friend. In the dreams, people become prototypes, referred to as "fictitious replicas" of people he has known, or else they might themselves be wearing a mask, masquerading, as in the "Nazis dressed up as members of a rap band." People he dislikes are seen as constipated, "evil, pushy, snotty people" who are self-righteous and arrogant like his father. People might be "talking a lot and saying very little. Empty speech is such a great defense. Also a great time waster. Makes the other person zone out. Great defense," he says. "I've used it plenty. I think I know when I do it. But a lot of it here is heard by the speaker and the listener as wise."

Other early themes are of places that are beautiful but redolent with anxiety, particularly when others are there. There are also places that are "shabby, shoddy, and kind of dirty . . . always quite mediocre," or else "dreary, drab, depressing—represents slow death to me." There is "crappy beer" that is "not very satisfying" and insubstantial food that has neither taste nor substance. A recurrent theme is of an elusive beauty that is spoiled by human contact, a sense of "being surrounded [that] is based on the feeling of others having the power or other forces having the power." John reports that this feeling is similar to what happens to him when confronted with impossible choices. I suggest that meaningless choices are impossible to make because there is no way to discriminate, despite the sense that life depends on that very possibility. He says he keeps "thinking that the choices I make are going to have some future ramification I can't know about in advance that could affect my whole life."

A recurring theme in his dreams is of a *secret knowledge*, the sense that there are meanings that have been eluding him that are essential to his survival. Early failures had left him unsure of his own mind or capacities, dependent on his mother for knowledge he had no way of obtaining. Rather than being able to use others in the service of his own learning, he was continually at risk of being used by others in relation to intentions that did not take into account his needs, interests, or desires. He could find no refuge, no place of safety in a world in which the keys to the meanings on which life was based were hidden, known only to others. We can see in this image a dilemma Freud (1909/1955a) pointed to in the case of Little Hans, in which the phobic, obsessive defenses develop in relation to the truths the young boy cannot learn from his father and so they remain as enigmatic meanings that entice and tantalize him without any way of finding the keys. Even at that time, Freud sensed that the young child needed truth from his parents as a way of being able to more reflectively organize the experiences that otherwise merely tantalized and frightened him.

In John's dreams, he often finds himself within a structure that is supposed to provide knowledge but feels more like a prison. His early dreams show his fear of the aggression inside of him but, as time goes by, his aggression seems key to his survival. Much like the hero's quest in the labyrinth, for John, murders often get rid of a hazard in his path. Locating this pattern in his history, I am reminded of Winnicott's (1971) description of the child's need to be able to kill the parent and have them not retaliate, to find them still standing. "I feel that a lot of things have stood in the way—situations which have blocked me in the past, which is why I am so fussy about leaving here prepared," he says. "I think it is a healthy release that I am able to kill people in my dreams."

We learn to distinguish and manage feelings as they are recognized and managed by others. In this way, feelings become meaningful signals rather than problems. But John's anger was so unacceptable to his parents that he learned to suppress it at all costs. It was only over time, as we worked to normalize and recognize his feelings as they emerged in context, that John began to emerge from the dream-become-nightmare that was grounded in his inability to rely on his own internal compass to guide him in his life. He began to recognize that the secret knowledge was only secret because he had been looking outside for what could only be found within.

Taking seriously the images and meanings we gleaned from the repetitive tropes in his dreams helped John to recognize his own values, preferences, and desires, and to begin to allow these to guide his life. He became aware of the need to build his own library of lived meanings: "We needed more room for an *archive*," he said, this term notably marking the crucial juncture between authority and the social order that allows meaning to be made (Derrida, 1996). To build an archive to which he can find the keys, he has needed to be able to organize meanings through his own authority in relation to a social order that can engage with him toward refining those meanings.

This transition from external to internal authority surfaced notably in one pivotal dream: John is searching for secret knowledge and learns that he can find it in a hut nearby. He enters the hut and is surprised to find that the secret knowledge is not what he had imagined, but rather is something that he already knows. That dream helped us recognize that his fear that the knowledge he seeks is in the hands of others does not mean that is the case. Rather, his anxiety keeps him searching in the wrong places for something he will not find there. He begins to see how he locates and mislocates aspects of his own being and experience. Referring to "fictitious people," he says, "the missing person is the equivalent of secret knowledge."

As John recognizes the possibility of actually learning, he is able to build on his knowledge. In one dream, he uses familiar images but reconfigures them into a coherent story in which he is trying to understand what has gone wrong. He is doing research at the family home, trying to understand the calamity that has befallen the children of the house, a calamity that now threatens the world. In this dream, we see John's story of a childhood gone awry because of forces outside of his control. We also, however, see that story as it plays out in a wider panorama of lost children trying to find their way, and how dangerous childhood aggression, neither tamed nor understood, can be. I say, "Secret knowledge has been a mysterious allure to you, but, in some ways, it is a dead end." "My health felt so bad," he replies. "Could it be my body becoming my own prey because I treated it so badly? I am eager to get it all cleansed."

Images also emerge of people betraying one another by becoming caught in social convention. "The primary message of the dream is my disappointment in people," he says, "that people act really shitty and make excuses." He is tantalized by a formula for success that he can sense, but the path eludes him. "We needed more room for an archive," he says. "There was a certain way I could pull the sheets over me in bed that leaves me more room and allows me to acquire a larger section of land." His awareness of his own possibilities and inherent value grows, even though he cannot entirely believe in them.

In one dream, he creates art that doctors would like to have: "The doctors had been clients, but now they were just collectors of memorabilia." At that point, I wonder to what extent we have become coconspirators in the collection of memorabilia and to what extent he is outgrowing me. John is finally learning to confront authority in his daily life and to ask questions about the legitimacy of such authority. Finding his own authority to make decisions and demands in relation to his own needs and values forces a confrontation with the limits of secret knowledge: that we are each inevitably limited in what we can know and need to be open to what we might learn from others without overriding our own sensibilities.

As John struggled to find and believe in his own authority, the possibility of building a life became both tantalizing and terrifying. In his dreams, he struggled with the perplexing question of how he might come back from suspended animation to a life worth living. Relying on his own mind required his ability to take a stand regarding his own needs and values and to tolerate the possibility of being opposed by the needs and values of others. In this vivid dream, John transposes his difficulties with his father into those of a friend called "M":

> M and I are at a fictitious ARC [the Austen Riggs Center]. The building reminds me of high school. I'm in a third-floor art studio. M just got a package of dollhouses from her father. She hates him. I thought it was really cool, and I wanted to put them together. There were five beautiful wooden houses in the mail, unassembled. She wants to leave them in common areas to see if they get assembled because they were given to her by an asshole. I wanted to purify them by assembling them together.

From the safe distance of someone else's relationship with a toxic father, John can contemplate putting the pieces together in his own way. Being in charge of constructing his own life story in his own way offers the possibility of purification. Decontaminating the story-as-given affords him access to the legacy that had been bequeathed to him as he uses his own secret knowledge to decipher the texts.

And yet, truly believing in himself does not come easily. In his dreams at this point in time, he plays with the possibility that stealing might be the only means for obtaining what he needs. Much like the trope of killings in previous dreams, stealing may be a way of taking back his rightful authority in this transitional phase in which the shadow of the external authority still looms large. He says,

> I wanted to steal a very important manuscript, perhaps occult, from the library. The floor is grated, the steps are at an angle. I entice someone who has the keys to work with me. They give me the keys. I shrink them, and they fall through the grates and die. They have tiny sunglasses. They put them in my hand, so I have the sunglasses and the keys. There is the excitement of I'm going to be robbing this building later, excited anticipation.
>
> Sitting at a table in an enclosed dining room with people from different times of my life, all passing around notes that look like fortune cookie fortunes. Sometimes I am able to intercept a note or look over someone's shoulder. There are stairs that go up to a different level. That motif of a dining room and steps going down, I've dreamt it before. It's an aesthetically pleasing setup—very dreamlike, strange but not sinister. There is the secret knowledge motif—the lack of secrecy with the notes—also the sloppiness of the spelling—trying to tell me something.

He dreams of sitting at a table "with people coming in and out and someone singing a narrative of each person." We see him marking that there are differences among people and that each person is a legitimate individual in their own right.

In these dreams, hopeful images collide with fears-turned-nightmares. Despite his growing knowledge, there is still the fear that he might step out and find that there is no solid ground on which to stand. It is still not clear to what extent the danger is external or internal. So much of his life has been spent believing in his own incapacity that he cannot quite shake the inherent truth value of that idea:

> I was back in the apartment, but this time, there's two levels, three large rooms. I've noticed there's a cat I seem to be following in recent dreams. I acknowledge I'm in a dream, like "I'm back here." It almost felt like mystical travel, like I traveled here by dreaming. It's like very clean, very organized, tons of stuff in it but easy to explore. I have the feeling, this has all been given to me, it's mine to explore but I don't know where to start. The cat is not there to help or hinder.

We see in this dream the thought that someone might be company without being "the guide," the possibility that he might have support without being utterly dependent and subsumed. We find ourselves in the territory of the use of the object as John learns how to be sufficiently separate that he can also choose to rely on others in ways he finds useful without undermining or betraying himself. In this way, the trope of the betrayal from without can now be discussed in the more complicated terms of the betrayal from within. In this new universe, each person carries their own weight and might have to deal with their own complicity in events.

As John dreams of an old witch who provides him with a safe place and then dies, we could wonder in what ways I was that old witch who provides him with a safe space in which to feel his own feelings and to speak freely. John was faced with the need to kill me off, to leave me behind and move forward with his own life. In that way, this dream served as a poignant reminder of the immanence of ending, an ending afforded by John's newfound ability to know and make use of his own mind. That ability enables him to use others without losing himself in the process.

Through the dream images, John has reconstructed the universe from one that had been dire, deadly, and incomprehensible into one in which various truths could be confronted and worked through. The tenor of our work shifted profoundly with more eye contact and more humor. As John contemplated a future that seemed both desirable and possible, his greater ease was palpable. There was, as Julian Barnes (2011) put it, *the sense of an ending*.

Finally taking a stand against the hoarding that had become its own nightmare, John begins burning papers that had become truly discriminable as debris. He describes feeling a lightness of being he could never have imagined. The urgency of attachment relieves, and, like the transitional object, I can see that I will be left behind. As we end our work together, he still has all the appointment cards he has collected from me over the years. I hope he will, at some point, be able to burn those as well and trust in what he has internalized from the years we spent in intensive study of—and increasingly playful engagement with—the images in his dreams. Years later, I hear he is doing well, finally able to make use in his waking life of the extraordinary creativity we encountered in his dreams.

CONCLUSION

In this chapter, we have tracked ways in which theory can be a useful resource for working with dreams, particularly with those lost within their selves and with little other access to their own creative potential. In the following chapter, I again make use of a clinical case to look at ways in which psychoanalysis can open up possibilities when trauma has foreclosed development. Because trauma can freeze time, I address in particular the issue of psychic time.

14 TRAUMA, RESILIENCE, AND PSYCHIC TIME

In the previous chapter, we discussed how we might make use of dreams and field theory in our work with those whose development has been foreclosed. In this chapter, we turn our attention to the issue of psychic time and ways in which meanings and possibilities can be transformed over time. In addition to looking from the side, looking backward can enable a person to be more fully present in their life and experience.

TROUBLING PSYCHOANALYSIS

Lacan (1964/1977e) has troubled our ideas about psychoanalysis and the possibility of cure or healing, turning our attention to our own desire. To the extent that we are unaware or uninterested in what motivates us in inviting a person into our consulting room, our unconscious desires are even more free to wreak havoc. Lacan, along with Winnicott and others, pointed to the problem of the false self that underlies the desire to discover not ourselves, but rather some better, "new and improved" version, in line with ideas of what is desirable in the eyes of the other. This pursuit leaves us ever further off-balance, like a malformed wheel.

https://doi.org/10.1037/0000455-015
Echoes of Trauma: Meaning and Identity in Psychoanalysis, by M. Charles

What I like about Lacan is that he challenges us to resist taking the word of others for truth, and instead be open to encountering truth where we find it—our own or that of the other—and amend our ideas as we bump into obstructions. To this end, he transformed Freud's ego, superego, and id into his ideas of the *Imaginary*—the realm of individual experience, ideas and meanings, the inevitable idiosyncrasy of the individual's constructions and points of view; the *Symbolic*—the realm of consensual meanings where agreement makes communication possible; and the *Real*—whatever is left over, what we run into at the edges of what we know from experience and from what we learn from others. Lacan's *Real* includes, importantly, the residual meanings from the unconscious that push back at us but are not fully accessible to conscious awareness, the realm of the embodied truths and implicit meanings we have been discussing.

Psychoanalysis has also been troubled by its very push into existence. Opposing the prevailing ideas of the time has resulted in pressured meanings that need to be released from the contexts of their construction so we might free ourselves from outdated constraints and make our own meanings. This process of ongoing construction is essential for the development of ideas and requires that we try to look from the side or backward at our own constructions and recognize the particular contexts in which they are embedded to disentangle the personal, cultural, and historical from the more universal elements.

As Bion (1977) noted, binocular vision shows us more than we can see from any single perspective. Although Freud (1895/1966) needed to oppose ideas of the time to make way for the insights that were developing through his explorations, he was also inevitably thinking through the lenses of his time. Over time, those willing and able to share their own ideas expanded the field in ways that invite us to adopt Freud's (1900/1953b, 1910/1957a) *method of exploration* rather than merely follow whatever conclusions he came to along the way. Whatever use it is put to, psychoanalysis is best viewed as a method and a process, a lens through which to organize our understandings, not as a lexicon of prescribed meanings or dogmatic prescriptions.

In contemporary times, much of what has seemed true is open for further exploration. That very openness, and the uncertainty that accompanies it, invites us to close down as we try to find some anchors we can rely on. That regressive pull toward safety is important to recognize if we are also going to be intrepid and search for meaning in our work with those who come to us seeking assistance. We use our training as a conceptual map through which to organize our insights, but we always need to be open to the singularity of the person before us. Perhaps more than ever, people need room to learn and to grow, a free space in which to explore possibilities and face what is most difficult to face in themselves and in others. The psychoanalytic practitioner is in a good position to open up that type of space to the extent that they have traversed it themselves. To that end, our journeys into our own minds, hearts, and beings are at the core of the work, but theory can also help us be open to possibilities if we can carry it loosely and consider it rather than be constrained by it. That is the spirit in which I offer you this volume: a spirit of collective inquiry, knowing that this is at heart a personal journey, but one with implications for us all as fellow travelers on a course of self-discovery.

Along with those issues previously mentioned, psychoanalysis has been troubled by a tendency to become lodged in binaries. I imagine this is inevitable. Learning depends on developing categories to begin to make sense of the complexities. One binary that perhaps was inevitable was Freud's relationship with women: the *dark continent* of otherness he referred to and stumbled over (Freud, 1926/1959). With respect to that divide in our beginnings, I would like to offer a quote from Hélène Cixous, from 1976, on what remains secret in women. She said, "Her shameful sickness is that she resists death, that she makes trouble" (Cixous et al., 1976, p. 876). I think we have not made nearly enough trouble, and everyone suffers from that lack. The trauma of repression of women is the backdrop in Western culture, entangled with the repression in men that turns toward the obsessive in terrible ways. This fundamental splitting leaves us in the position Lacan (1975–1976/2016) pointed to in suggesting that what we stumble over is the idea that something has been taken away, foreclosed to us, which leaves us tripping over what is missing rather than trying to discover it.

In our journey tracking the impact of trauma on identity, we have seen how the most destructive force waylaying development in children often comes from failures in mourning that leave parents unreliably available to attend to the needs of the child, the type of small-t, complex trauma that impedes growth. The overwhelming flooding of affect attendant to failures in parental containment becomes a precursor for later feelings of shame, humiliation, and alienation. These feelings, then, as they arise later in life, point to internal deficits in ways that invite hopelessness and helplessness, further obstructing the ability to find oneself within an evolving life story. In contrast, Lacan's (1964/1977e) ideas regarding our reluctance to face our own limits invite us to consider ways in which the failures in mourning that impede growth may be linked with enigmatic messages from the parent regarding the impossibility of finding a valued place in the world (Laplanche, 1997).

In this regard, Freud's early work may have led us astray. In fact, he seemed to have a blind spot for the impact of potentially traumatic factors he had good reason to be aware of (Blum, 2007). His focus, instead, was on how we move from a preliminary self-focus toward the interpersonal engagement that underlies both resilience and the capacity to care. That capacity, as Winnicott (1971) taught us, requires our ability to stand as a separate self in relation to others who can keep their own grounding. No real care is possible without sufficient sturdiness to recognize both sameness and difference, as Cixous et al. (1976) suggested, to move past convention and fly.

Our models evolve within the metaphors driving meaning in our times. Current times push past Freud's (1914/1958d) ideas of primary narcissism toward a kaleidoscopic, holographic, associative view of meanings through which the part reveals the whole, a perspective in line with Lacan's (1964/1977e) ideas of the unconscious structuring of meaning that may become visible but not overcome. Much as DNA drives development, known through its expressions, the structuring of our being is similarly enigmatic but also recognizable—if we track the patterns. Psychoanalysis takes a stand for the meaning at the core of human being and behavior. At the intersection of the particular structurings that shape the individual and the impediments to development occasioned by trauma, we find the person positioned such that the particularities of their unique being make themselves known through their manifestations.

NACHTRÄGLICHKEIT

We have noted ways in which a view from the side can help us recognize those particularities, but Freud's cases also show the importance of the backward glance that can disrupt the story as it has been told, leaving room for realization of information left out. Early on, Freud (1895/1966) introduced the idea of *Nachträglichkeit*, translated as "deferred action" or, in Lacan's terms, *afterwardsness*, the *après-coup*. We see this process in Winnicott's (1974) descriptions of the fear of the breakdown that has already happened and in Lacan's (1964/1977e) diagrams of the shift backward from the point of exigency. This push for false reassurance as the person ignores what continues to be excluded from the story invites the clinician's disruption as a technical tool that marks the enactment. Laplanche (1997) took up this issue in the enigmatic message that can only be recognized in retrospect, illuminating unintegrated aspects of experience that have driven development.

For Freud, Nachträglichkeit refers to events whose meanings are deferred to a subsequent point in time that renders them meaningful, that makes "possible a different understanding of what was remembered" (Freud, 1895/1966, p. 356). Lacan (1953/1977b) was the first to highlight Freud's particular conceptualization of psychic temporality and causality in the case of the Wolf Man. Laplanche and Pontalis (1968) then recognized this process as a general mechanism in psychoanalysis, which they termed the *après-coup*.

For Faimberg (2007), Freud's views of Nachträglichkeit are subversive in shifting our view of meaning-making from the linear to one that is more respectful of the constructive aspects of this project. With this idea in mind, she focused on this constructive aspect of Nachträglichkeit that can occur as meanings shift and are reinterpreted through the analytic process. In this regard, she saw Winnicott's (1974) ideas formulated as the fear of the breakdown that has already happened as "paradigmatic of this broader concept of Nachträglichkeit" (p. 1222). Adding to these ideas what we know from Kristeva (1986), Aulagnier (2001), and Laplanche (1997) regarding meanings that cannot be parsed because they register affectively without the words through which they might be contextualized, we are in a better position to understand some of the sequelae of complex trauma and how putting the story together can help to alleviate its impact.

In Laplanche's (1997) formulation, the child receives enigmatic messages that cannot be parsed, in part because the child cannot yet formulate meanings from the world of the adult, but often the adult is not even aware of some of the nuances of the nonverbal communications. These transmitted meanings remain unconscious but profoundly impactful, in part because they cannot be recognized, responded to, softened, or attenuated. Following Lacan, Laplanche (1997) stressed the importance of respecting the inevitable alienness of the other in relation to whatever is real. In this way, he made space for the unconscious of each of us such that "the adult transmits a message . . . he 'makes a sign' from his own unconscious" (p. 660). "The analytic situation, as long as it is maintained and well beyond the theories that are given of it, bears witness to the upheaval caused in the individual by a renewed confrontation with the enigma of the other" (Laplanche, 1997, p. 663). For Laplanche, then, the centrality of the message from the other is always there, however we may read it. Our ideas about those messages may be seen as projections, coming from our own imaginaries, but their origins are not in us. This paradox results in a felt sense of truth, according to Lacan (1971–1972/2018), because the knowledge received at this level seems to occur at the level of the soul.

Creativity, from Laplanche's perspective, is set in motion by the enigmatic call from the other. "Cultural activity is an opening out on to the other, an address to the other . . . related to that opening caused *by* the other" (Laplanche, 1997, p. 664). If we can find our position in relation to the very alienness of the address by the other, then, suggested Laplanche, we may have a very different relation to inspiration and, with it, to our own creative capacities. From that position, we become informed or impacted by the other rather than constrained or defined in relation to a projected other.

CASE ILLUSTRATION

To enter into this territory together, I begin with a brief clinical vignette from the case of Sophia, a woman whose trauma occurred later in life and who had been afforded sufficient grounding in her early years that she was able to regain her bearings and achieve insight into even the troubles that were only revealed in retrospect. From that point, she could also recognize the insidious misrecognitions from early childhood that had contributed to her suffering.

Sophia, an immigrant, came to treatment in her late forties, frightened by a 2-year descent into a suicidal depression so compelling that, despite her devotion to her family, she tried to kill herself three times. Having finally found some relief from the darkness that enveloped her, she was terrified that it might return. In the brief time of our work together, it seemed that Sophia found sufficient containment to find herself within the traumatic narrative rather than merely being lost in it.

At one point, she tells me that she has been listening to podcasts by Tara Brach. A particular line has remained with her: "Through the wound is the place where the light enters." Brach had linked that line to a quote from Leonard Cohen, which Sophia misquotes as: "In the broken pieces, light shines through." "I like that," she says.

I recognize this line as coming from Cohen's song "Anthem" (L. Cohen, 1992). The line goes: "There is a crack, a crack in everything. That's how the light gets in." Leonard Cohen's lyrics come back to me:

> Ring the bells that still can ring
> Forget your perfect offering.
> There is a crack, a crack in everything
> That's how the light gets in.

Sophia thinks lovingly of these cracks that allow the light in, which brings to my mind *Kintsugi*, which means "golden joinery," coming from the art of repairing broken pottery with lacquer and gold, suggesting that even though something may be damaged, it may still be valuable and have meaning. Kintsugi affirms the beauty of imperfection and impermanence, a metaphor for the aesthetic and human values of growth and transformation.

The next day, Sophia says,

> Throughout the weeks here, I really feel my self-love is back. I feel it strongly. I'm more thinking about me. How being alive is a miracle, and spending the rest of my life in a meaningful way, and the quote I made you: That's how the light gets in.

Going back to Lacan again, there is the idea that we avoid recognizing our damage and our lack, which is also our particularity. If we can accept it, we might find a way to live in the world as ourselves. But we tend to stumble over the fact of our limit, either looking for a way past it or to avoid being faced with it. Looking for a way past it is the neurotic solution; avoiding being faced with it is the perverse. Lacan (1953/1977b) located the unconscious as a structural process—like a language, which is particular in its manifestations but universal in its rules. Like prions, proteins that incorrectly replicate themselves, the body creates a template that organizes us in relation to those early, rhythmic patterns referred to by Kristeva (1986) and Milner (1987), and then, separately, we create a story about it. From this perspective, psychoanalysis becomes a process whereby the story is deconstructed sufficiently that the light might show through the cracks.

It is precisely through these cracks in the story as it has evolved that we encounter aspects of experience that remain unintegrated. The symptom marks a meaning that is troubling without being parsable (Lacan, 1962–1963/2014), leaving people seeking a cure for what ails them. But even this idea of cure, of healing, is ensconced in ideas that Lacan (1975–1976/2016) suggested may obscure what is really at stake. Rather, I think that what is at stake is the ability to encounter the pushback and be interested in it so that we might, perhaps, learn something more. Much like Bion's (1977) conceptualization of *O*, a real that we can touch but never quite stay in, there is a psychoanalytic notion of becoming that does not offer a resting place.

I think of another line from Leonard Cohen, something about "comes as a refugee" that I think relates to love. Checking into it, I find that this, too, comes from the song "Anthem": "Every heart, every heart, to love will come, but like a refugee" (L. Cohen, 1992). There is something in this that seems right to me.

I think of Sophia, a foreigner in this land, who, I think, was mistreated in part because she was a refugee. There is an insidious disparagement of difference that festers under cover of darkness. Shining a light on it requires recognizing how we are all implicated in the stereotyped meaning structures of internal racism (Davids, 2011). I encounter Sophia as a refugee from a health care system that seemed to see her as so hopeless and dangerous that their only offer of "cure" was to shock her brain for a year even though no benefit was derived. That she came to me with any hope left was, indeed, both a miracle and a tribute to her capacity for love that affords her some faith in a humanity that has in so many ways failed her.

Sophia muses on her mother but, in many ways, she might be speaking about herself: "She had a tough life. And yet she's so strong, objective, loving—it's amazing." Leonard Cohen comes back to me:

> Ring the bells that still can ring
> Forget your perfect offering.
> There is a crack, a crack in everything
> That's how the light gets in.

Sophia intuitively recognizes in Tara Brach's words a meaning that calls to her soul and replenishes her, but without necessarily understanding why. This process seems to be a fundamentally creative one, as Laplanche (1997) described it, the type of opening out that is set in motion by the enigmatic call from the other "related to that opening caused *by* the other" (p. 664). If we can find our position in relation to the very alienness of the address by the other, suggested Laplanche, we may have a very different relation to inspiration and, with it, to our own creative capacities. In our clinical work, it is important to be able to support the work being done so that the person might more easily become informed or impacted by another rather than constrained or defined in relation to a projected other.

LOOKING BACKWARD

In looking at the case of Sophia, we find a woman who in many ways sits at the opposite end of the character continuum from the narcissist. Her Achilles' heel was to have focused too much on care for others. When her own needs became compelling, she was unable to orient toward them and lost herself in the process. Finding herself again was laborious, but she was sufficiently object-related to be able to use her experiences of self and other to find answers to her questions regarding what had happened.

Engaging empathically with others who found themselves cast as various characters in her own developmental drama, Sophia was able to see herself and others in these various roles and to integrate a complex understanding that allowed for mourning, working through, and repair. Her empathic recognition of the plights of those around her who are damaged by life and inhibited in their experience is an important reminder to those of us in the "caring" professions that we can only be useful to others to the extent that we can find our common humanity and recognize the limits of what we can know or do for another human being.

Notably, as a refugee, Sophia found herself between two cultures, neither of which entirely embraced the whole of her being or desires (Tummala-Narra, 2019). This fact required respect from those who intended to offer assistance so that our efforts did not so easily cover over important aspects of her being. In some ways, emigration from her home of origin had resulted in cracks in the story that had been constructed through the lens of that culture. These cracks enabled her to imagine possibilities for herself that had seemed out of reach and out of place. From the perspective of this culture, however, there were differences in value that needed to be cracked into so that Sophia could organize her sense of self in world in ways that were true to the amalgam of values she had inherited and adopted.

CONCLUSION

When trauma has impeded the development of a coherent self capable of meeting and recovering from life's challenges, the individual is inevitably off-balance, living in fear of the truth that will reveal their smallness and insufficiency. Our job is to recognize this fear empathically, hold it, and speak to it in ways that recognize its legitimacy as one stopping point in a journey that is ongoing. Essential to an empathic position is that, for some individuals, it is precisely the light of insight through the crack—which might ultimately provide relief—that feels most dangerous. Perhaps it is with these individuals that we most need to have in mind Bion's (1990) insight regarding the harshness of the light of our illuminations. This insight reminds us that, at times, what is needed is to allow the darkness to deepen sufficiently to allow the cracks to be discerned, tolerated, and embraced.

There are many perils in our path in working with such vulnerable individuals. With those caught off-balance within themselves, we need to be able to ride the waves of defensive, wounded vulnerability to build relational resilience within the person and within the relationship. In doing such work, it is important to keep in mind the emptiness at the core of that world—and to be empathic with the plight of one so terribly alone—so that we can discern the light that shines within and the meanings and values on which that light depends.

We need heroes. And mentors. People who believe in us. When that function is not filled early on, it becomes difficult to believe in the believer. That difficulty results in a terrible isolation that we must be able to be empathic toward, and resilient in the face of, to continue to cross the divides. In contrast, when the trauma has occurred later, we need to be able to recognize the resilience lying in wait and find once again the person who has lost themselves, to provide a scaffolding through which they can accustom themselves to the light of their own insights and the beauty of their own particularity: their own soul.

To be believed in, we must believe in ourselves, grounded in our own histories, our own embodied experience, our own truths. At the outer limit of the rational, we find the unconscious reservoir that holds our creative potential. If we can stand in that space, we find, standing with us, along with our more familiar psychoanalytic fathers, Hélène Cixous, Nina Coltart, Marian Milner, Joyce McDougall, Julia Kristeva, and all our other psychoanalytic mothers, reminding us that, in standing as ourselves and opposing the dogmatic turn, we shine a light toward personhood for those who have lost their way and need to find not our insights, but rather their own.

EPILOGUE

Instruments in Need of Fine-Tuning

In this volume, we traced the development of the capacities to feel, to think, and to be. As we come to the end of this investigation, we are reminded that we, too, as clinicians, are continually developing these capacities in ourselves as we journey alongside our fellow travelers. I hope that you will carry what you have learned gently, in the background, as you continue to engage deeply and learn from your own experience. We often hear that we are instruments in need of fine-tuning, and I think that is a wonderful metaphor for this work. It allows us to refine our craft and still be susceptible to misattunements and wrong notes. It is in the being human with those who come to work with us that possibilities emerge.

If we really take seriously what we are learning about mirror neurons in the context of the developmental and attachment literature, we see that people develop most fully in relation to one another when there is an attentive being who recognizes their responsibility to the person in need of care. From that vantage point, in the clinical encounter I offer what I can, learning in real time how the other person responds to these offerings, both accommodating to and speaking about what I think I am learning. From that place, truly astonishing things can occur.

https://doi.org/10.1037/0000455-016
Echoes of Trauma: Meaning and Identity in Psychoanalysis, by M. Charles

This stance, however, at times requires the breaking of boundaries that have good reason to remain in place. I am not talking, of course, about the absolute boundaries that cannot be transgressed, but rather the more convenient boundaries that help us end a session on time or keep our own personal interests out of the playing field. The problem of crossing these other, more uncertain lines is that we will need to reestablish them at the appropriate time. In coming up against an externally imposed constraint that seems to violate a pressing need in the moment, we need sufficient wherewithal to be able to make a meaningful choice without incurring disaster.

These pressures were prevalent in my very early work with a young woman in her early twenties with an extensive history of trauma and neglect. My supervisor at the time saw her as "borderline" in a way that was linked with such contempt that I found I could not even keep her in mind in our conversations. I soon learned to present my other cases to him instead, and she ultimately grew into an extraordinary being, capable of creative work and meaningful relationships.

When I met Siobhan, she was lost, not only in her own development, but also within the world of diagnoses that marked her as hopelessly damaged. In trying to meet her needs, I often found myself in liminal spaces that felt dangerous in relation to "rules" but essential in terms of human decency. There are moments when the press for extra session times needs to be managed and moments when the time needs to be offered. But then, we need to be prepared for the time when the offering becomes proof of something we are not willing to agree with, when the extra time is not needed for the work, but rather has become a form of self-soothing reassurance or an illegitimate demand that obstructs growth rather than furthers it. That is when interpretation needs to come back into play so that we are not fostering dependency or offering false promises, but rather marking the dilemma as we see it. Learning these lessons through real-time experience has prepared me for the work I am now doing with Caroline.

Caroline is a woman in her sixties, who has come to me after many decades of intensive work trying to overcome the sequelae of early trauma and neglect. Caroline sought me out because she had encountered me in the past and carried some sense that I might be up to the task at hand. Most recently, she has been using mind-altering substances to help break through the wall she finds herself behind and is looking for someone to help her make sense of her journeys.

It has been an odd and intense ride because she alternately enacts her trauma and speaks about it. It has taken some time for me to get my bearings, find my place, and begin to make offerings that are in alignment with her needs. Often, I do not know precisely what she is communicating or whether my job is to witness or to speak. Through it all, Caroline's respect for my limits and appreciation of my honesty have helped me sustain my engagement and push past my fears. As we speak out loud from our adult selves about difficult encounters, we help to arm ourselves for the more difficult journeys into the psychic spaces she is trying to explore.

A breakthrough occurred recently, after I had finally registered that she needed me, not merely to recognize what was being depicted before me, but to speak to it as best I might. This demanded fortitude on my part, to tolerate whatever reactions might result, including irritation, anger, or derision. Initially, I erred (properly, I think) on the side of respecting her own knowledge of herself, her needs, desires, and intentions, so that I might learn her language. However, a moment came when it seemed that Caroline was hurting herself in relation to what seemed to be false premises. "You seem to be trying to evacuate the trauma forcefully as a way of rebirthing yourself. But I think that the path need not be through suffering," I said. That seemed to be the interpretation that *touched,* in Sirois's (2012) sense of the term. Her face and whole being seemed to soften as she took in that idea. The next day, she marked, aloud, its importance, a touchstone to hold onto as she tried to forge a different path.

We never know what a person needs when we first encounter them. But we can learn if we are sufficiently open. I find that those I work with are generous in tolerating whatever needs to be tolerated in their encounters with me. I think that generosity stems from their sense that I am trying, as best I can, to have integrity in my dealings with them. I need not be any more clever or even available in a given moment than I am able to be. But I do need to show up when they need me. Speaking from one's own experience invites greater authenticity in precisely those moments when the path is not clear.

I now return to the vignette in Chapter 12 of my granddaughter, who at age 1 was learning to become herself in relation to a mother who offered herself to be modeled in relation to a young child who has been able to obtain attention when she needs it. Now, at age 11, she is able to mark injustice and speak to it with great authority. Her brother is a quieter, gentler being but is absolutely intrepid in his own way. These children mark the legitimacy of everything I have been trying to teach you in this volume.

As the child of traumatically unavailable parents, despite their very best intentions, I was left to wander the earth in search of enigmatic meanings that tantalized and tortured me. My husband gave me a loving home, and psychoanalysis gave me meaning structures through which to repair and reclaim the possibilities that had remained elusive. My grandchildren, with their shining lights, are testaments to the absolute value of these efforts. Keeping them in mind helps me face the ongoing challenges posed in these clinical journeys. I offer these words to you in the hope that they might serve you in this way as well. We all need lights in the darkness, and, at times, as Bion has reminded us, we must soften our lights and find our way in the darkness.

There is a truth to each person's life. As we learn to live from that place, there are reverberations for all those around us.

References

Abraham, N., & Torok, M. (1994). *The shell and the kernel: Vol. 1. Renewals of psychoanalysis* (N. T. Rand, Ed. & Trans., pp. 171–176). The University of Chicago Press. (Original work published 1975)

Adams, G., Fryberg, S. A., Garcia, D. M., & Delgado-Torres, E. U. (2006). The psychology of engagement with indigenous identities: A cultural perspective. *Cultural Diversity & Ethnic Minority Psychology, 12*(3), 493–508. https://doi.org/10.1037/1099-9809.12.3.493

Adenzato, M., Todisco, P., & Ardito, R. B. (2012). Social cognition in anorexia nervosa: Evidence of preserved theory of mind and impaired emotional functioning. *PLOS ONE*. Advance online publication. https://doi.org/10.1371/journal.pone.0044414

Aisenstein, M. (2006). The indissociable unity of psyche and soma: A view from the Paris Psychosomatic School. *The International Journal of Psychoanalysis, 87*(3), 667–680. https://doi.org/10.1516/0VBX-1HGY-T86R-P5CB

Akhtar, S. (1989). Narcissistic personality disorder. Descriptive features and differential diagnosis. *The Psychiatric Clinics of North America, 12*(3), 505–529. https://doi.org/10.1016/S0193-953X(18)30411-8

Akhtar, S. (1995). A third individuation: Immigration, identity, and the psychoanalytic process. *Journal of the American Psychoanalytic Association, 43*(4), 1051–1084. https://doi.org/10.1177/000306519504300406

American Psychiatric Association. (2013). *Diagnostic and statistical manual of mental disorders* (5th ed.). https://doi.org/10.1176/appi.books.9780890425596

Amianto, F., Bertorello, A., Migliore, F., Abbate-Daga, G., & Fassino, S. (2016). Alexithymia in anorexia and bulimia: Ubiquitous and primary trait? *Cogent Psychology, 3*(1), Article 1185994. https://doi.org/10.1080/23311908.2016.1185994

Apollon, W., Bergeron, D., & Cantin, L. (2002). *After Lacan: Clinical practice and the subject of the unconscious*. State University of New York Press. https://doi.org/10.1353/book4575

Apprey, M. (2024). *Transgenerational haunting in psychoanalysis: Toxic errands*. Routledge.

Arlow, J. A. (1987). The dynamics of interpretation. *The Psychoanalytic Quarterly*, *56*(1), 68–87. https://doi.org/10.1080/21674086.1987.11927166

Atkinson, J. (2002). *Trauma trails, recreating song lines: The transgenerational effects of trauma in Indigenous Australia*. Spinifex Press.

Aulagnier, P. (2001). *The violence of interpretation: From pictogram to statement*. Brunner-Routledge.

Aulagnier, P. (2015). Birth of a body, origin of a history. *The International Journal of Psychoanalysis*, *96*(5), 1371–1401. https://doi.org/10.1111/1745-8315.12345

Bankier, B., Aigner, M., & Bach, M. (2001). Alexithymia in *DSM-IV* disorder: Comparative evaluation of somatoform disorder, panic disorder, obsessive-compulsive disorder, and depression. *Psychosomatics*, *42*(3), 235–240. https://doi.org/10.1176/appi.psy.42.3.235

Baraitser, L. (2023). Passivity and gender: Psychical inertia and maternal stillness. *The International Journal of Psychoanalysis*, *104*(5), 912–926. https://doi.org/10.1080/00207578.2023.2255470

Barnes, J. (2011). *The sense of an ending*. Random House.

Bateman, A. W. (1998). Thick- and thin-skinned organisations and enactment in borderline and narcissistic disorders. *The International Journal of Psycho-Analysis*, *79*(1), 13–25.

Beebe, B., Lachmann, F., & Jaffe, J. (1997). Mother–infant interaction structures and presymbolic self- and object representations. *Psychoanalytic Dialogues*, *7*(2), 133–182. https://doi.org/10.1080/10481889709539172

Beebe, B., & Lachmann, F. M. (1988). The contributions of mother–infant mutual influence to the origins of self and object representations. *Psychoanalytic Psychology*, *5*(4), 305–337. https://doi.org/10.1037/0736-9735.5.4.305

Beebe, B., & Lachmann, F. M. (1994). Representation and internalization in infancy: Three principles of salience. *Psychoanalytic Psychology*, *11*(2), 127–165. https://doi.org/10.1037/h0079530

Beebe, B., & Lachmann, F. M. (1998). Co-constructing inner and relational processes: Self and mutual regulation in infant research and adult treatment. *Psychoanalytic Psychology*, *15*(4), 480–516. https://doi.org/10.1037/0736-9735.15.4.480

Beebe, B., Rustin, J., Sorter, D., & Knoblauch, S. (2003). An expanded view of intersubjectivity in infancy and its application to psychoanalysis. *Psychoanalytic Dialogues*, *13*(6), 805–841. https://doi.org/10.1080/10481881309348769

Belkin, M. (2021a). Intersectionality and psychoanalysis. *Contemporary Psychoanalysis*, *57*(2), 163–164. https://doi.org/10.1080/00107530.2021.1934808

Belkin, M. (2021b). Towards an intersectional psychoanalysis of race, gender, and sexuality. *Contemporary Psychoanalysis*, *57*(2), 206–227. https://doi.org/10.1080/00107530.2021.1935033

Beneduce, R. (2016). Traumatic pasts and the historical imagination: Symptoms of loss, postcolonial suffering, and counter-memories among African migrants. *Transcultural Psychiatry, 53*(3), 261–285. https://doi.org/10.1177/1363461516645079

Benzies, K., Tough, S., Edwards, N., Mychasiuk, R., & Donnelly, C. (2011). Aboriginal children and their caregivers living with low income: Outcomes from a two-generation preschool program. *Journal of Child and Family Studies, 20*(3), 311–318. https://doi.org/10.1007/s10826-010-9394-3

Bernardi, R., & Eidlin, M. (2018). Thin-skinned or vulnerable narcissism and thick-skinned or grandiose narcissism: Similarities and differences. *The International Journal of Psychoanalysis, 99*(2), 291–313. https://doi.org/10.1080/00207578.2018.1425599

Bick, E. (1968). The experience of the skin in early object-relations. *The International Journal of Psycho-Analysis, 49*(2), 484–486.

Bilotta, E., Carcione, A., Fera, T., Moroni, F., Nicolò, G., Pedone, R., Pellecchia, G., Semerari, A., & Colle, L. (2018). Symptom severity and mindreading in narcissistic personality disorder. *PLOS ONE, 13*(8). Advance online publication. https://doi.org/10.1371/journal.pone.0201216

Bion, W. R. (1959). Attacks on linking. *The International Journal of Psychoanalysis, 40*, 308–315.

Bion, W. R. (1961). *Experiences in groups: And other papers*. Routledge.

Bion, W. R. (1962). *Learning from experience*. Heinemann.

Bion, W. R. (1963). *Elements of psychoanalysis*. Heinemann.

Bion, W. R. (1965). *Transformations*. Heinemann.

Bion, W. R. (1967a). Notes on memory and desire. *Psychoanalytic Forum, 2*, 271–280.

Bion, W. R. (1967b). *Second thoughts: Selected papers on psycho-analysis*. Jason Aronson.

Bion, W. R. (1970). *Attention and interpretation*. Jason Aronson.

Bion, W. R. (1977). *Seven Servants*. Jason Aronson.

Bion, W. R. (1980). *Bion in New York and São Paolo*. Clunie Press.

Bion, W. R. (1989). *Two papers: The "Grid" and "Caesura"* (pp. 3–33). Karnac Books. (Reprinted from *Two papers: The "Grid" and "Caesura,"* 1977, Imago Editora)

Bion, W. R. (1990). *Brazilian lectures: 1973, São Paolo: 1974, Rio de Janeiro/São Paolo*. Routledge.

Bion, W. R. (1992). *Cogitations*. Karnac Books.

Black-Gutman, D., & Hickson, F. (1996). The relationship between racial attitudes and social-cognitive development in children: An Australian study. *Developmental Psychology, 32*(3), 448–456. https://doi.org/10.1037/0012-1649.32.3.448

Blum, H. P. (2007). Little Hans: A centennial review and reconsideration. *Journal of the American Psychoanalytic Association, 55*(3), 749–765. https://doi.org/10.1177/00030651070550030201

Bowen, M. (1978). *Family therapy in clinical practice*. Jason Aronson.

Bower, G. H. (1981). Mood and memory. *American Psychologist, 36*(2), 129–148. https://doi.org/10.1037/0003-066X.36.2.129

Brance, K., Chatzimpyros, V., & Bentall, R. P. (2024). Social identity, mental health and the experience of migration. *British Journal of Social Psychology*. Advance online publication. https://doi.org/10.1111/bjso.12745

Breuer, J., & Freud, S. (1955). Studies on hysteria. In J. Strachey (Ed. & Trans.), *The standard edition of the complete psychological works of Sigmund Freud* (Vol. 2, pp. 1–335). The Hogarth Press. (Original work published 1895)

Brockmeyer, T., Pellegrino, J., Münch, H., Herzog, W., Dziobek, I., & Friederich, H.-C. (2016). Social cognition in anorexia nervosa: Specific difficulties in decoding emotional but not nonemotional mental states. *International Journal of Eating Disorders, 49*(9), 883–890. https://doi.org/10.1002/eat.22574

Bromberg, P. M. (1983). The mirror and the mask: On narcissism and psychoanalytic growth. *Contemporary Psychoanalysis, 19*(2), 359–387. https://doi.org/10.1080/00107530.1983.10746614

Bronstein, C. (2011). On psychosomatics: The search for meaning. *The International Journal of Psychoanalysis, 92*(1), 173–195. https://doi.org/10.1111/j.1745-8315.2010.00388.x

Brown, M., & Charles, M. (Eds.). (2019a). *Women & psychosis: Multidisciplinary perspectives*. Lexington Books.

Brown, M., & Charles, M. (Eds.). (2019b). *Women and the psychosocial construction of madness*. Lexington Books.

Bucci, W. (1997). Symptoms and symbols: A multiple code theory of somatization. *Psychoanalytic Inquiry, 17*(2), 151–172. https://doi.org/10.1080/07351699709534117

Bucci, W. (2001). Pathways of emotional communication. *Psychoanalytic Inquiry, 21*(1), 40–70. https://doi.org/10.1080/07351692109348923

Bucci, W. (2002). The referential process, consciousness, and the sense of self. *Psychoanalytic Inquiry, 22*(5), 766–793. https://doi.org/10.1080/07351692209349017

Bucci, W. (2018). The primary process as a transitional concept: New perspectives from cognitive psychology and affective neuroscience. *Psychoanalytic Inquiry, 38*(3), 198–209. https://doi.org/10.1080/07351690.2018.1430966

Bucci, W., Maskit, B., & Murphy, S. (2016). Connecting emotions and words: The referential process. *Phenomenology and the Cognitive Sciences, 15*(3), 359–383. https://doi.org/10.1007/s11097-015-9417-z

Burke, H. M., Davis, M. C., Otte, C., & Mohr, D. C. (2005). Depression and cortisol responses to psychological stress: A meta-analysis. *Psychoneuroendocrinology, 30*(9), 846–856. https://doi.org/10.1016/j.psyneuen.2005.02.010

Campbell, J. (1949). *The hero with a thousand faces*. Princeton University Press.

Carignani, P. (2012). I. The body in psychoanalysis. *British Journal of Psychotherapy, 28*(3), 288–318. https://doi.org/10.1111/j.1752-0118.2012.01299.x

Caruth, C. (1991). Unclaimed experience: Trauma and the possibility of history. *Yale French Studies*, *79*, 181–192. https://doi.org/10.2307/2930251

Carvalho, R. (2012). II. A brief introduction to the thought of Armando B. Ferrari. *British Journal of Psychotherapy*, *28*(4), 413–434. https://doi.org/10.1111/j.1752-0118.2012.01300.x

Cassirer, E. (1957). *The philosophy of symbolic forms: Vol. 3. The phenomenology of knowledge*. Oxford University Press.

Charles, M. (2000a). Convex and concave, Part I: Images of emptiness in women. *American Journal of Psychoanalysis*, *60*(1), 5–27. https://doi.org/10.1023/A:1001823827655

Charles, M. (2000b). The intergenerational transmission of unresolved mourning: Personal, familial, and cultural factors. *Samīkṣa*, *54*, 65–80.

Charles, M. (2001). The language of the body: Allusions to self-experience in women's poetry. *Psychoanalytic Psychology*, *18*(2), 340–364. https://doi.org/10.1037/0736-9735.18.2.340

Charles, M. (2002a). Bion's Grid: A tool for transformation. *The Journal of the American Academy of Psychoanalysis*, *30*(3), 429–445. https://doi.org/10.1521/jaap.30.3.429.21971

Charles, M. (2002b). *Patterns: Building blocks of experience*. The Analytic Press.

Charles, M. (2003). On faith, hope, and possibility. *The Journal of the American Academy of Psychoanalysis and Dynamic Psychiatry*, *31*(4), 687–704. https://doi.org/10.1521/jaap.31.4.687.23000

Charles, M. (2004). *Constructing realities: Transformations through myth and metaphor* (pp. 85–93). Brill. https://doi.org/10.1163/9789401202367_010

Charles, M. (2006). Silent scream: The cost of crucifixion—Working with a patient with an eating disorder. *The Journal of the American Academy of Psychoanalysis and Dynamic Psychiatry*, *34*(2), 261–285. https://doi.org/10.1521/jaap.2006.34.2.261

Charles, M. (2010). When cultures collide: Myth, meaning, and configural space. *Modern Psychoanalysis*, *34*(1), 26–47.

Charles, M. (2012). *Working with trauma: Lessons from Bion and Lacan*. Jason Aronson.

Charles, M. (2014). The intergenerational transmission of trauma: Effects on identity development in Aboriginal people. In N. Tracey (Ed.), *Transgenerational trauma and the Aboriginal preschool child: Healing through intervention* (pp. 133–152). Rowman & Littlefield.

Charles, M. (2018). A Kleinian/Bionian perspective. In M. Charles (Ed.), *Comparative psychoanalysis: Defining terms and building bridges* (pp. 75–96). Routledge.

Charles, M. (2019). The dream and the image: Creative transformations in psychoanalytic space. *American Journal of Psychoanalysis*, *79*(2), 174–195. https://doi.org/10.1057/s11231-019-09194-2

Charles, M. (2020). Borderline: A diagnostic straightjacket? *Free Associations: Psychoanalysis and Culture, Media, Groups. Politics, 78,* 50–65. https://www.freeassociations.org.uk/FA_New/OJS/index.php/fa/article/view/328/437

Charles, M. (2021a). Creative transformations: The establishment, the mystic and the aesthetic drive. In M. Brown & R. S. Brown (Eds.), *Emancipatory perspectives on madness: Psychological, social, and spiritual dimensions* (pp. 152–167). Routledge.

Charles, M. (2021b). Meaning, metaphor, and metabolization: The case of eating disorders. *American Journal of Psychoanalysis, 81*(4), 444–466. https://doi.org/10.1057/s11231-021-09324-9

Charles, M. (2023). Working psychoanalytically with the family as an adjunct to individual treatment. *Psychoanalytic Social Work,* 1–27. https://doi.org/10.1080/15228878.2023.2198650

Charles, M. (2024). Somatization and symbolization. *The American Journal of Psychoanalysis, 84,* 57–78. https://doi.org/10.1057/s11231-024-09441-1

Civitarese, G. (2005). Fire at the theatre: (Un)reality of/in the transference. *The International Journal of Psychoanalysis, 86*(5), 1299–1316. https://doi.org/10.1516/EQ54-C5GF-LL64-1NUX

Civitarese, G. (2006). Dreams that mirror the session. *The International Journal of Psychoanalysis, 87*(3), 703–723. https://doi.org/10.1516/CQUL-BUPN-30QQ-XQ88

Civitarese, G. (2015). Transformations in hallucinosis and the receptivity of the analyst. *The International Journal of Psychoanalysis, 96*(4), 1091–1116. https://doi.org/10.1111/1745-8315.12242

Civitarese, G., & Ferro, A. (2013). The meaning and use of metaphor in analytic field theory. *Psychoanalytic Inquiry, 33*(3), 190–209. https://doi.org/10.1080/07351690.2013.779887

Cixous, H., Cohen, K., & Cohen, P. (1976). The laugh of the Medusa. *Signs, 1*(4), 875–893. https://doi.org/10.1086/493306

Cohen, A. (2024). This is who I am: Psychotherapy with gender questioning and transgender adolescents. *Journal of Child Psychotherapy, 50*(1), 145–165. https://doi.org/10.1080/0075417X.2023.2279638 (Correction published 2024, *Journal of Child Psychotherapy, 50*(1), p. 1. https://doi.org/10.1080/0075417X.2024.2329426)

Cohen, L. (1992). Anthem [Song]. On *The future*. Columbia.

Coltart, N. (1992). *Slouching towards Bethlehem*. The Guilford Press.

Constable, M. D., Rajsic, J., Welsh, T. N., & Pratt, J. (2019). It is not in the details: Self-related shapes are rapidly classified but their features are not better remembered. *Memory & Cognition, 47*(6), 1145–1157. https://doi.org/10.3758/s13421-019-00924-6

Cook, C. C. H. (2004). Psychiatry and mysticism. *Mental Health, Religion & Culture, 7*(2), 149–163. https://doi.org/10.1080/13674670310001602436

Craig, A. D. (Bud). (2009). How do you feel—Now? The anterior insula and human awareness. *Nature Reviews Neuroscience, 10*(1), 59–70. https://doi.org/10.1038/nrn2555

Crociani-Windland, L., & Charles, M. (2022a). Editorial. *Journal of Psychosocial Studies, 15*(2), 83–86. https://doi.org/10.1332/147867321X16575521436529

Crociani-Windland, L., & Charles, M. (Eds.). (2022b). Repositioning the maternal: An intimate pedagogy [Special issue]. *Journal of Psychosocial Studies, 15*(2).

Curtis, W. J., & Cicchetti, D. (2003). Moving research on resilience into the 21st century: Theoretical and methodological considerations in examining the biological contributors to resilience. *Development and Psychopathology, 15*(3), 773–810. https://doi.org/10.1017/S0954579403000373

da Rocha Barros, E. M. (2000). Affect and pictographic image: The constitution of meaning in mental life. *The International Journal of Psychoanalysis, 81*(6), 1087–1099. https://doi.org/10.1516/0020757001600435

da Rocha Barros, E. M., & da Rocha Barros, E. L. (2011). Reflections on the clinical implications of symbolism. *The International Journal of Psychoanalysis, 92*(4), 879–901. https://doi.org/10.1111/j.1745-8315.2011.00402.x

Davids, M. F. (2011). *Internal racism: A psychoanalytic approach to race and difference.* Bloomsbury Academic.

Davis, J. L. (2014). Triangulating the self: Identity processes in a connected era. *Symbolic Interaction, 37*(4), 500–523. https://doi.org/10.1002/symb.123

Davis, K. (2012). Tensions of identity in a networked era: Young people's perspectives on the risks and rewards of online self-expression. *New Media & Society, 14*(4), 634–651. https://doi.org/10.1177/1461444811422430

Davis, M. S., & Marsh, L. (1986). Self-love, self-control, and alexithymia: Narcissistic features of two bulimic adolescents. *American Journal of Psychotherapy, 40*(2), 224–232. https://doi.org/10.1176/appi.psychotherapy.1986.40.2.224

Davoine, F., & Gaudillière, J. M. (2004). *History beyond trauma: Whereof one cannot speak, thereof one cannot stay silent*. Other Press.

de M'Uzan, M. (2019). Interpreting: For whom, and why? *The International Journal of Psychoanalysis, 100*(4), 736–743. https://doi.org/10.1080/00207578.2018.1489573

Decety, J., & Moriguchi, Y. (2007). The empathic brain and its dysfunction in psychiatric populations: Implications for intervention across different clinical conditions. *BioPsychoSocial Medicine, 1*, Article 22. https://doi.org/10.1186/1751-0759-1-22

Derrida, J. (1996). *Archive fever: A Freudian impression* (E. Prenowitz, Trans.). University of Chicago Press.

Dimaggio, G., Procacci, M., Nicolò, G., Popolo, R., Semerari, A., Carcione, A., & Lysaker, P. H. (2007). Poor metacognition in narcissistic and avoidant personality disorders: Four psychotherapy patients analysed using the Metacognition Assessment Scale. *Clinical Psychology & Psychotherapy, 14*(5), 386–401. https://doi.org/10.1002/cpp.541

Dimaggio, G., Semerari, A., Falcone, M., Nicolò, G., Carcione, A., & Procacci, M. (2002). Metacognition, states of mind, cognitive biases, and interpersonal cycles: Proposal for an integrated narcissism model. *Journal of Psychotherapy Integration, 12*(4), 421–451. https://doi.org/10.1037/1053-0479.12.4.421

Dozio, E., Feldman, M., Bizouerne, C., Drain, E., Laroche Joubert, M., Mansouri, M., Moro, M. R., & Ouss, L. (2020). The intergenerational transmission of trauma: The effects of PTSD in mother–infant interactions. *Frontiers in Psychiatry, 11*. Advance online publication. https://doi.org/10.3389/fpsyt.2020.480690

Ekman, P. (1982). *Emotion in the human face*. Cambridge University Press.

Eliot, T. S. (1971). *Four quartets*. Houghton Mifflin Harcourt. (Original work published 1943)

Faimberg, H. (2007). A plea for a broader concept of Nachträglichkeit. *The Psychoanalytic Quarterly, 76*(4), 1221–1240. https://doi.org/10.1002/j.2167-4086.2007.tb00303.x

Fairbairn, W. R. D. (1952). *Psychoanalytic studies of the personality*. Routledge.

Feldman, M. (1993). The dynamics of reassurance. *The International Journal of Psycho-Analysis, 74*(2), 275–285.

Feldman, M. (1997). Splitting and projective identification. In R. E. Schafer (Ed.), *The contemporary Kleinians of London* (pp. 119–140). International Universities Press.

Feldman, R. (2006). From biological rhythms to social rhythms: Physiological precursors of mother-infant synchrony. *Developmental Psychology, 42*(1), 175–188. https://doi.org/10.1037/0012-1649.42.1.175

Feldman, R. (2007). Parent–infant synchrony and the construction of shared timing: Physiological precursors, developmental outcomes, and risk conditions. *The Journal of Child Psychology and Psychiatry, 48*(3–4), 329–354. https://doi.org/10.1111/j.1469-7610.2006.01701.x

Feldman, R. (2010). The relational basis of adolescent adjustment: Trajectories of mother–child interactive behaviors from infancy to adolescence shape adolescents' adaptation. *Attachment & Human Development, 12*(1–2), 173–192. https://doi.org/10.1080/14616730903282472

Felman, S. (1993). *What does a woman want? Reading and sexual difference*. The Johns Hopkins University Press. https://doi.org/10.56021/9780801846175

Fernald, A. (1993). Approval and disapproval: Infant responsiveness to vocal affect in familiar and unfamiliar languages. *Child Development, 64*(3), 657–674. https://doi.org/10.2307/1131209

Ferrari, A. B. (2004). *From the eclipse of the body to the dawn of thought*. Free Associations Press.

Ferro, A. (2002). *In the analyst's consulting room* (P. Slotkin, Trans.). Brunner-Routledge.

Ferro, A. (2009). Transformations in dreaming and characters in the psychoanalytic field. *The International Journal of Psychoanalysis, 90*(2), 209–230. https://doi.org/10.1111/j.1745-8315.2009.00131.x

Field, T. (1992). Infants of depressed mothers. *Development and Psychopathology, 4*(1), 49–66. https://doi.org/10.1017/S0954579400005551

Fischbein, J. E. (2011). Psychosomatics: A current overview. *The International Journal of Psychoanalysis, 92*(1), 197–219. https://doi.org/10.1111/j.1745-8315.2010.00389.x

Fivush, R. (2007). Maternal reminiscing style and children's developing understanding of self and emotion. *Clinical Social Work Journal, 35*(1), 37–46. https://doi.org/10.1007/s10615-006-0065-1

Fivush, R., Habermas, T., Waters, T. E. A., & Zaman, W. (2011). The making of autobiographical memory: Intersections of culture, narratives and identity. *International Journal of Psychology, 46*(5), 321–345. https://doi.org/10.1080/00207594.2011.596541

Flasbeck, V., Juckel, G., & Brüne, M. (2021). Evidence for altered neural processing in patients with borderline personality disorder: A review of event-related potential studies. *Journal of Psychophysiology, 35*(3), 163–185. https://doi.org/10.1027/0269-8803/a000271

Flavell, J. H. (2004). Theory-of-mind development: Retrospect and prospect. *Merrill-Palmer Quarterly, 50*(3), 274–290. https://doi.org/10.1353/mpq.2004.0018

Fogel, A. (1992). Movement and communication in human infancy: The social dynamics of development. *Human Movement Science, 11*(4), 387–423. https://doi.org/10.1016/0167-9457(92)90021-3

Fonagy, P., & Allison, E. (2014). The role of mentalizing and epistemic trust in the therapeutic relationship. *Psychotherapy, 51*(3), 372–380. https://doi.org/10.1037/a0036505

Fonagy, P., & Allison, E. (2023). Beyond mentalizing: Epistemic trust and the transmission of culture. *The Psychoanalytic Quarterly, 92*(4), 599–640. https://doi.org/10.1080/00332828.2023.2290023

Fonagy, P., & Bateman, A. (2008). The development of borderline personality disorder—A mentalizing model. *Journal of Personality Disorders, 22*(1), 4–21. https://doi.org/10.1521/pedi.2008.22.1.4

Fonagy, P., Gergely, G., & Jurist, E. L. (Eds.). (2002). *Affect regulation, mentalization and the development of the self.* Routledge. https://doi.org/10.4324/9780429471643

Fonagy, P., & Luyten, P. (2009). A developmental, mentalization-based approach to the understanding and treatment of borderline personality disorder. *Development and Psychopathology, 21*(4), 1355–1381. https://doi.org/10.1017/S0954579409990198

Ford, J. D. (2008). Trauma, posttraumatic stress disorder, and ethnoracial minorities: Toward diversity and cultural competence in principles and practices. *Clinical Psychology, 15*(1), 62–67. https://doi.org/10.1111/j.1468-2850.2008.00110.x

Freedman, N., & Lavender, J. (2002). On desymbolization: The concept and observations on anorexia and bulimia. *Psychoanalysis & Contemporary Thought, 25*(2), 165–199.

Freud, S. (1953a). Fragment of an analysis of a case of hysteria. In J. Strachey (Ed. & Trans.), *The standard edition of the complete psychological works of Sigmund Freud* (Vol. 7, pp. 3–122). The Hogarth Press. (Original work published 1905)

Freud, S. (1953b). The interpretation of dreams. In J. Strachey (Ed. & Trans.), *The standard edition of the complete psychological works of Sigmund Freud* (Vols. 4/5, pp. xi–627). The Hogarth Press. (Original work published 1900)

Freud, S. (1955a). Analysis of a phobia in a five-year-old boy. In J. Strachey (Ed. & Trans.), *The standard edition of the complete psychological works of Sigmund Freud* (Vol. 10, pp. 3–149). The Hogarth Press. (Original work published 1909)

Freud, S. (1955b). Beyond the pleasure principle: Group psychology and other works. In J. Strachey (Ed. & Trans.), *The standard edition of the complete psychological works of Sigmund Freud* (Vol. 18, pp. 3–274). The Hogarth Press. (Original work published 1920)

Freud, S. (1955c). Notes upon a case of obsessional neurosis. In J. Strachey (Ed. & Trans.), *The standard edition of the complete psychological works of Sigmund Freud* (Vol. 10, pp. 151–320). The Hogarth Press. (Original work published 1909)

Freud, S. (1955d). Studies on hysteria: The psychotherapy of hysteria. In J. Strachey (Ed. & Trans.), *The standard edition of the complete psychological works of Sigmund Freud* (Vol. 2, pp. 253–305). The Hogarth Press. (Original work published 1895)

Freud, S. (1957a). Five lectures on psycho-analysis. In J. Strachey (Ed. & Trans.), *The standard edition of the complete psychological works of Sigmund Freud* (Vol. 11, pp. 3–56). The Hogarth Press. (Original work published 1910)

Freud, S. (1957b). On narcissism: An introduction. In J. Strachey (Ed. & Trans.), *The standard edition of the complete psychological works of Sigmund Freud* (Vol. 14, pp. 67–102). The Hogarth Press. (Original work published 1914)

Freud, S. (1958a). The dynamics of transference. In J. Strachey (Ed. & Trans.), *The standard edition of the complete psychological works of Sigmund Freud* (Vol. 12, pp. 97–108). The Hogarth Press. (Original work published 1912)

Freud, S. (1958b). Formulations on the two principles of mental functioning. In J. Strachey (Ed. & Trans.), *The standard edition of the complete psychological works of Sigmund Freud* (Vol. 12, pp. 213–226). The Hogarth Press. (Original work published 1911)

Freud, S. (1958c). Recommendations to physicians practising psycho-analysis. In J. Strachey (Ed. & Trans.), *The standard edition of the complete psychological works of Sigmund Freud* (Vol. 12, pp. 109–120). The Hogarth Press. (Original work published 1912)

Freud, S. (1958d). Remembering, repeating and working through. In J. Strachey (Ed. & Trans.), *The standard edition of the complete psychological works of Sigmund Freud* (Vol. 12, pp. 145–156). The Hogarth Press. (Original work published 1914)

Freud, S. (1959). The question of lay analysis. In J. Strachey (Ed. & Trans.), *The standard edition of the complete psychological works of Sigmund Freud* (Vol. 20, pp. 177–258). The Hogarth Press. (Original work published 1926)

Freud, S. (1961). The ego and the id. In J. Strachey (Ed. & Trans.), *The standard edition of the complete psychological works of Sigmund Freud* (Vol. 19, pp. 1–66). The Hogarth Press. (Original work published 1923)

Freud, S. (1964). Constructions in analysis. In J. Strachey (Ed. & Trans.), *The standard edition of the complete psychological works of Sigmund Freud* (Vol. 23, pp. 255–269). The Hogarth Press. (Original work published 1937)

Freud, S. (1966). Project for a scientific psychology. In J. Strachey (Ed. & Trans.), *The standard edition of the complete psychological works of Sigmund Freud* (Vol. 1, pp. 283–397). The Hogarth Press. (Original work published 1895)

Friedlander, S. R. (1991). "Why do (don't) you ask?" Transference and the desire (not) to know. *American Journal of Psychoanalysis, 51*(2), 117–135. https://doi.org/10.1007/BF01252168

Fryberg, S. A., & Markus, H. R. (2003). On being American Indian: Current and possible selves. *Self and Identity, 2*(4), 325–344. https://doi.org/10.1080/714050251

Gadamer, H.-G. (1975). *Truth and method.* Continuum.

Gallese, V. (2005). Being like me: Self–other identity, mirror neurons, and empathy. In S. Hurley & N. Chater (Eds.), *Perspectives on limitation: Vol. 1. From neuroscience to social science—Vol. 1. Mechanisms of limitation and limitation in animals.* The MIT Press. https://doi.org/10.7551/mitpress/5330.003.0004

Gallese, V. (2009). Mirror neurons, embodied simulation, and the neural basis of social identification. *Psychoanalytic Dialogues, 19*(5), 519–536. https://doi.org/10.1080/10481880903231910

Gallese, V. (2013). Mirror neurons, embodied simulation and a second-person approach to mindreading. *Cortex, 49*(10), 2954–2956. https://doi.org/10.1016/j.cortex.2013.09.008

Gallese, V. (2014). Bodily selves in relation: Embodied simulation as second-person perspective on intersubjectivity. *Philosophical Transactions of the Royal Society B, 369*(1644), Article 20130177. https://doi.org/10.1098/rstb.2013.0177

Gallese, V., Eagle, M. N., & Migone, P. (2007). Intentional attunement: Mirror neurons and the neural underpinnings of interpersonal relations. *Journal of the American Psychoanalytic Association, 55*(1), 131–175. https://doi.org/10.1177/00030651070550010601

Gallese, V., & Goldman, A. (1998). Mirror neurons and the simulation theory of mind-reading. *Trends in Cognitive Sciences, 2*(12), 493–501. https://doi.org/10.1016/S1364-6613(98)01262-5

García Salas, J. (2018). Interpretation as a misunderstanding. *Scandinavian Psychoanalytic Review, 41*(1), 37–43. https://doi.org/10.1080/01062301.2018.1534772

Gergely, G., & Watson, J. S. (1996). The social biofeedback theory of parental affect-mirroring: The development of emotional self-awareness and self-control in infancy. *The International Journal of Psycho-Analysis, 77*(6), 1181–1212.

Gerzi, S. (2005). Trauma, narcissism and the two attractors in trauma. *The International Journal of Psychoanalysis, 86*(4), 1033–1050. https://doi.org/10.1516/2TTK-G0TL-9DWL-UHWY

Gesell, A. (1933). Maturation and the patterning of behavior. In C. Murchison (Ed.), *A handbook of child psychology* (2nd ed., rev., pp. 209–235). Clark University Press.

Gilboa-Schechtman, E., Avnon, L., Zubery, E., & Jeczmien, P. (2006). Emotional processing in eating disorders: Specific impairment or general distress related deficiency? *Depression and Anxiety, 23*(6), 331–339. https://doi.org/10.1002/da.20163

Gorrell, S., & Murray, S. B. (2019). Eating disorders in males. *Child and Adolescent Psychiatric Clinics of North America, 28*(4), 641–651. https://doi.org/10.1016/j.chc.2019.05.012

Green, A. (1986). *On private madness*. International Universities Press.

Green, A. (1998). The primordial mind and the work of the negative. *The International Journal of Psycho-Analysis, 79*(4), 649–665.

Green, A. (2002). A dual conception of narcissism: Positive and negative organizations. *The Psychoanalytic Quarterly, 71*(4), 631–649. https://doi.org/10.1002/j.2167-4086.2002.tb00020.x

Grotstein, J. S. (1995). Orphans of the "real": I. Some modern and postmodern perspectives on the neurobiological and psychosocial dimensions of psychosis and other primitive mental disorders. *Bulletin of the Menninger Clinic, 59*(3), 287–311.

Grotstein, J. S. (2000). *Who is the dreamer who dreams the dream? A study of psychic presences*. Routledge. https://doi.org/10.4324/9780203779927

Grotstein, J. L. (2009). *But at the same time and on another level: Vol. 1. Psychoanalytic theory and technique in the Kleinian/Bonian mode.* Routledge.

Gunnar, M. R., & Fisher, P. A. (2006). Bringing basic research on early experience and stress neurobiology to bear on preventive interventions for neglected and maltreated children. *Development and Psychopathology, 18*(3), 651–677. https://doi.org/10.1017/S0954579406060330

Hammack, P. L., & Manago, A. M. (2024). The psychology of sexual and gender diversity in the 21st century: Social technologies and stories of authenticity. *American Psychologist*. Advance online publication. https://doi.org/10.1037/amp0001366

Hartung, T., & Steinbrecher, M. (2018). From somatic pain to psychic pain: The body in the psychoanalytic field. *The International Journal of Psychoanalysis, 99*(1), 159–180. https://doi.org/10.1111/1745-8315.12651

Heimann, P. (1950). On counter-transference. *The International Journal of Psycho-Analysis, 30*, 81–84.

Herbert, B. M., Herbert, C., & Pollatos, O. (2011). On the relationship between interoceptive awareness and alexithymia: Is interoceptive awareness related to emotional awareness? *Journal of Personality, 79*(5), 1149–1175. https://doi.org/10.1111/j.1467-6494.2011.00717.x

Heriot-Maitland, C. P. (2008). Mysticism and madness: Different aspects of the same human experience? *Mental Health, Religion & Culture, 11*(3), 301–325. https://doi.org/10.1080/13674670701287680

Hinshelwood, R. D. (1999). Countertransference. *The International Journal of Psycho-Analysis, 80*(4), 797–818. https://doi.org/10.1516/0020757991598927

Horney, K. (1950). *Neurosis and human growth: The struggle toward self-realization*. W. W. Norton.

Horney, K. (1967). *Feminine psychology*. W. W. Norton.

Isaacs, S. (1948). The nature and function of phantasy. *The International Journal of Psycho-Analysis, 29*, 73–97.

Jaffe, J., Beebe, B., Feldstein, S., Crown, C. L., & Jasnow, M. D. (2001). Rhythms of dialogue in infancy: Coordinated timing in development. *Monographs of the Society for Research in Child Development, 66*(2), i–viii, 1–132.

Jenkinson, P. M., Taylor, L., & Laws, K. R. (2018). Self-reported interoceptive deficits in eating disorders: A meta-analysis of studies using the eating disorder inventory. *Journal of Psychosomatic Research, 110*, 38–45. https://doi.org/10.1016/j.jpsychores.2018.04.005

Johnson, C. L. (1981). Psychoanalysis, shamanism and cultural phenomena. *The Journal of the American Academy of Psychoanalysis, 9*(2), 311–318. https://doi.org/10.1521/jaap.1.1981.9.2.311

Joseph, B. (1985). Transference: The total situation. *The International Journal of Psychoanalysis, 66*, 447–454.

Joseph, B. (1997). Projective identification: Some clinical aspects. In R. E. Schafer (Ed.), *The contemporary Kleinians of London* (pp. 100–116). International Universities Press.

Kafka, F. (1971). In the penal colony. In N. H. Glatzer (Ed.), *Franz Kafka: The complete stories* (pp. 140–167). Schocken Books. (Original work published 1919)

Katz, S. M. (2013). *Metaphor and fields: Common ground, common language, and the future of psychoanalysis*. Routledge. https://doi.org/10.4324/9780203072318

Katznelson, H., Falkenström, F., Daniel, S. I. F., Lunn, S., Folke, S., Pedersen, S. H., & Poulsen, S. (2020). Reflective functioning, psychotherapeutic alliance, and outcome in two psychotherapies for bulimia nervosa. *Psychotherapy, 57*(2), 129–140. https://doi.org/10.1037/pst0000245

Kealy, D., Laverdière, O., Cox, D. W., & Hewitt, P. L. (2023). Childhood emotional neglect and depressive and anxiety symptoms among mental health outpatients: The mediating roles of narcissistic vulnerability and shame. *Journal of Mental Health, 32*(1), 24–32. https://doi.org/10.1080/09638237.2020.1836557

Keats, J. (1899). *The complete poetical works and letters of John Keats* (H. E. Scudder, Ed.). Houghton, Mifflin and Company.

Kernberg, O. (1965). Notes on countertransference. *Journal of the American Psychoanalytic Association, 13*(1), 38–56. https://doi.org/10.1177/000306516501300102

Kernberg, O. F. (1970). A psychoanalytic classification of character pathology. *Journal of the American Psychoanalytic Association, 18*(4), 800–822. https://doi.org/10.1177/000306517001800403

Kernberg, O. F. (2014). An overview of the treatment of severe narcissistic pathology. *The International Journal of Psychoanalysis, 95*(5), 865–888. https://doi.org/10.1111/1745-8315.12204

Klein, M. (1946). Notes on some schizoid mechanisms. *The International Journal of Psycho-Analysis, 27*(3–4), 99–110.

Klein, M. (1952). The origins of transference. *The International Journal of Psycho-Analysis, 33*(4), 433–438.

Klein, M. (1975). Envy and gratitude. In M. Klein (Ed.), *The writings of Melanie Klein: Vol. 3. Envy and gratitude and other works, 1946–1963* (pp. 1–24). Delacorte Press. (Original work published 1957)

Klein, M. (1981a). The importance of symbol-formation in the development of the ego. In R. E. Money-Kyrle (Ed.), *The writings of Melanie Klein: Vol. 1: Love, guilt and reparation and other works, 1921–1945* (pp. 219–232). Hogarth Press. (Original work published 1930)

Klein, M. (1981b). Mourning and its relation to manic-depressive states. In R. E. Money-Kyrle (Ed.), *The writings of Melanie Klein: Vol. 1. Love, guilt and reparation and other works, 1921–1945* (pp. 344–369). Hogarth Press. (Original work published 1940)

Knox, J. (2009). Mirror neurons and embodied simulation in the development of archetypes and self-agency. *The Journal of Analytical Psychology, 54*(3), 307–323. https://doi.org/10.1111/j.1468-5922.2009.01782.x

Kohut, H. (1966). Forms and transformations of narcissism. *Journal of the American Psychoanalytic Association, 14*(2), 243–272. https://doi.org/10.1177/000306516601400201

Kohut, H. (1977). *The restoration of the self*. International Universities Press.

Koss-Chioino, J. D. (2003). Jung, spirits and madness: Lessons for cultural psychiatry. *Transcultural Psychiatry, 40*(2), 164–180. https://doi.org/10.1177/1363461503402002

Kristeva, J. (1982). *Powers of horror: An essay on abjection* (L. S. Roudiez, Trans.). Columbia University Press. https://doi.org/10.7312/kris21457-004 (Original work published 1980)

Kristeva, J. (1986). *The Kristeva reader* (T. Moi, Ed.). Columbia University Press.

Krystal, H. (1988). *Integration and self-healing: Affect, trauma, alexithymia*. The Analytic Press.

Lacan, J. (1974–1975). *Seminar XII: RSI* [Speech audio recording]. C. Gallagher (Trans.). https://soundcloud.com/lacan-in-ireland/sets/rsi

Lacan, J. (1977a). The directions of the treatment and the principles of its power. In *Écrits: A selection* (A. Sheridan, Trans.; pp. 226–280). W. W. Norton & Company. (Original work published 1958)

Lacan, J. (1977b). The function and field of speech and language in psychoanalysis. In *Écrits: A selection* (A. Sheridan, Trans.; pp. 30–113). W. W. Norton & Company. (Original work published 1953)

Lacan, J. (1977c). The mirror stage as formative of the I as revealed in psychoanalytic experience. In *Écrits: A selection* (A. Sheridan, Trans.; pp. 1–7). W. W. Norton & Company. (Original work published 1949)

Lacan, J. (1977d). On a question preliminary to any possible treatment of psychosis. In *Écrits: A selection* (A. Sheridan, Trans.; pp. 179–225). W. W. Norton & Company. (Original work published 1955–1956)

Lacan, J. (1977e). *The seminar of Jacques Lacan: Book XI. The four fundamental concepts of psychoanalysis* (J.-A. Miller, Ed.; A. Sheridan, Trans.). W. W. Norton & Company. (Original work published 1964)

Lacan, J. (1977f). The subversion of the subject and the dialectic of desire in the Freudian unconscious. In *Écrits: A selection* (A. Sheridan, Trans.; pp. 292–325). W. W. Norton & Company. (Original work published 1960)

Lacan, J. (1988). *The seminar of Jacques Lacan: Book II. The ego in Freud's theory and in the technique of psychoanalysis, 1954–1955* (J.-A. Miller, Ed.; S. Tomaselli, Trans.). W. W. Norton & Company. (Original work published 1954–1955)

Lacan, J. (1993). *The seminar of Jacques Lacan: Book III. The psychoses, 1955–1956* (R. Grigg, Trans.). W. W. Norton & Company. (Original work published 1955–1956)

Lacan, J. (2014). *The seminar of Jacques Lacan: Book X. Anxiety, 1962–1963* (J.-A. Miller, Ed.; A. R. Price, Trans.). Polity Press. (Original work published 1962–1963)

Lacan, J. (2016). *The seminar of Jacques Lacan: Book XXIII. The sinthome* (A. R. Price, Trans.). Polity Press. (Original work published 1975–1976)

Lacan, J. (2018). *. . . or worse: The seminar of Jacques Lacan: Book XIX* (J.-A. Miller, Ed.; A. R. Price, Trans.). Polity Press. (Original work published 1971–1972)

LaCapra, D. (1999). Trauma, absence, loss. *Critical Inquiry, 25*(4), 696–727. https://doi.org/10.1086/448943

Lakoff, G., & Johnson, M. (1980). *Metaphors we live by*. University of Chicago Press.

Lane, R. D., Solms, M., Weihs, K. L., Hishaw, A., & Smith, R. (2020). Affective agnosia: A core affective processing deficit in the alexithymia spectrum. *BioPsychoSocial Medicine, 14*(1), Article 20. https://doi.org/10.1186/s13030-020-00184-w

Laplanche, J. (1995). Seduction, persecution, revelation. *The International Journal of Psycho-Analysis, 76*(4), 663–682.

Laplanche, J. (1997). The theory of seduction and the problem of the other. *The International Journal of Psycho-Analysis, 78*(4), 653–666.

Laplanche, J., & Pontalis, J.-B. (1968). Fantasy and the origins of sexuality. *The International Journal of Psycho-Analysis, 49*(1), 1–18.

Lawton, P. N. (2005). Love and justice: Lévinas' reading of Buber. In C. E. Katz (Ed.), *Lévinas and the question of religion* (pp. 212–219). University of Illinois Press.

LeDoux, J. E. (1999). Psychoanalytic theory: Clues from the brain. *Neuropsychoanalysis, 1*(1), 44–49. https://doi.org/10.1080/15294145.1999.10773244

LeDoux, J. E. (2002, April 12). *Trauma, dissociation and conflict: The space where neuroscience, cognitive science and psychoanalysis overlap* [Symposium contribution]. 22nd Annual Spring Meeting of the Division of Psychoanalysis of the American Psychological Association, New York, NY, United States.

Leikert, S. (2021). Encapsulated body engrams and somatic narration—Integrating body memory into psychoanalytic technique. *The International Journal of Psychoanalysis, 102*(4), 671–688. https://doi.org/10.1080/00207578.2021.1927044

Levenson, E. A. (1978). Two essays in psychoanalytic psychology. *Contemporary Psychoanalysis, 14*(1), 1–30. https://doi.org/10.1080/00107530.1978.10745519

Levenson, E. A. (2009). The enigma of the transference. *Contemporary Psychoanalysis, 45*(2), 163–178. https://doi.org/10.1080/00107530.2009.10745994

Lévinas, E. (1991a). *Otherwise than being or beyond essence* (A. Lingis, Trans.). Springer-Science+Business Media. (Original work published 1974)

Lévinas, E. (1991b). *Totality and infinity: An essay on exteriority* (A. Lingis, Trans.). Kluwer Academic Publishers. (Original work published 1969)

Lewin, B. (1951). *The psychoanalysis of elation*. Hogarth Press.

Lifton, R. J. (1995). *The protean self: Human resilience in an age of fragmentation*. Basic Books.

Lima, A. R., Mello, M. F., Andreoli, S. B., Fossaluza, V., de Araújo, C. M., Jackowski, A. P., Bressan, R. A., & Mari, J. J. (2014). The impact of healthy parenting as a protective factor for posttraumatic stress disorder in adulthood: A case-control study. *PLOS ONE, 9*(1), Article e87117. https://doi.org/10.1371/journal.pone.0087117

Liotti, G. (2004). Trauma, dissociation, and disorganized attachment: Three strands of a single braid. *Psychotherapy, 41*(4), 472–486. https://doi.org/10.1037/0033-3204.41.4.472

Lippmann, P. (2000). *Nocturnes: On listening to dreams*. Routledge.

Littlewood, R., & Dein, S. (2013). Did Christianity lead to schizophrenia? Psychosis, psychology and self reference. *Transcultural Psychiatry, 50*(3), 397–420. https://doi.org/10.1177/1363461513489681

Loewenstein, R. M. (1956). Some remarks on the role of speech in psychoanalytic technique. *The International Journal of Psycho-Analysis, 37*(6), 460–468.

Lombardi, R. (2008). The body in the analytic session: Focusing on the body–mind link. *The International Journal of Psychoanalysis, 89*(1), 89–110. https://doi.org/10.1111/j.1745-8315.2007.00008.x

Lombardi, R. (2009). Body, affect, thought: Reflections on the work of Matte Blanco and Ferrari. *The Psychoanalytic Quarterly, 78*(1), 123–160. https://doi.org/10.1002/j.2167-4086.2009.tb00388.x

Lombardi, R. (2017). *Body–mind dissociation in psychoanalysis: Development after Bion*. Routledge.

Lombardi, R. (2018). Beyond the psychosexual: The body–mind relationship discussion of "somatic experiencing." *Psychoanalytic Dialogues, 28*(5), 629–639. https://doi.org/10.1080/10481885.2018.1506226

Lorenzer, A. (2016). Language, life praxis and scenic understanding in psychoanalytic therapy. *The International Journal of Psychoanalysis, 97*(5), 1399–1414. https://doi.org/10.1111/1745-8315.12601

Luyten, P., Campbell, C., & Fonagy, P. (2020). Borderline personality disorder, complex trauma, and problems with self and identity: A social-communicative approach. *Journal of Personality, 88*(1), 88–105. https://doi.org/10.1111/jopy.12483

Lyons-Ruth, K. (2003). Dissociation and the parent–infant dialogue: A longitudinal perspective from attachment research. *Journal of the American Psychoanalytic Association, 51*(3), 883–911. https://doi.org/10.1177/00030651030510031501

Lysaker, P. H., Carcione, A., Dimaggio, G., Johannesen, J. K., Nicolò, G., Procacci, M., & Semerari, A. (2005). Metacognition amidst narratives of self and illness in schizophrenia: Associations with neurocognition, symptoms, insight and quality of life. *Acta Psychiatrica Scandinavica, 112*(1), 64–71. https://doi.org/10.1111/j.1600-0447.2005.00514.x

Lysaker, P. H., Dimaggio, G., Daroyanni, P., Buck, K. D., LaRocco, V. A., Carcione, A., & Nicolò, G. (2010). Assessing metacognition in schizophrenia with the metacognition Assessment scale: Associations with the social cognition and object relations scale. *Psychology and Psychotherapy, 83*(3), 303–315. https://doi.org/10.1348/147608309X481117

Lysaker, P. H., Erickson, M., Buck, K. D., Procacci, M., Nicolò, G., & Dimaggio, G. (2010). Metacognition in schizophrenia spectrum disorders: Methods of assessment and associations with neurocognition and function. *European Journal of Psychiatry, 24*(4), 220–226. https://doi.org/10.4321/S0213-61632010000400004

Lysaker, P. H., Erickson, M., Ringer, J., Buck, K. D., Semerari, A., Carcione, A., & Dimaggio, G. (2011). Metacognition in schizophrenia: The relationship of mastery to coping, insight, self-esteem, social anxiety, and various facets of neurocognition. *British Journal of Clinical Psychology, 50*(4), 412–424. https://doi.org/10.1111/j.2044-8260.2010.02003.x

Lysaker, P. H., Kukla, M., Leonhardt, B. L., Hamm, J. A., Schnakenberg Martin, A., Zalzala, A. B., Gagen, E. C., & Hasson-Ohayon, I. (2020). Meaning, integration, and the self in serious mental illness: Implications of research in metacognition for psychiatric rehabilitation. *Psychiatric Rehabilitation Journal, 43*(4), 275–283. https://doi.org/10.1037/prj0000436

Main, M., & Hesse, E. (1990). Parent's unresolved traumatic experiences are related to infant disorganized/disoriented attachment status: Is frightened and/or frightening parental behavior the linking mechanism? In M. Greenberg, D. Cicchetti, & E. M. Cummings (Eds.), *Attachment in the preschool years: Theory, research, and intervention* (pp. 161–182). University of Chicago Press.

Mancia, M. (1989). The dream as an internal language of memory. *Rivista di Psicoanalisi, 35*(2), 328–350.

Mancia, M. (2008). The early unrepressed unconscious in relation to Matte-Blanco's thought. *International Forum of Psychoanalysis, 17*(4), 201–212. https://doi.org/10.1080/08037060701676359

Mangold, J. (Director). (1999). *Girl interrupted* [Film]. Columbia Pictures, Red Wagon Productions, 3 Arts Entertainment.

Marty, P. (1958). The allergic object relationship. *The International Journal of Psychoanalysis, 39*(2–4), 98–103.

Marty, P. (1968). A major process of somatization: The progressive disorganization. *The International Journal of Psycho-Analysis, 49*(2), 246–249.

Marty, P., M'Uzan, M. D. E., & David, C. (1963). *L'Investigation Psychosomatique* [*Psychosomatic investigation*]. Presses Universitaires de France.

Matte-Blanco, I. (1975). *The unconscious as infinite sets: An essay in bi-logic*. Routledge.

Mayes, L., Fonagy, P., & Target, M. (Eds.). (2007). *Developmental science and psychoanalysis: Integration and innovation*. Karnac Books.

McDougall, J. (1974). The psychosoma and the psychoanalytic process. *The International Review of Psycho-Analysis, 1*(4), 437–459.

McDougall, J. (1978). *Plea for a measure of abnormality*. International Universities Press.

McDougall, J. (1985). *Theaters of the mind*. Basic Books.

McDougall, J. (1989). *Theaters of the body: A psychoanalytic approach to psychosomatic illness*. W. W. Norton & Company.

McGilchrist, I. (2009). *The master and his emissary: The divided brain and the making of the Western world*. Yale University Press.

Meissner, W. W. (1979). Narcissistic personalities and borderline conditions: A differential diagnosis. *The Annual of Psychoanalysis, 7*, 171–202.

Meltzer, D. (1968). Terror, persecution, dread—A dissection of paranoid anxieties. *The International Journal of Psycho-Analysis, 49*(2), 396–401.

Meltzer, D. (1984). *Dream-life*. Clunie Press.

Miller, A. E., Racine, S. E., & Klonsky, E. D. (2021). Symptoms of anorexia nervosa and bulimia nervosa have differential relationships to borderline personality disorder. *Eating Disorders, 29*(2), 161–174. https://doi.org/10.1080/10640266.2019.1642034

Miller, P. (2015). Piera Aulagnier, an introduction: Some elements of her intellectual biography. *The International Journal of Psychoanalysis, 96*(5), 1355–1369. https://doi.org/10.1111/1745-8315.12409

Milner, M. (1969). *The hands of the living god*. Hogarth Press.

Milner, M. (1987). *The suppressed madness of sane men: Forty-four years of exploring psychoanalysis*. Routledge. https://doi.org/10.4324/9780203013748

Mitrani, J. L. (1995). Toward an understanding of unmentalized experience. *The Psychoanalytic Quarterly, 64*(1), 68–112. https://doi.org/10.1080/21674086.1995.11927444

Mitrani, J. L. (2001). "Taking the transference": Some technical implications in three papers by Bion. *The International Journal of Psychoanalysis, 82*(6), 1085–1104. https://doi.org/10.1516/JECN-FBNV-TUUE-NUHX

Modell, A. H. (2005). Emotional memory, metaphor, and meaning. *Psychoanalytic Inquiry, 25*(4), 555–568. https://doi.org/10.2513/s07351690pi2504_9

Modell, A. H. (2009). Metaphor—The bridge between feelings and knowledge. *Psychoanalytic Inquiry, 29*(1), 6–11. https://doi.org/10.1080/07351690802246890

Morrison, A. (1983). Shame, ideal self, and narcissism. *Contemporary Psychoanalysis, 19*(2), 295–318. https://doi.org/10.1080/00107530.1983.10746610

Muller, J. P. (2007). A view from Riggs: treatment resistance and patient authority-IV: Why the pair needs the third. *The Journal of the American Academy of Psychoanalysis and Dynamic Psychiatry, 35*(2), 221–241. https://doi.org/10.1521/jaap.2007.35.2.221

Murray, L., & Trevarthen, C. (1985). Emotional regulation of interactions between two-month-olds and their mothers. In T. M. Field & N. A. Fox (Eds.), *Social perspectives in infants* (pp. 177–197). Ablex.

Nagy, E., & Molnár, P. (2004). *Homo imitans* or *Homo provocans*? Human imprinting model of neonatal imitation. *Infant Behavior and Development, 27*(1), 54–63. https://doi.org/10.1016/j.infbeh.2003.06.004

Neal, D. W., Bufford, R. K., Charles, M., & Thurston, N. (2023). Metacognitive changes in individuals with severe mental disorders in response to psychoanalytic therapy. *International Journal for the Advancement of Scientific Psychoanalytic Empirical Research (JASPER), 5*(1), 5–40.

O'Loughlin, M., & Charles, M. (2015). *Fragments of trauma and the social production of suffering: Trauma, history, and memory*. Rowman & Littlefield.

Oldershaw, A., Startup, H., & Lavender, T. (2019). Anorexia nervosa and a lost emotional self: A psychological formulation of the development, maintenance, and treatment of anorexia nervosa. *Frontiers in Psychology, 10*, Article 219. https://doi.org/10.3389/fpsyg.2019.00219

Palser, E. R., Palmer, C. E., Galvez-Pol, A., Hannah, R., Fotopoulou, A., & Kilner, J. M. (2018). Alexithymia mediates the relationship between interoceptive sensibility and anxiety. *PLOS ONE, 13*(9), Article e0203212. https://doi.org/10.1371/journal.pone.0203212

Papoušek, M., Bornstein, M. H., Nuzzo, C., Papoušek, H., & Symmes, D. (1990). Infant responses to prototypical melodic contours in parental speech. *Infant Behavior and Development, 13*(4), 539–545. https://doi.org/10.1016/0163-6383(90)90022-Z

Parker, I. (2005). Lacanian discourse analysis in psychology: Seven theoretical elements. *Theory & Psychology*, *15*(2), 163–182. https://doi.org/10.1177/0959354305051361

Parsons, M. (2007). Raiding the inarticulate: The internal analytic setting and listening beyond countertransference. *The International Journal of Psychoanalysis*, *88*(6), 1441–1456. https://doi.org/10.1516/T564-G13J-400H-2W23

Patsalides, B., & Patsalides, A. (2001). "Butterflies caught in the network of signifiers": The goals of psychoanalysis according to Jacques Lacan. *The Psychoanalytic Quarterly*, *70*(1), 201–230. https://doi.org/10.1002/j.2167-4086.2001.tb00596.x

Pedersen, S. H., Poulsen, S., & Lunn, S. (2015). Eating disorders and mentalization: High reflective functioning in patients with bulimia nervosa. *Journal of the American Psychoanalytic Association*, *63*(4), 671–694. https://doi.org/10.1177/0003065115602440

Petkova, V. I., & Ehrsson, H. H. (2008). If I were you: Perceptual illusion of body swapping. *PLOS ONE*, *3*(12), Article e3832. https://doi.org/10.1371/journal.pone.0003832

Phinney, J. S. (1991). Ethnic identity and self-esteem: A review and integration. *Hispanic Journal of Behavioral Sciences*, *13*(2), 193–208. https://doi.org/10.1177/07399863910132005

Pick, I. B. (1985). Working through in the countertransference. *The International Journal of Psycho-Analysis*, *66*(2), 157–166.

Prefit, A.-B., Cândea, D. M., & Szentagotai-Tătar, A. (2019). Emotion regulation across eating pathology: A meta-analysis. *Appetite*, *143*, Article 104438. https://doi.org/10.1016/j.appet.2019.104438

Puttevils, L., Vanderhasselt, M.-A., Horczak, P., & Vervaet, M. (2021). Differences in the use of emotion regulation strategies between anorexia and bulimia nervosa: A systematic review and meta-analysis. *Comprehensive Psychiatry*. Advance online publication. https://doi.org/10.1016/j.comppsych.2021.152262

Racker, H. (2007). The meanings and uses of countertransference. *The Psychoanalytic Quarterly*, *76*(3), 725–777. https://doi.org/10.1002/j.2167-4086.2007.tb00277.x

Ramis, H. (Director). (1993). *Groundhog day* [Film]. Columbia Pictures; A Sony Pictures Entertainment Company.

Reiser, L. W. (1990). The oral triad and the bulimic quintet: Understanding the bulimic episode. *The International Review of Psychoanalysis*, *17*(2), 239–248.

Richter, M., Mota, S., Hater, L., Bratek, R., Goltermann, J., Barkhau, C., Gruber, M., Repple, J., Storck, M., Blitz, R., Grotegerd, D., Masuhr, O., Jaeger, U., Baune, B. T., Dugas, M., Walter, M., Dannlowski, U., Buhlmann, U., Back, M., & Opel, N. (2023). Narcissistic dimensions and depressive symptoms in patients across mental disorders in cognitive behavioural therapy and in psychoanalytic interactional therapy in Germany: A prospective cohort study. *The*

Lancet Psychiatry, 10(12), 955–965. https://doi.org/10.1016/S2215-0366(23)00293-6

Ricoeur, P. (1970). *Freud and philosophy: An essay on interpretation*. The University of Chicago Press.

Rivera, G. N., Christy, A. G., Kim, J., Vess, M., Hicks, J. A., & Schlegel, R. J. (2019). Understanding the relationship between perceived authenticity and well-being. *Review of General Psychology, 23*(1), 113–126. https://doi.org/10.1037/gpr0000161

Riviere, J. (2019). *The inner world and Joan Riviere: Collected Papers 1928–1958* (A. Hughes, Ed.). Routledge. https://doi.org/10.4324/9780429482083

Romano, F. (2013). Anorexia and bulimia: Two aspects of adolescence. *British Journal of Psychotherapy, 29*(1), 5–24. https://doi.org/10.1111/j.1752-0118.2012.01301.x

Rosenfeld, H. (1971). A clinical approach to the psychoanalytic theory of the life and death instincts: An investigation into the aggressive aspects of narcissism. *The International Journal of Psycho-Analysis, 52*(2), 169–178.

Rosenfeld, H. (1987). *Impasse and interpretation: Therapeutic and anti-therapeutic factors in the psychoanalytic treatment of psychotic, borderline, and neurotic patients*. Tavistock/Routledge.

Rothstein, A. (1979). The theory of narcissism: An object-relations perspective. *Psychoanalytic Review, 66*(1), 35–47.

Sander, L. (1977). The regulation of exchange in the infant-caretaker system and some aspects of the context–content relationship. In M. Lewis & L. Rosenblum (Eds.), *Interaction, conversation, and the development of language* (pp. 133–156). John Wiley & Sons.

Schafer, R. E. (Ed.). (1997). *The contemporary Kleinians of London*. International Universities Press.

Schmidt Neven, R. (2005). Under fives counselling: Opportunities for growth, change, and development for children and parents. *Journal of Child Psychotherapy, 31*(2), 189–208. https://doi.org/10.1080/00754170500221642

Schore, A. (2012). *Affect regulation and the origin of the self: The neurobiology of emotional development*. Psychology Press. https://doi.org/10.4324/9781410604163

Schore, A. N. (1994). *Affect regulation and the origin of the self: The neurobiology of emotional development*. Lawrence Erlbaum Associates.

Schore, A. N. (2003). *Affect regulation & the repair of the self*. W. W. Norton & Company.

Schore, J. R., & Schore, A. N. (2008). Modern attachment theory: The central role of affect regulation in development and treatment. *Clinical Social Work Journal, 36*(1), 9–20. https://doi.org/10.1007/s10615-007-0111-7

Schulte-Rüther, M., Markowitsch, H. J., Fink, G. R., & Piefke, M. (2007). Mirror neuron and theory of mind mechanisms involved in face-to-face interactions: A functional magnetic resonance imaging approach to empathy. *Journal of Cognitive Neuroscience, 19*(8), 1354–1372. https://doi.org/10.1162/jocn.2007.19.8.1354

Schwartz, H. J. (1986). Bulimia: Psychoanalytic perspectives. *Journal of the American Psychoanalytic Association, 34*(2), 439–462. https://doi.org/10.1177/000306518603400209

Segal, H. (1957). Notes on symbol formation. *The International Journal of Psycho-Analysis, 38*(6), 391–397.

Seikkula, J., Aaltonen, J., Alakare, B., Haarakangas, K., Keränen, J., & Lehtinen, K. (2006). Five-year experience of first-episode nonaffective psychosis in open-dialogue approach: Treatment principles, follow-up outcomes, and two case studies. *Psychotherapy Research, 16*(2), 214–228. https://doi.org/10.1080/10503300500268490

Semerari, A., Carcione, A., Dimaggio, G., Falcone, M., Nicolò, G., Procacci, M., & Alleva, G. (2003). How to evaluate metacognitive functioning in psychotherapy? The Metacognition Assessment Scale and its applications. *Clinical Psychology & Psychotherapy, 10*(4), 238–261. https://doi.org/10.1002/cpp.362

Semerari, A., Carcione, A., Dimaggio, G., Nicoló, G., Pedone, R., & Procacci, M. (2005). Metarepresentative functions in borderline personality disorder. *Journal of Personality Disorders, 19*(6), 690–710. https://doi.org/10.1521/pedi.2005.19.6.690

Semerari, A., Carcione, A., Dimaggio, G., Nicolò, G., & Procacci, M. (2007). Understanding minds: Different functions and different disorders? The contribution of psychotherapy research. *Psychotherapy Research, 17*(1), 106–119. https://doi.org/10.1080/10503300500536953

Shapira-Berman, O. (2022). When should we not interpret? The analyst's transformative act as a vital contribution to the patient's sense of being real and alive. *Psychoanalytic Perspectives, 19*(3), 309–326. https://doi.org/10.1080/1551806X.2022.2097514

Simonsen, C. B., Jakobsen, A. G., Grøntved, S., & Kjaersdam Telléus, G. (2020). The mentalization profile in patients with eating disorders: A systematic review and meta-analysis. *Nordic Journal of Psychiatry, 74*(5), 311–322. https://doi.org/10.1080/08039488.2019.1707869

Sirois, F. (2012). The role and importance of interpretation in the talking cure. *The International Journal of Psychoanalysis, 93*(6), 1377–1402. https://doi.org/10.1111/j.1745-8315.2012.00650.x

Skårderud, F. (2007). Eating one's words, part II: The embodied mind and reflective function in anorexia nervosa—Theory. *European Eating Disorders Review, 15*(4), 243–252. https://doi.org/10.1002/erv.778

Sroufe, L. A. (2005). Attachment and development: A prospective, longitudinal study from birth to adulthood. *Attachment & Human Development, 7*(4), 349–367. https://doi.org/10.1080/14616730500365928

Steiner, J. (1985). Turning a blind eye: The cover-up for Oedipus. *The International Review of Psychoanalysis, 12*(2), 161–172.

Stern, D. N. (1985). *The interpersonal world of the infant: A view from psychoanalysis and developmental psychology*. Basic Books.

Stern, D. N., Bruschweiler-Stern, N., Harrison, A. M., Lyons-Ruth, K., Morgan, A. C., Nahum, J. P., Sander, L. W., & Tronick, E. Z. (1998). The process of therapeutic change involving implicit knowledge: Some implications of developmental observations for adult psychotherapy. *Infant Mental Health Journal, 19*(3), 300–308. https://doi.org/10.1002/(SICI)1097-0355(199823)19:3<300::AID-IMHJ5>3.0.CO;2-P

Stern, D. N., Sander, L. W., Nahum, J. P., Harrison, A. M., Lyons-Ruth, K., Morgan, A. C., Bruschweiler-Stern, N., & Tronick, E. Z. (1998). Non-interpretive mechanisms in psychoanalytic therapy: The "something more" than interpretation. *The International Journal of Psycho-Analysis, 79*(5), 903–921.

Strachey, J. (1969). The nature of the therapeutic action of psychoanalysis. *The International Journal of Psycho-Analysis, 50*(3), 275–292.

Strenger, C. (2003). The self as perpetual experiment: Psychodynamic comments on some aspects of contemporary urban culture. *Psychoanalytic Psychology, 20*(3), 425–440. https://doi.org/10.1037/0736-9735.20.3.425

Strenger, C. (2005). *The designed self: Psychoanalysis and contemporary identities*. The Analytic Press.

Strober, M., & Humphrey, L. L. (1987). Familial contributions to the etiology and course of anorexia nervosa and bulimia. *Journal of Consulting and Clinical Psychology, 55*(5), 654–659. https://doi.org/10.1037/0022-006X.55.5.654

Strober, M., Lampert, C., Morrell, W., Burroughs, J., & Jacobs, C. (1990). A controlled family study of anorexia nervosa: Evidence of familial aggregation and lack of shared transmission with affective disorders. *International Journal of Eating Disorders, 9*(3), 239–253. https://doi.org/10.1002/1098-108X(199005)9:3<239::AID-EAT2260090302>3.0.CO;2-7

Stubley, J., & Young, L. (2021). *Complex trauma: The Tavistock model*. Routledge. https://doi.org/10.4324/9781003227182

Suomi, S. J. (2011). Risk, resilience, and gene-environment interplay in primates. *Journal of the Canadian Academy of Child and Adolescent Psychiatry, 20*(4), 289–297. https://www.ncbi.nlm.nih.gov/pmc/articles/PMC3222572/

Symington, N. (1983). The analyst's act of freedom as agent of therapeutic change. *The International Review of Psychoanalysis, 10*(3), 283–291.

Symington, N. (1993). *Narcissism: A new theory*. Karnac Books.

Tasca, G. A., & Balfour, L. (2014). Attachment and eating disorders: A review of current research. *International Journal of Eating Disorders, 47*(7), 710–717. https://doi.org/10.1002/eat.22302

Thibeault, M. A., Stein, G. L., & Nelson-Gray, R. O. (2018). Ethnic identity in context of ethnic discrimination: When does gender and other-group orientation increase risk for depressive symptoms for immigrant-origin young adults? *Cultural Diversity & Ethnic Minority Psychology, 24*(2), 196–208. https://doi.org/10.1037/cdp0000174

Thorne, A. (2000). Personal memory telling and personality development. *Personality and Social Psychology Review*, *4*(1), 45–56. https://doi.org/10.1207/S15327957PSPR0401_5

Tomkins, S. S. (1978). Script theory: Differential magnification of affects. *Nebraska Symposium on Motivation*, *26*, 201–236.

Tomkins, S. S. (1982). Affect theory. In J. Aronoff, A. I. Rabin, & R. A. Zucker (Eds.), *The emergence of personality* (pp. 147–216). Springer Publishing Co.

Tower, L. E. (1956). Countertransference. *Journal of the American Psychoanalytic Association*, *4*(2), 224–255. https://doi.org/10.1177/000306515600400202

Trevarthen, C. (2005). First things first: Infants make good use of the sympathetic rhythm of imitation, without reason or language. *Journal of Child Psychotherapy*, *31*(1), 91–113. https://doi.org/10.1080/00754170500079651

Tronick, E. (2007). *The neurobehavioral and social-emotional development of infants and children*. W. W. Norton & Company.

Tronick, E. (2022). Trauma never occurs only once: Being traumatized by a slap is like making meaning of the game of peek-a-boo. *Psychoanalytic Dialogues*, *32*(6), 661–673. https://doi.org/10.1080/10481885.2022.2138083

Tronick, E., & Reck, C. (2009). Infants of depressed mothers. *Harvard Review of Psychiatry*, *17*(2), 147–156. https://doi.org/10.1080/10673220902899714

Tronick, E. Z. (1989). Emotions and emotional communication in infants. *American Psychologist*, *44*(2), 112–119. https://doi.org/10.1037/0003-066X.44.2.112

Tummala-Narra, P. (2019). Working with immigrants and refugees in psychodynamic psychotherapy. In D. Kealy & J. S. Ogrodniczuk (Eds.), *Contemporary psychodynamic psychotherapy: Evolving clinical practice* (pp. 281–294). Elsevier Academic Press.

Tummala-Narra, P. (2020). Intersectionality in the immigrant context. In M. Belkin & C. White (Eds.), *Intersectionality and relational psychoanalysis: New perspectives on race, gender, and sexuality* (pp. 119–143). Routledge/Taylor & Francis Group. https://doi.org/10.4324/9780429344312-9

Tustin, F. (1984). Autistic shapes. *The International Review of Psychoanalysis*, *11*(3), 279–290.

van Ijzendoorn, M. H., Schuengel, C., & Bakermans-Kranenburg, M. J. (1999). Disorganized attachment in early childhood: Meta-analysis of precursors, concomitants, and sequelae. *Development and Psychopathology*, *11*(2), 225–249. https://doi.org/10.1017/S0954579499002035

Van Nieuwenhove, K., & Meganck, R. (2019). Interpersonal features in complex trauma etiology, consequences, and treatment: A literature review. *Journal of Aggression, Maltreatment & Trauma*, *28*(8), 903–928. https://doi.org/10.1080/10926771.2017.1405316

Vanheule, S. (2011). *The subject of psychosis: A Lacanian perspective*. Palgrave MacMillan. https://doi.org/10.1057/9780230355873

Vardy, M. M., & Kaplan, B. M. (2008). Christ/Messiah delusions revisited: Toward an anthropological definition of religious delusions. *Psychoanalytic Review*, *95*(3), 473–487. https://doi.org/10.1521/prev.2008.95.3.473

Verhaeghe, P. (1999). The collapse of the father and its effect on gender roles. *Psychoanalysis, Culture & Society, 4*(1), 18–30.

Verhaeghe, P., & Vanheule, S. (2005). Actual neurosis and PTSD: The impact of the other. *Psychoanalytic Psychology, 22*(4), 493–507. https://doi.org/10.1037/0736-9735.22.4.493

Verhaeghe, P., Vanheule, S., & De Rick, A. (2007). Actual neurosis as the underlying psychic structure of panic disorder, somatization, and somatoform disorder: An integration of Freudian and attachment perspectives. *The Psychoanalytic Quarterly, 76*(4), 1317–1350. https://doi.org/10.1002/j.2167-4086.2007.tb00306.x

Vlahaki, I. (2012). "Two in a body": From the mother's anorexia to the daughter's bulimia. *International Forum of Psychoanalysis, 21*(3–4), 195–201. https://doi.org/10.1080/0803706X.2012.657675

Watson, E. (2022). Gender transitioning and variance in children and adolescents: Some temporal and ethical considerations. *The Psychoanalytic Study of the Child, 75*(1), 184–190. https://doi.org/10.1080/00797308.2021.1975460

Welch-Ross, M. K. (1995). An integrative model of the development of autobiographical memory. *Developmental Review, 15*(3), 338–365. https://doi.org/10.1006/drev.1995.1013

Wermke, K., & Mende, W. (2009). Musical elements in human infants' cries: In the beginning is the melody. *Musicae Scientiae, 13*(2_Suppl.), 151–175. https://doi.org/10.1177/1029864909013002081

Williams, G. (1997). Reflections on some dynamics of eating disorders: "No entry" defences and foreign bodies. *The International Journal of Psycho-Analysis, 78*(5), 927–941.

Wilson, M. (2013). Desire and responsibility: The ethics of countertransference experience. *The Psychoanalytic Quarterly, 82*(2), 435–476. https://doi.org/10.1002/j.2167-4086.2013.00036.x

Winnicott, D. W. (1955). Metapsychological and clinical aspects of regression within the psycho-analytical set-up. *The International Journal of Psycho-Analysis, 36*(1), 16–26.

Winnicott, D. W. (1965). Communicating and not communicating leading to a study of certain opposites. In *The maturational processes and the facilitating environment: Studies in the theory of emotional development* (pp. 179–192). The Hogarth Press. (Original work published 1963)

Winnicott, D. W. (1971). *Playing and reality*. Routledge.

Winnicott, D. W. (1974). Fear of breakdown. *The International Review of Psycho-analysis, 1*(1–2), 103–107.

Zackheim, L. (2007). Alexithymia: The expanding realm of research. *Journal of Psychosomatic Research, 63*(4), 345–347. https://doi.org/10.1016/j.jpsychores.2007.08.011

Index

A

B

C

D

E

F

M

N

O

P

V

W

About the Author

Marilyn Charles, PhD, ABPP, is a psychologist and psychoanalyst at the Austen Riggs Center, Co-Chair of the Association for the Psychoanalysis of Culture and Society (APCS) and Scholar of the British Psychoanalytic Council. A training analyst at the Chicago Center for Psychoanalysis and international coordinator of the psychoanalytic track at Universidad de Monterrey, she is on faculty at Boston Graduate School of Psychoanalysis and Harvard Medical School. Research interests include creativity, metacognition, and the intergenerational transmission of trauma. A contributing editor of *Psychoanalysis, Culture and Society* and a member of several editorial boards, Marilyn is actively engaged in mentoring future generations of psychoanalytic scholars, clinicians, and researchers. She is also an artist, a poet, and a writer, who has presented her work nationally and internationally, publishing more than 100 articles and book chapters and five books: *Patterns: Building Blocks of Experience; Constructing Realities: Transformations Through Myth and Metaphor*; *Learning from Experience: a Guidebook for Clinicians*; *Working with Trauma: Lessons from Bion and Lacan*; *Psychoanalysis and Literature: The Stories We Live*; and five edited volumes: *Introduction to Contemporary Psychoanalysis*; *Fragments of Trauma and the Social Production of Suffering* (with Michael O'Loughlin); *Women and Psychosis and Women and the Psychosocial Construction of Madness* (with Marie Brown); and *The Importance of Play in Early Childhood Education: Psychoanalytic, Attachment, and Developmental Perspectives* (with Jill Bellinson).